INDEX ON CENSORSHIP

VOLUME 32 • NO 2 • APRIL 2003 • ISSUE 207

Sangatte refugee centre, northern France, 2001.
Credit: Matias Costa, Panos

WEBSITE NEWS UPDATED WEEKLY
WWW.INDEXONCENSORSHIP.ORG • CONTACT@INDEXONCENSORSHIP.ORG
TEL: 020 7278 2313 • FAX: 020 7278 1878

CONTENTS

MOVING POPULATIONS

URSULA OWEN

As we go to press, the US-led coalition is at war with Iraq. The threat has been there for months, and with it the calculations indicating the staggering likely humanitarian cost for Iraq. Six hundred thousand refugees are predicted by UNHCR. Meanwhile, applications from asylum seekers in Britain last year topped 100,000 for the first time, Iraqis and Afghans representing the highest numbers. Will the Labour government, in the aftermath of a war it supports, stick with its stated aim of reducing the number of applications to half by September?

Public debate on immigration in Britain is mostly vicious, couched sometimes in the hysterical language of mindless media, sometimes in what Toni Morrison calls the 'malign language of law-without-ethics'. The effect has been to create damaging stereotypes, not least those of the 'genuine' and the 'bogus' asylum seeker – new versions of the Victorian concept of the deserving and undeserving poor. Refugees and asylum seekers are calculated to be only 0.5 per cent of the total UK population. Many of them are digging our gardens, cleaning our kitchens, looking after our children: often their earnings are below the minimum wage.

No one denies that migration is a highly contentious issue, involving conflicting interests and difficult moral and practical questions, especially for rich countries such as the UK. Positions have become polarised. The 'cosmopolitans' view nation states and national identities as disabling anachronisms, and think that the dangerous aspect of the asylum issue is tabloid hysteria. Others, the 'ethnic nationalists', want to defend the purity of their nation against all foreigners and believe that abuse of Britain's asylum laws is the greatest threat to our country.

Index looks at these polarities, and attempts to steer a different course, to start a debate on migration free of rhetoric and stereotypes, showing how immensely complex the realities are. Our contributors write about identities and subversion of borders (p60), about who comes to Europe and why (p42), about blurred distinctions between refugees and economic migrants (p107). We report on internal migrations in China (p120), women trafficked for sex in Europe (p87), the population movements created by the end of the Soviet Empire (p82), illegal migrants in Israel (p112), UK media coverage of immigration (p184); and we profile Leicester, a city of migration par excellence (p125).

Is it right to restrict immigration? Is immigration a burden on Western economies or a necessary economic support for our ageing populations? Is migration a human right? Such questions will become even more urgent in the near future. ❑

IN TIME OF WAR

Nasiriyah, Southern Iraq, March 2003: captured US Army cook, Specialist Shoshana Johnson of the 507th Maintenance Company, based out of Fort Bliss, Texas, quizzed by Iraqi TV for a film later rebroadcast by al-Jazeera TV, but not – at the request of the military authorities – by US or British TV networks. Credit: AFP

Entirely by coincidence, on 26 March *Index on Censorship* honoured the Qatari-based satellite TV station al-Jazeera with a special award for its courage in circumventing censorship of view, exactly at the moment the network was facing a storm of condemnation for broadcasting film of dead and detained British and US soldiers.

But that was just one airburst in a conflict that has become the testing ground for the strategy – and laws – that will guide the conduct of war for the next 50 years.

The role of the media, state propaganda, international laws of war, the future of the multinational process, concepts of alliances, even the culture of warfare and the conceptualisation of victory and defeat – all are under question. And all this in a war fought in front of the eyes of billions of people allowed to see, but prevented from understanding.

What follows is only the start. ❏

PRESSED INTO MILITARY SERVICE

ROHAN JAYASEKERA

WILL A POST-WAR IRAQI MEDIA
COME UNDER THE AUTHORITY OF
A US MILITARY GOVERNMENT?

The pace of modern war is a real trial for a quarterly magazine. *Index on Censorship* had barely put out its first post-11 September issue when it found itself encamped in Afghanistan working with the Institute for War & Peace Reporting on a three-month media support programme. There, the ruthless expediency of US political strategy in Afghanistan was clear to see. But we could still conclude that the independent media and their supporters were working well together in Kabul.

Index on Censorship may soon be in Iraq – seeking practical means to support the diversity, viability and the independence of the post-war Iraqi media, lobbying for a fair legal framework for its operation with our partners at Article 19 and working on training networks with IWPR again.

Yet we may face unexpected opposition on the ground. From the US Army. As we go to press, Washington is preparing for sole control of Iraqi civilian life without recourse to the UN, under the direct command of US Army Lt-General John Abizaid and Jay Garner, the retired US general who directs the Pentagon's new Office of Reconstruction and Humanitarian Assistance. His team will oversee emergency relief and refugees, long-term planning for roads, rail and waterways, economic development and the removal of senior officials of Saddam's Ba'ath Party in the manner of the massive US Army-directed 'de-Nazification' process in post-World War II Germany.

So, considering that particular model, what about the post-war Iraqi media? Post-World War II German media were rigorously controlled by the remarkable but little known US Major-General Alexis McClure. His wartime Psychological Warfare Division (PWD) provided 'consolidation propaganda', designed 'to gain the cooperation of the German population in restoring essential services, and to create a public opinion favourable to post-war Allied aims'. (US Army 'psyops' squads have the same objective in Iraq today.) After 1945, PWD was renamed the Information Control Divi-

Kabul 2002: Rohan Jayasekera (with beard) at work with Afghan journalists.
Credit: Tony Borden

sion (ICD) and by July 1946 McClure could tell Time-Life vice-president CD Jackson: 'We now control 37 newspapers, six radio stations, 314 theatres, 642 [cinemas], 101 magazines, 237 book publishers, 7,384 book dealers and printers, and conduct about 15 public opinion surveys a month, as well as publish one newspaper with 1,500,000 circulation . . . run the Associated Press of Germany and operate 20 library centres . . . The job is tremendous.' Making its first attempt at post-war nation-building since post-war Germany, does the US aim to repeat McClure's strategy in post-war Iraq? Well, *it's a secret*, of course. But when we get there we'll find out. And let you know. ❏

TALKING DIRTY TO AMERICA

SHEILA MACVICAR

AN ESTIMATED 22 PER CENT
OF AMERICANS GET THEIR DAILY
NEWS FROM TALK RADIO

Talk radio is a peculiarly American phenomenon, featuring much rhetoric and not a lot of substance; high-volume noise often combined with the absence of facts. My recent voyage into this world taught me that it is also a place where prejudices and stereotypes are passed off as real information.

I was asked to promote, on half a dozen or so talk radio shows, a documentary I prepared for CNN called *The Arab Street*, the result of an eight-day journey overland from Amman to Damascus and on to Beirut, sampling public opinion in this part of the Arab world as the US, Britain and their partners lurched towards war.

My first call was to a West Coast morning duo called Young and Elder; nationally syndicated, they came together after not quite making it as comedians. I talked about what people had told me of their fears of war and US objectives. They asked, 'So did you have to walk three paces back all covered up in black?' If I'd been on camera, viewers would have seen my jaw drop. No, I replied, I wasn't quite dressed for a day at the beach in California, but then, how many places on the planet can you appear in public wearing only a few tiny triangles?

There was the syndicated talk-show host out of Washington; ranked by *USA Today* as one of the 25 most influential in the US, who demanded: 'Don't they get it? Without us, they'll be riding camels again.' Or the talk-show host who wanted to know whether I was frightened talking to Arabs.

Much of this could have been amusing. But a recent Gallup poll, released in January 2003, found that 22 per cent of those surveyed in the US said that they got their news every day from talk radio, more than double the percentage just four years ago.

Al Rantel, of KABC-740AM, and a talk radio host himself, said: 'Let's not kid ourselves. talk radio is entertainment. I'm flattered that many people trust talk radio to get their information.' But, he added, talk radio is 'a three-hour editorial. People should know talk radio is opinion and commentary and we are not unbiased.'

It's one thing to engage in domestic political ranting over the airwaves (the vast majority of talk radio hosts consider themselves to be Republicans), and another to indulge in ignorance, prejudice and even racism.

'It's not producing an informed democracy,' said Amy Mitchell, at the Project for Excellence in Journalism, a group that strives to improve journalistic standards.

Talk radio, and an increasing reliance on editorial opinion dressed up as infotainment, is failing to help people understand, failing to give them the factual basis which they can use to evaluate the issues of the day. It is also reinforcing deeply held stereotypes born out of ignorance.

Long beyond 11 September, it seems that many Americans do not yet understand the deep wellspring of anger in the Middle East. This includes middle-class professionals who admire much about the US, were often educated there, and who are deeply disturbed by US policy, especially the Israeli–Palestinian conflict, described to me by Jordan's foreign minister as 'the central conflict in the region'.

I listened to young, Western-educated Arabs talk of their belief that America is entering into a new colonialist era of occupation. The question of democracy? No one with whom I spoke believed the US had any interest in promoting democracy in the region, and they would not support any 'democracy' that was imposed.

People in the region talk of the concepts of Jeffersonian and Wilsonian democracy, concepts that I would wager have been lost to most Americans, or at least those who listen to talk radio, and their hosts. Graduates of US universities told me that they were now ashamed to be seen to be supporters of more democracy in the region. That was now perceived as 'doing America's work', in the words of one key regional adviser.

These are complicated and difficult issues, in complicated and difficult times. It would seem that 22 per cent and growing of the American population could be better served. ❑

Sheila MacVicar *is a CNN correspondent*

DODGING THE FIRST AMENDMENT

JOANNE MARINER

PENTAGON WARLORD RICHARD PERLE
VOWS TO SUE OVER SUGGESTIONS THAT
WAR IS GOOD FOR HIS BUSINESS, BUT
LOOKS TO BRITISH COURTS FOR LEGAL
ADVANTAGES DENIED HIM IN THE US

Seymour Hersh, the celebrated investigative journalist, is no stranger to the pressures of reporting on controversial issues during wartime. After the verdict was handed down in the criminal prosecution of the My Lai massacre, a story he broke during the Vietnam War, he felt so threatened by angry soldiers that he went into hiding.

It is a telling sign of the times that Hersh is once again under attack for his reporting. Last week, just as Hersh was giving a speech in which he publicly warned that journalists were frightened and intimidated, senior Pentagon adviser Richard Perle was telling the New York *Sun* that he planned to file suit against Hersh for libel.

Another sign of the times (or perhaps just a hallmark of the Bush administration): Perle has a strategy for evading constitutional protections against this action. Although Perle is an American, Hersh is an American and the magazine in which Hersh printed his allegedly defamatory article is published in the United States, Perle told the *Sun* that he would file suit in Britain. Known as the 'libel capital of the world' because of its plaintiff-friendly rules on defamation, Britain has nothing remotely comparable to the First Amendment's protections for freedom of the press.

In the US courts, Perle would have to prove that Hersh's statements were false and that they were made with 'actual malice', making it likely that his suit would be dismissed in the early stages of litigation. In England, where the law establishes a rebuttable presumption that a defamatory statement is false, Perle stands a far better chance of dragging Hersh into a long and costly court battle.

Perle, a former assistant secretary of defence in the Reagan administration, was chairman of the influential Defense Policy Board, an advisory panel to the Defense Department. He is also a businessman, serving as managing partner of a private venture capital firm called Trireme Partners that invests primarily in companies that deal in goods and services related to national security.

Last January, as reported in an article that Hersh published in the *New Yorker*, Perle may have inappropriately mixed his public and private roles. The article states that Perle met Saudi arms trader Adnan Khashoggi and another Saudi businessman for lunch on 3 January in the French city of Marseilles.

On the menu was a discussion of the upcoming war and, according to the two Saudis, whom Hersh interviewed, the opportunities for investment in Perle's company. Hersh's article does not directly accuse Perle of wrong-doing.

Perle, who has been credited as the intellectual force behind the Iraq war, insists that his hawkish views are not up for sale. While Hersh does not challenge him on this point, he suggests that Perle should take greater care to insulate his foreign policy connections from his financial dealings.

Hersh's *New Yorker* article was published in early March, and Perle's response was swift and vicious. Questioned on CNN on 9 March, Perle said Hersh was 'the closest thing American journalism has to a terrorist'. The day after he told the MSNBC show *Hardball:* 'If any reasonable lawyer tells me there's a prospect of winning a case, I would be delighted to sue Sy Hersh.'

No reasonable lawyer would advise a suit in the US, given the First Amendment's robust protections on freedom of speech. Thus, from the standpoint of legal strategy, Perle's forum-shopping preferences are understandable. If Perle were to bring suit in the US, he would face daunting obstacles. First, given his prominent role in shaping foreign policy, he would be considered a public figure. Second, under the more stringent First Amendment protections applicable to libel suits against public figures, Perle would have the burden of proving that Hersh made the allegedly defamatory statements with actual malice.

To prove actual malice, Perle would have to show that Hersh knew that the statements were false or that he had a reckless disregard for their truth or falsity. Under these standards, it is likely that the suit would be dismissed on a motion for summary judgement. Interviewed by the *Washington Post*, Hersh noted that Perle has yet to specify a single inaccuracy in Hersh's article. Yet one of the beauties of British libel law, from the plaintiff's perspective, is that the failure to show falsity is no bar to a successful lawsuit.

Under British law, any published statements that negatively affect a person's reputation are presumed to be false. In contrast to the American constitutional rule, the burden is on the defendant to prove that the statements are true. Even more important, in terms of the viability of the suit, British libel law does not distinguish between private persons and public figures, and extends no special protection to criticisms directed at members of the latter category. Because it so clearly favours plaintiffs, English libel law has drawn the criticism of the European Court of Human Rights. More to the point, from Perle's perspective, is that US courts have frequently refused to enforce English libel judgements against American defendants, opposing them on public policy grounds.

In a 1992 case, a New York state court set out the reasoning behind such a refusal. The First Amendment's protections on speech and the press, the court explained, 'would be seriously jeopardised by the entry of foreign libel judgements granted pursuant to standards deemed appropriate in England but considered antithetical to the protections afforded the press by the US Constitution'.

Although Perle's planned lawsuit would stand a much greater chance of success were it to be filed in Britain rather than in the US, it is still a gamble. The British courts, which have shown a recent impatience with such overt forum-shopping strategies, could refuse to hear the case on the ground that US courts would provide a more suitable forum. A jury in Britain might give him a hard time for who he is and what he represents. And, should he lose, he would be liable for Hersh's costs.

Whatever the outcome of the suit, Perle's threat to file it has already sent a chilling message to the American press. The stakes are high. Already the most divisive US military intervention since Vietnam, the war in Iraq will place heavy demands on journalists' skill and integrity. With courageous investigative reporting more than ever necessary, it is no time to subject American journalists to British rules. ❑

Joanne Mariner is a human rights lawyer based in New York

(As we go to press, Richard Perle said he was resigning from the chairmanship of the Defense Policy Board but had agreed to remain a board member. Ed)

WATCHING FROM THE SIDELINES
ABDUL MOHAMMED & ALEX DE WAAL

AFRICA'S REASONS TO FEAR
THE CONSEQUENCES OF THE
ATTACK ON IRAQ

A rich industrialised nation with the most modern military technology attacks and invades an impoverished nation in another continent, deaf to the cries of unfairness in the world's chambers of diplomacy. Ethiopians will recognise a defining moment from their history, and a moment of betrayal that discredited the League of Nations and helped set in motion the lawless descent into the greatest conflagration of our age, World War II.

There are more differences between fascist Italy's unprovoked invasion of Ethiopia and the US-led attack on Iraq than there are similarities. Iraq has been repeatedly sanctioned by the United Nations for its intransigence and unreadiness to bend to the requests of the world community. It is Iraq, not the US and its allies, that has used chemical weapons. Saddam Hussein is a thug who has ruled a republic of fear, not a modernising emperor appealing to the conscience of the world to resist colonialism. And America has not abandoned its democratic constitution in favour of fascism.

But there is one compelling similarity between these two defining events, a lifetime apart. A powerful nation feels that it has the power and privilege to tear up the rules governing the conduct of international affairs, and to use force recklessly in pursuit of its aims, casually dismissive of the consequences. The world will not weep at the demise of the Iraqi dictator, and we will all join the Iraqi people in their jubilation at the end of their three-decade-long nightmare of tyranny and war.

But the world is justifiably apprehensive when the sole superpower decides carelessly to discard six decades of painstaking diplomatic and political labour in building the norms and institutions of multilateralism. The moral language of liberation and destroying weapons of mass destruction cannot hide the irreducible illegality of what the US and Britain intend to do. Where will this road lead? The US spends as much on what it calls 'defence' as the next 20 ranked nations put together. The Pentagon's annual budget is US$366 billion, slightly exceeding the combined GNP of all the nations of sub-Saharan Africa (which the World Bank last estimated at US$354 billion). But does this enable it to police the world on its own terms?

Effective policing depends on a consensus in the community to keep the law. The police can do their job only if most of the citizens are law-abiding and cooperative. If a community descends into anarchy, the sheriff simply becomes a vigilante cowboy, arbitrarily dispensing retribution, dependent on instilling fear to deter his adversaries. This is the miscalculation of the American administration: they are making the world a more lawless and thus more dangerous place. Countries that have paid the price of lawlessness clothed in higher motives have seen the dangers. The US, its judgement clouded by the trauma of 11 September, and Britain, which should know better, have arrogantly ignored their calls for moderation.

The multilateral system is decidedly imperfect, and one of its most notorious flaws is its reluctance to take effective action against governments that kill and torture their own citizens under the camouflage of 'national sovereignty'. The constant tinkering with the system, and the proliferation of talking shops, engenders impatience and scepticism. But, to improve upon Churchill's dictum that 'jaw jaw' is better than 'war war', 'jaw jaw jaw jaw' is better than 'quick war'.

For all its flaws, the current system provides incentives for a troublesome regime to become a recognised law-abiding member of the international community. It is precisely because there are benefits – both material rewards and the intangible but no less important factor of national pride – that come from being a recognised member of the world community that states such as Libya and Syria have abandoned terrorism, and Sudan is negotiating an end to its civil war.

Without these rewards, potential rogue states have every reason to act as North Korea is now doing, and acquire nuclear weapons and threaten a first strike against any that appears too threatening. Will we only appreciate the value of these subtle pieces of multilateral furniture when they have been jettisoned?

Nowhere is this lesson more important than in Africa, which has suffered more than its fair share of troublemakers. The African Union is just in the very process of developing a common security doctrine to be adopted at the next summit in Maputo in July.

While Africa struggles to establish a basic framework of common responsibility for peace and security, the very fount of these principles is being

poisoned by unilateralism. It will take energetic, sustained and rapid reme-
dial action by the US and Britain to salvage these vital principles, if multilateralism is not to be cut adrift in a world of cynical realpolitik.

Advocates of the US neo-imperial occupation of Iraq like to point out
that an American general oversaw the transformation of militaristic imperial
Japan into a pacific democracy. What they overlook is that this transformation was built upon financial generosity and an order of magnitude greater
than anything envisaged by the parsimonious Republicans now in power in
Washington and, more important still, it was achieved in the context of the
US-led building of the United Nations system that promised to 'save future
generations from the scourge of war'.

Can a US-imposed 'democracy' in Iraq prosper, while Western governments mortgage the country's oil wealth to pay for a reconstruction they do
not want to fund themselves? Can it survive when the implicit slogan for
international relations is 'might is right'? Not even the US State Department
believes so. Its internal paper on the subject, 'No Dominoes', was leaked to
the press on the same day that the US president announced that a democratic Iraq under US tutelage would be a model for the region.

Another historical parallel is the Opium War, inflicted upon China by
the great powers of the day, led by Britain. The latter's aim: to 'open up'
China to commerce, on extractive terms dictated by the imperial armies, to
'protect' their citizens, and to ensure that what had been the world's greatest
nation state would be subjugated. China retained its nominal independence,
but was humiliated and demoralised, and for more than a century it was
wracked by war and famine. Already humiliated by Israel's crushing of the
Palestinians with impunity, the Arab and Muslim countries most likely face
an immediate future shaped by the politics of rage.

Sub-Saharan Africa is a spectator in the Iraqi crisis, as well as an injured
bystander in the 'war on terrorism'. But let us not assume that this war
has no effect on the African continent. The economic impact could be
disastrous.

Should, for example, the price of oil double, then countries that already
struggle to pay for the bare minimum of fuel to keep their economies functioning will face a serious recession. International aid funds may not be
massively diverted to pay for the reconstruction costs in Iraq – it didn't
happen last year with Afghanistan, perhaps illustrating the unreadiness of the
developed countries to foot any sort of rehabilitation bill. But the sustained
political attention that is needed to address Africa's multiple crises, including

debt, unfair terms of trade, HIV/Aids and ongoing conflict, will surely be depleted.

Perhaps, in the short term, the political repercussions will not be great.

Doubtless there will be violent demonstrations in northern Nigeria, and the Sudan government may be compelled to go slow on the peace process with the SPLA. In Ethiopia, the fabric of tolerance that has allowed the country to be a model of peaceful coexistence between Christians and Muslims will no doubt remain strong. But who can tell what 'unknown unknowns' lurk in this explosive mix? What new fundamentalisms may emerge? What opportunities for peaceful resolution of conflict will be forgone?

It's salutary to recall that the Somali government collapsed during the 1991 Gulf War, and the sole US or European response was to evacuate their nationals by helicopter. A little more diplomatic attention – such as Ethiopia received just four months later – and Somalia's last decade might have been very different. Another unanticipated and unforeseeable consequence of the elder Bush's war.

Since the fascist invasion of 1935, Africa has suffered whenever international law has been undermined or ignored. Multilateralism and international consensus-building has been Africa's greatest friend. Africa has much to fear from the reckless vigilantism that is passing for international law enforcement in Washington and London. The world has reason to listen to Africa's hard-learned lessons that peace, democracy and development cannot be imposed by might. ❏

Abdul Mohammed *is the chair of InterAfrica Group, Addis Ababa*
Alex de Waal *is director of Justice Africa*

A version of this article was first published in the Sub-Saharan Africa Informer *on 21 March*

FOXY BUSINESS

JULIAN PETLEY

WHEN DID DIVERSITY EVER EQUAL
IMPARTIALITY? IT DIDN'T, BUT IT HAS
BECOME THE COVER FOR ANY KIND
OF 'POLEMICAL' — AKA BIASED —
BROADCASTING

Although British broadcasting is mercifully free from the strident editorial-ising that characterises most of the UK press, it hasn't always escaped charges of bias. Back in the days when media studies still had a critical edge, books such as *The Manufacture of News, Putting 'Reality' Together* and the various *Bad News* studies from the Glasgow University Media Group argued that broadcast news and current affairs programmes, for all their apparent impartiality and balance, actually presented a largely establishment-friendly view of the world. More recently, this charge has been taken up by radical journalists such as John Pilger and Nick Cohen, and it's a constant theme of Noam Chomsky's formidable output.

Now the question of impartiality has been raised by rather less radical commentators in the shape of Damian Tambini and Jamie Cowling in *New News: Impartial Broadcasting in the Digital Age*, a collection they edited for the Institute for Public Policy Research, and Ian Hargreaves and James Thomas in *New News, Old News*, an account of research undertaken for the Broadcasting Standards Commission and Independent Television Commission.

Why this renewed interest? According to Tambini: 'Despite the success of the British approach to impartiality in broadcasting, the regulations that guarantee it will have to change if the UK traditions of independent, accurate, impartial broadcasting are to survive.' The need for reform arises both from changes to the broadcasting ecology and wider political shifts: 'The market is fragmenting and becoming more competitive whilst commercial concerns are tainting the news values of all broadcasters. At the same time, politics is changing in ways that challenge UK news regulation, focused as it is on a narrow range of party balance.'

On the broadcasting front, increased competition has meant, according to Tambini, that 'news is increasingly presented to attract an audience, rather than to reflect formal notions of the public interest and impartiality'.

This is not something the IPPR authors welcome, although they acknowledge it as a challenge to be faced. Additionally, they also recognise that it may become increasingly difficult, although not impossible, for Ofcom (the new regulatory body established by the Communications Bill that will merge the Independent Television Commission, Broadcasting Standards Commission, Oftel, Radio Authority and Radio Communications Agency) to enforce impartiality regulations for a plethora of channels, including foreign-language and niche channels, some of which are not even aimed at UK audiences.

When it comes to the political side of things, it is obvious that impartiality codes designed essentially to ensure fair treatment between the two major established political parties are ill suited to deal with political issues in an era in which, for an increasing number of people, the play of forces at Westminster no longer constitutes what they regard as politics. This has meant, among other things, that questions are increasingly being asked about the media filters through which the UK public experience their political life. Tambini sums up these concerns by asking if 'regulation for broadcasting impartiality [is] responsible for a ritualised, adversarial presentation of politics that in fact contributes to public disengagement?' He and Cowling conclude that, partly thanks to these rules, 'we are ill prepared to cope with the complexity of politics in the new century, and the institutions of impartiality regulation run the risk of becoming irrelevant or, worse, obliging journalists to focus on ritualised formal politics when the real story, and the real challenge for public information, is elsewhere'.

Broadcasting's apparent inability to deal adequately with a changed political environment and the role played in this by current impartiality regulations also concern *New News, Old News*. This reports that the overall level of television national news consumption has fallen by 5.6 per cent since 1994, in spite of an 80 per cent increase of supply on the five main terrestrial channels. ITV has experienced a 23 per cent decline, and the biggest fall-offs in viewing (14 per cent) have been among the 25–34 age group and social groups C2DE. People are increasingly 'spotlight chasing' – dipping into 24-hour news channels when a major story such as 9/11 breaks – or using the internet. Only 16 per cent of those questioned regarded themselves as regular current affairs viewers, and between 1994 and 2002 the current affairs audience fell by 31.7 per cent while current affairs output dropped by almost 12 per cent.

On the other hand, however, 92 per cent of those who took part in the survey thought that the principle of accuracy in news was very important, and 71 per cent took the same view about impartiality. Interestingly, 88 per cent of those in multi-channel homes thought impartiality a good thing, compared with 93 per cent in non-multi-channel homes. *New News, Old News* states that this particular finding adds weight to the view that 'there may be the first signs of a growing volume of dissent from this long-established principle as viewers enjoy greater choice. This may be an early warning sign that Parliament and regulators should be ready to understand and respond to a shifting view and to encourage innovation rather than stifle it.' It's also significant that only 64 per cent of those among the Asian and black communities thought impartiality a good thing, 'perhaps reflecting a view amongst these communities that broadcast news is not impartial in its reporting of issues of concern to them'.

In what ways, then, do the authors of these studies think that the impartiality regulations might be changed to meet some of the concerns they raise? According to Tambini and Cowling, the BBC, ITC and Radio Authority codes should encourage a broader approach to balance, one that does not necessarily require a focus on each major party's stance on every issue. In particular, 'a greater emphasis should be placed on the need for impartiality in relation to a range of expert opinions, the problem of corporate interests, single-issue groups and competing scientific opinions'. In their view, 'the provision of accurate, impartial news to the citizen and the requirement for due impartiality should be retained for all broadcast services which are not an active purchase . . . The principles guiding content regulation in general are that the services that are most public, most invasive, most pervasive and most influential should be subject to most regulation in the public interest. As the market develops for niche services, Ofcom should periodically consult the public on whether to relax the impartiality obligations on those services with less market share.'

What this in effect means is that 'there will be a role in the future for polemical channels. It is possible that polemical channels, if correctly regulated, could widen the diversity of voice in British broadcasting.'

Hargreaves and Thomas reach broadly similar conclusions, arguing that 'in a time of diminished party loyalties, impartiality should be more broadly defined, to require that broadcasters provide even-handed treatment of issues of race, science, environment, health and any other matter of public controversy'. However, they explicitly reject relaxation of the impartiality regulations based on the notion of 'active purchase' because, in the digital future, so many channels are likely to be 'active purchases', and because they feel that it is unclear 'what amounts to an "active purchase" in a satellite television environment where services are bundled together for sale to consumers'.

None the less, given that their survey shows that significant numbers of the young and of Britain's ethnic groups feel that broadcast news does not represent them adequately, 'it may be that a more opinionated style of broadcast news, originated from well outside the UK broadcasting mainstream, is helpful in the overall news mix, so long as consumers are aware what they are getting and which services conform to impartiality rules and which do not. The time has come when a range of experimentation should be encouraged.' In their view, therefore, 'the most sensible course is to create an opening for Ofcom to recommend to the Secretary of State variation in the impartiality rules, where channels involved are of minority interest and where they do not threaten the central, impartial reputation of mainstream UK television news.'

It is unfortunate, to put it mildly, that such thoughtful analyses of the political shortcomings of news and current affairs programmes should conclude with recommendations that are guaranteed only to make matters considerably worse. Why? Because they will allow Rupert Murdoch to do to British broadcasting what he has already done to the British press: namely, force all other market players to compete with him on his own debased terms. For Murdoch is absolutely itching to turn Sky News into a British version of his rabidly populist Fox News which, even before its post-9/11 transformation into a cheerleader for war, was dubbed by Freedom and Accuracy in Reporting (FAIR) 'the most biased name in news'.

This is not paranoid fantasy. Both BSkyB and News International used the consultation process leading up to the Communications Bill to lobby for relaxation of the current broadcasting content regulations, and their submissions are easily viewable on the Department of Culture, Media and Sport's website. Or turn to a recent edition of the *British Journalism Review* to find *Sun* pundit Richard Littlejohn complaining that at Sky News 'we'd never been able to make the programme we intended. If Sky News could emulate its US sister Fox News, which has wiped the floor with CNN with opinion-driven "fair and balanced" coverage, ratings would soon shoot past the Astra satellite. But the regulators won't allow it.' Nor does the Communications

Bill permit partisan news. However, given that the bill specifically instructs Ofcom to minimise regulatory burdens, and given that Murdoch clearly interprets the impartiality regulations as highly burdensome, it is safe to assume that intense pressure for these to be removed from Sky News will be one of the main tasks of the formidable Murdoch lobbying machine (of which his papers are a crucial part) once the bill becomes law this summer.

There is, of course, nothing remotely 'fair and balanced' about Fox News: in its very choice of pundits, interviewees and stories, quite apart from the way in which those stories are treated, it is, as FAIR puts it, 'the central hub of the conservative movement's well-oiled media machine'. In other words, it's just like Murdoch's papers. Take, for example, the way in which the *Sunday Times* used the publication of the IPPR and BSC/ITC studies shamelessly to lobby on behalf of its proprietor's interests. On 17 November it ran a piece by Andrew Sullivan headlined 'Let's hear it for prejudiced television news' and calling for 'an injection of honest bias, US-style'. Fox is represented as 'an antidote to the liberalism endemic to much of the rest of television', and the 'pseudo-objective networks' are condemned for their 'suffocating liberalism'. Turning to the UK, Sullivan complains that 'nobody I knew in my generation who had anything good to say about Margaret Thatcher went in to the BBC. Why should we be shocked today to find that, two decades later, news coverage reflects this view of the world?' He continues: 'Watching the BBC when I visit Britain is an eye-opener. The soft anti-Americanism, the unreflective Third World-ism, the facile assumption that old-style statist politics on the environment are correct, the instinctual loathing of Israel, the benevolent multiculturalism, the equation of the European Union with the future all reflect an effortless left-liberal viewpoint.' Sullivan concludes that while 'there's room for a left-leaning network in Britain . . . what's wrong is the pretence that the BBC is somehow neutral, objective or balanced. And what makes this doubly wrong is that it's paid for by the licence fee. I can see why people in a free society should tolerate a television channel that promotes a viewpoint with which they disagree. I don't see why they should also be forced to pay for it and then be denied the opportunity to have an alternative by specious regulations over something ludicrously called balance.'

Few people would, I think, recognise the BBC from Sullivan's caricature but, of course, he has to peddle this kind of nonsense in order to put the argument that there needs to be an alternative news source to the BBC. By tirelessly insisting that all other news providers are driven by liberal bias, Fox

News executives attempt the impossible intellectual conjuring trick of casting the rabid Fox as the centrist voice of reason. The truth of the matter is, quite simply, that the mainstream media in the US appear overly liberal only when viewed from a vertiginously conservative perspective. As FAIR points out, their ideology is, in fact, staunchly centrist, and rarely do they proselytise for left-wing or even overtly progressive values. They do, however, like British broadcasters, try to uphold the traditional journalistic values of fairness, accuracy, independence of judgement and – yes – impartiality. Right-wing journalism, on the other hand, seems to regard its mission in life as tirelessly to evangelise on behalf of the conservative world view and to excoriate all unbelievers as the spawn of Satan.

Can anyone seriously believe that the shortcomings of British television news and current affairs programmes are really going to be remedied by injecting the kind of brutishly populist news values that make Fox such a disgrace to broadcast journalism – and which have already given the UK some of the worst newspapers in the world? Newspapers whose readership has fallen by 25 per cent in the last 40 years, and which, according to a recent Eurobarometer poll, are trusted by a mere 24 per cent of the population. ❏

Julian Petley is chair of the Campaign for Press and Broadcasting Freedom

THE ORANGE INDEX DEBATE

PANELLISTS KAMILA SHAMSIE, HOWARD JACOBSON AND PETER HITCHENS DISAGREE PROFOUNDLY OVER THE RIGHT TO FREEDOM OF MOVEMENT

MIGRATE OR DIE:

Should freedom of movement be a human right?

MIGRATE OR DIE

KAMILA SHAMSIE

'EVERYONE HAS THE RIGHT TO SEEK AND TO ENJOY IN OTHER COUNTRIES ASYLUM FROM PERSECUTION' — UNIVERSAL DECLARATION OF HUMAN RIGHTS, ARTICLE 14

'Bogus asylum seekers'. What does the term mean? It means: here are people who want refuge in Britain but (oh, perfidy!) can't prove they were forced to leave their countries in fear for their lives – torture, imprisonment or some equally hideous fate.

It means, quite probably, they're just economic migrants – people who have come to the UK to leech off its social services, take jobs and public housing away from its residents, create massive crowding in its urban centres. And all this while remaining wilfully un-British.

Is it possible to counter these claims by insisting that economic deprivation is itself a form of persecution? That it falls under Article 14 of the UN Declaration of Human Rights? Is it possible to argue that the threat of starvation, of malnourishment, of being forced to send your children to work in factories and farmlands from the age of three, is evidence of the 'cruel and inhumane' treatment of a particular group – the poor and downtrodden of a nation? Can persecution in the passive – indifference, incompetence, venality – be just as insidious and sinister as its more familiar active form? The persecution that is driven by a focused, malignant intent – armed men breaking down your door, for instance.

Yes. And yes again.

If a nation fails to provide its citizens with an existence worthy of human dignity, who can argue with their right to seek it out elsewhere? But of course, the argument against the free movement of economic migrants never explicitly denies people the right to leave their countries of nationality and go elsewhere – the argument merely says let the elsewhere be not-here.

Those who seek to restrict economic migration will doubtless say: 'It's not that we think people should starve, or children be forced to inhale toxic fumes in factories without ventilation; we're just saying it's not our problem. We're just saying, we need to put ourselves first, or we'll be flooded.'

Oh, yes. The flood of refugees. The great onslaught.

What great onslaught?

No one can convincingly argue that Britain today is collapsing under the weight of asylum seekers. All the hysteria is around the projections, the fear of a trend being established that will lead to all sorts of horrors. Well, for every projection there's a counter-projection. For every insistence that London will be overrun with asylum seekers placing unreasonable demands on the city's infrastructure and causing its collapse, others point out that ageing populations and static growth rates, combined with an increase in white-collar workers, mean there's a need for economic migration to fill the gaps that are being created.

What, really, is the fear at the heart of the anti-immigrant discourse?

Is it that the entire population of the developing world will arrive in the UK? Unlikely. Asylum seekers are more likely to go to the nearest place of refuge – because it's cheaper to get there and because it's closer to home in ways that mitigate the process of alienation. While sections of the UK press last year were claiming that the UK had become a haven for asylum seekers, the country with the greatest refugee crisis was Afghanistan. Only 9,000 came to the UK; over 200,000 went to Pakistan.

As the UK isn't exactly surrounded by nations on the cusp of famine and economic disaster it seems unlikely that it's going to face anything like the problems Pakistan faced through the 1980s and 1990s when the official Afghan refugee numbers crossed the 3 million mark in the space of 15 years – with the United Nations High Commission for Refugees acknowledging that vast numbers of refugees who crossed the porous border were simply never counted. Having lived in Pakistan through this time, I've more than once wondered why it is that I hear so much more about the asylum seeker crisis in the UK than I ever did in Pakistan – a country far less able than the UK to cope with such a sharp influx of refugees.

And the answer, the simple unmistakable answer, lies in one word that is at the very heart of this asylum argument: race.

The natives are coming. For God's sake, don't let them in.

At university I studied eighteenth- and nineteenth-century imperial texts in which the portrayal of Africans, Asians and Arabs as inferior and in need of civilising bolstered claims to imperial expansion. Today, I can still hear the same language in discussions of asylum seekers. The difference is that now it's not being used as an incentive to go out and conquer the world, but rather as a reason to erect the barricades and keep the world out.

It's worth mentioning that there is a connection between those days of Empire and the current state of the world. Between 1947 and 1974, as the British pulled out of their colonies, arbitrarily created administrative boundaries became national boundaries, resulting in states with inbuilt instability. This would be problematic in the best of circumstances, but in the post-Empire world of the Cold War it was disastrous. The post-colonial states became pawns for the USSR and the USA, their governments (often undemocratic) bolstered with the economic and military aid they desperately needed precisely because of their inherent instability.

And when the Cold War ended, the superpowers rapidly pulled out, cutting off the aid, leaving nations such as Somalia and Rwanda and Afghanistan to implode.

I don't raise this to evoke imperial guilt, but to assert the need for responsibility and an understanding of how this absurdly imbalanced world of ours got to be the way it is and why all those asylum seekers are compelled to risk their lives to go to countries that might just be able to restore to them that basic requirement – human dignity.

Where does all this leave us? In a world of consequences. As the past has brought Britain to this present – this complicated present without easy answers but with an absolute need clearly to see and state the problems that exist without hiding behind a smokescreen of racist imagery and apocalyptic predictions – so the choices Britain makes now will define the arguments of the next decades. The most crucial choice that seems to be facing the Western world at this point is whether or not to let fear govern decisions.

Should fear of the outsider, of the possible-terrorist, of foreign leeches govern this nation's choices as it defines itself in a rapidly changing world?

Is it better to turn away 1,000 people who only want security and who will work for it, than risk letting in one whose purpose in coming here is altogether more nefarious?

Is it better to cling to already outdated ideas of who you are and what you look like than to accept that there is a need to redefine what it means to be British in the twenty-first century?

There is much that needs to be worked out in the migration debate – but it must start with this belief: if you lock the doors, you only lock yourself in. ❏

Kamila Shamsie's *most recent book is* Kartography *(Bloomsbury, 2002)*

HOME, HEIMAT, HAIMISH

HOWARD JACOBSON

I WAS BROUGHT UP NOT TO TRY THE
NERVES OF THOSE WHO WERE NOT AS
I AM, TO WHOM WE OWED OUR SAFETY,
AND WHO, AT THE VERY LEAST, WERE
HERE BEFORE WE WERE

It is a terrible thing to love only yourself, to rejoice only in the reflection you see in the faces of those who look and think like you. It is a pathology.

It is a wonderful thing to love others more than yourself, to be happy only when your own likeness is expunged – but it, too, is a pathology.

Between these two pathologies we clatter about our business, making or not making war, loving or not loving our enemy, welcoming or not welcoming that ultimate otherness-figure – the migrant.

I myself have migration in my blood. I have a migrant's name. Jacobson. When my father's father's father fled the pogroms in the Ukraine he had no English with which to tell immigration officials in this country who he was. Mordechai ben Yakob was the best he could do. Mordechai son of Jacob. And sons of Jacob we became. So our family tree goes back three generations, and then the roots vanish from the earth. We are rooted in the process of migration.

I migrated, as it were a second time, in my early 20s, giving £10 to the Australian government who then shipped me in some comfort to Sydney. I wasn't fleeing war or torture – unless you call doing a PhD torture. I simply had an academic job to go to. So call me a 'career' migrant, which is a sort of subsection of economic migrant.

Since then, I have sometimes toyed with being at a loss as to where I belong and want to be, though I have never wanted to be in the Ukraine. You can develop a taste for migration: call it – for I am romantic about the condition – a migrancy of soul. Writers like that idea. 'Oh, to be in England now that April's there' – but you're not.

Home thoughts from abroad. In fact, I have no doubt where home is. I am English. I love the look of the country; relish and feel part of the national temperament; think of myself – pedantically – as a champion of the language; and admire the literature not always the right side of idolatry.

None of that, however, stops people occasionally writing to remind me that I am Jewish and therefore have the mark of Cain on me, by which they mean that I am destined to wander the earth for ever. Or until I accept Christ.

The latest of these reminders came last week, prompted, I suspect, not so much by something I had written as by the accompanying photograph. 'Many Jews,' I was reminded, 'have never integrated or assimilated into the countries which they entered – not even proselytised, thus causing friction, leading to unspeakable tragedies.'

Historically, of course, that is nonsense. The most 'unspeakable' tragedy to have befallen the Jews happened 60 years ago in Germany, where Jews had lined up to assimilate with almost unseemly haste. What caused the friction was not standoffishness but its very opposite. According to Nazi ideology, Jews had permeated German society to such a degree that they were undermining it. Like maggots in the dying body politic. Only the preferred metaphor was rats. The preferred metaphor in this country, for migrants in general, is flooding. Not as bad as infestation, but it bespeaks a similar fear of numbers. They will inundate us.

Nothing changes. There was talk of floods in England in the 1930s too. Yet here we still are, still English, still safe and dry . . . Still safeish, anyway.

Which isn't to say that the business of integration and assimilation is not problematic. I make no concessions to the prejudices of those who discern the mark of Cain on my brow, but it is true that while some Jews, as we say, 'mix in' with alacrity, some don't. So it is with Hindu, Chinese, Muslim communities. Partly you don't want to draw too much attention to yourself. You dig in, be good citizens, pay your taxes, go to war, even, for your new country, but do nothing to arouse the ire of those who might look upon you as unwelcome guests.

This is not only a matter of self-protection. It is also good manners. The idea that the migrant plays guest, initially, to someone else's host is alien, I suspect, to the spirit of the Universal Declaration of Human Rights; but there, precisely, is one of the problems of the 'right to asylum' – it de-humanises the give and take of migration, it undermines the virtues of magnanimity on the one hand and gratitude on the other.

Of course, when wars rage and persecution threatens, we cannot wait upon the uncertainties of other nations' hospitality. But this does not remove everything we mean by hospitality – goodwill, kindness, tolerance – from the equation. I was brought up not to try the nerves of those who were not as I am, to whom we owed our safety, and who, at the very least, were here before we were. That one cannot go about forever beholden, I agree, but I make this claim for the citizens of the country granting the asylum: their feelings in the matter are not irrelevant; their perturbations, while sometimes fanciful, are also sometimes real; and their scepticism, while a function of their suspiciousness, is no less a function of their intelligence.

I am not myself vexed because some migrants are in flight from poverty or even boredom, rather than torture. You don't like your own country? You don't like its climate or the films it make? Fine, I say. Come to ours. You are an economic migrant? Make yourself at home. Your desire to improve your material circumstances is laudable and in line with our political system. We all want to improve our material circumstances here.

But it's easy for me. I am not disadvantaged or neglected; the conditions of my life do not lead me into invidious comparison.

When it comes to issues of public safety, however, here in the detested West, I am one with everybody else. Our fears that we are making entry easy for people bent on our destruction are not allayed, either by the argument that only a small minority of them want to kill us, or that they will come in, anyway, by some other means. Inglorious such suspicions are, and unglamorous, compared to the romantic exile, the incumbent citizen, frightened for his life and property. But we should love others and our own equally. And attend to the anxieties of both. ❏

Howard Jacobson is a novelist and critic. His latest novel Who's Sorry Now? *is published in paperback by Vintage on 3 April. He writes a weekly column for the* Independent

THE END OF BRITAIN

PETER HITCHENS

WHAT IS THIS MULTICULTURAL SOCIETY IN
WHICH WE LIVE? PARALLEL LIVES STARING
AT EACH OTHER ACROSS THE UNMARKED
BOUNDARIES OF A CULTURAL DIVIDE

There is a strong moral case for strict border controls and severe limits on immigration. A country is the only unit in which it is possible for people to be effectively unselfish to their neighbours. Without its shared culture and loyalty, there can be no shared law, no shared willingness to pay taxes or accept authority, no free nation capable of protecting its own people from danger within and without, and of sheltering those fleeing from oppression elsewhere.

This argument often goes unsaid because of the semi-official ideological censorship now operating in most Western countries, which is called political correctness and which smears all dissenting views, usually as 'racist'. It is important that those genuinely concerned with freedom and with the defence of civilisation armour themselves against this foolish attempt to suppress free debate, and perhaps reconsider positions taken more because they are modish than because they are defensible with truth and reason.

The very idea that there can be such a person as a refugee or an asylum seeker depends on the existence of different countries that can be reached and of borders that can be crossed. If the whole globe were placed under the same authority, there would be nowhere on this earth that could shelter those who disagreed with that authority. But the existence of different countries is not enough. If they are to offer sanctuary to those persecuted elsewhere, some of those countries must have free institutions, the rule of law and a respect for freedom of speech and debate. What would be the use of fleeing, say, from North Korea to China?

Those conditions do not just appear by magic. Historically, those nations that have been able to create this sort of liberty – and to sustain it – have grown up in isolation from their neighbours. Almost all major civilisations have in fact developed behind physical barriers – oceans, deserts or mountains. These barriers do not necessarily isolate them from ideas or knowledge, any more than they isolate them from trade. It is ridiculous to suggest that a country that has no major immigration is therefore a closed and static society, or how can we explain the extraordinary flourishing of art, philosophy, science and knowledge in general in the British Isles between, say, 1500 and 1900?

However, these barriers can and do protect them from foreign invasion, from imperial repression and from enforced orthodoxy. The English common law, habeas corpus, the jury system, parliamentary democracy, the Anglican religious compromise and its accompanying tolerance, freedom of the press and the extraordinarily flexible and expressive English language in which these ideas were so effectively clothed would not have come into being except on these islands, or survived for long without the protection of the sea.

It is thanks to these unique developments, some of them exported to the USA, Canada, India, Australia and New Zealand, that this country has for centuries been a refuge. It is because we were able to preserve these things that we were able to re-export them more than once to Continental Europe, where a lack of natural borders made experiments in liberty a good deal more perilous. It is true that many other European countries now have comparable freedoms, but few have had them for an unbroken period of more than 50 years and several for even less. Liberty and law only really exist once they have taken root in the minds and lives of people and this takes time.

By the way, the survival of essentially English ideas of freedom elsewhere has often been something of a struggle, perhaps because other cultures and traditions are not so happy with them. The US Constitution is even now under grave threat from a serious assault on its principles in the Patriot Act, and in the shameful withdrawal of habeas corpus from the prisoners in Guantanamo Bay. Thomas Jefferson and the – English – gentlemen who drew up the Bill of Rights would, I think, be concerned and disturbed by these things.

To return to the main point, a society can be destabilised and upset by many things, invasion and subjugation being the most extreme. But mass movements of populations can have a similar effect – and certainly did so when Angles, Saxons and Jutes, not to mention Danes, arrived in what is now this country in the pre-Norman period. But it is quite false to describe, as some do, this country as a 'nation of immigrants'. Since 1066 it has been nothing of the kind. There have been several migrations, mostly highly successful but all limited and finite. The famous Huguenot immigration after 1681, for instance, totalled 50,000. About 250,000 Jews from Russia and Eastern Europe arrived here between 1880 and 1914. A further 60,000 Jews fled from the Nazis to Britain in the 1930s. Roughly 30,000 Asians fled from Uganda in the 1970s. Between 1955 and 1962, immigration from the entire British Commonwealth is thought to have totalled no more than 472,000.

None of these migrations was remotely as large, or as unlimited, as the current level of uncontrolled illegal immigration, which has been conservatively estimated at 100,000 a year and may well be greater, since official records are so inadequate.

Many of these past migrations were highly successful, though not all of them have been problem-free. In some places, early hopes of integration have been more or less abandoned and the children and grandchildren of migrants live in effectively segregated conditions, solitudes staring at each other across unmarked boundaries. Faced with this, many on the left have sought to make it permanent, seeking to transform Britain into what they call a multicultural society. But this has actually turned out to be a society with no culture at all, in which British history, traditions, customs and literature have been deliberately forgotten and even suppressed (a process I described in my 1999 book *The Abolition of Britain*). Continued uncontrolled immigration from cultures quite different from our own will accelerate this process. How long will English liberties, which make this country a place of asylum, survive this experience? I fear they are already weakening, as we cease to be a country and become no more than a place where various different people happen to live, without a history or a joint ideal. Who can want this? ❏

Peter Hitchens is a columnist with the Mail on Sunday, *UK*

**This is one of seven recent debates, set up by *Index* in universities around Britain, on subjects ranging from war reporting to drugs. The debates were sponsored by Orange
For full debates ⇨ www.orangeindex.co.uk**

'They that can give up essential liberty to obtain a little temporary safety deserve neither liberty nor safety' Benjamin Franklin

NOAM CHOMSKY ON
ROGUE STATES

EDWARD SAID ON
IRAQI SANCTIONS

LYNNE SEGAL ON
PORNOGRAPHY

... all in  INDEX

SUBSCRIBE & SAVE

UK and overseas

○ **Yes! I want to subscribe to *Index*.**

❐ 1 year (4 issues)   £32   Save 16%

❐ 2 years (8 issues)   £60   Save 21%

❐ 3 years (12 issues)   £84   **You save 26%**

Name

Address

B0B5

£ _____ enclosed.   ❐ Cheque (£)   ❐ Visa/MC   ❐ Am Ex   ❐ Bill me
(Outside of the UK, add £10 a year for foreign postage)

Card No.

Expiry   Signature

❐ I do not wish to receive mail from other companies.

INDEX

✉ Freepost: INDEX, 33 Islington High Street, London N1 9BR
☎ (44) 171 278 2313   Fax: (44) 171 278 1878
e tony@indexoncensorship.org

SUBSCRIBE & SAVE

North America

○ **Yes! I want to subscribe to *Index*.**

❐ 1 year (4 issues) $48   Save 12%

❐ 2 years (8 issues) $88   Save 19%

❐ 3 years (12 issues) $120   **You save 26%**

Name

Address

B0B5

$ _____ enclosed.   ❐ Cheque ($)   ❐ Visa/MC   ❐ Am Ex   ❐ Bill me

Card No.

Expiry   Signature

❐ I do not wish to receive mail from other companies.

 **INDEX**

 ✉ Freepost: INDEX, 708 Third Avenue, 8th Floor, New York, NY 10017
☎ (44) 171 278 2313   Fax: (44) 171 278 1878
e tony@indexoncensorship.org

Radio Free Maine

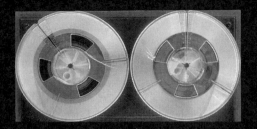

VOICES OF THE LEFT
UNEDITED & UNCENSORED

Radio Free Maine is an unparalleled living archive
of audio and video tapes featuring some of the
United States' most critical and dissenting voices.
NOAM CHOMSKY, HOWARD ZINN and **RALPH NADER**
recorded live at conferences and public appearances.

AUDIO TAPES
1–3 tapes: $10 each post paid to US • 4 or more: $8 each post paid to US
Postage: Canada and Mexico, add $1 per tape; all other countries, add $2

VIDEO TAPES
1–3 tapes: $20 each post paid to US • 4 or more: $19 each post paid to US
Postage: Canada and Mexico, add $2 per tape; all other countries, add $3

Payment (USA funds) must accompany order
Allow about two weeks for delivery
Free catalog with every order

For a catalog of **Radio Free Maine** audio and video tapes, please send
a self-addressed envelope, stamped with $1 postage

Please make check/money order payable to ROGER LEISNER and send to
P.O. BOX 2705, AUGUSTA, MAINE 04338

For more information go to www.radiofreemaine.com

Tarifa, Spain, 2001: African immigrants celebrate their safe arrival on European soil.
Credit: Stuart Franklin / Magnum Photos

DOUBLE CROSSINGS: MIGRATION NOW

RL STEVENSON SAID IT WAS BETTER TO TRAVEL HOPEFULLY THAN TO ARRIVE; TODAY'S MIGRANTS ARE LUCKY TO ARRIVE SAFELY

STRANGERS KNOW US BEST
FELIPE FERNÁNDEZ-ARMESTO

THE CARELESS BRITISH POSE A
GREATER THREAT TO BRITISHNESS
THAN ANY NUMBER OF WILLING
MIGRANTS TO THEIR SHORES

All history is the history of migrations. All of us got to where we are because we or our ancestors came from somewhere else. England's prehistoric 'Cheddar Man', according to DNA tests, still has local ancestors, 10,000 years after his death; but even he and his own progenitors reached what is now Britain only in the course of a long process of migration 'out of Africa', which peopled the recesses of the Earth. Humans have occupied just about every habitable environment on the planet for about 14,000 years, but migrations did not stop when they reached their present limits. Some peoples doubled back on themselves; others launched new endeavours across continents and oceans. Some migrations were violent and destructive, exploiting or extinguishing incumbent peoples and ways of life. Others helped host communities, bringing new skills, new vigour, demographic infill and fresh ideas.

Britain has generated destructive migrations to other parts of the world; indeed, the British have been responsible for some of the most conspicuous and disruptive mass migrations of the last half-millennium, exporting elites, reshuffling workforces, transporting slaves and indentured labour. But population movements that have ended up in Britain – even when they came with conquerors – have nearly always been broadly benign in their long-term effects. It seems incredible that people who pride themselves on descent from 'Saxon and Norman and Dane' should be unaware of the value of immigrants; or that zeal for barriers should thrive in a country so enriched in modern history by infusions, for instance, of Irish, Huguenots, Jews and black and Asian 'counter-colonists' from the former empire. Yet racism and migrant-phobia are rife. British governments, with remarkable consistency since the 1960s, have behaved towards would-be migrants with a repugnant mixture of hypocrisy, faithlessness, demagogy, moral indifference and outright cruelty. The present government is, by a clear margin, the worst of the lot, stimulating racism by means of insidious rhetoric, which turns refugees into 'bogus asylum seekers' and demonises 'economic migrants', who, in reality, are often the sort of go-ahead adventurers capitalism needs. Governments seem keener to appeal to that ineradicable British vice, xenophobia, than to that withering British virtue, a sense of fair play. Opposition to immigration is historically ignorant.

Now I do not want to deny that there is a rational case for immigration to be controlled – or, at least, for governments to have power to control it when necessary. Freedom of access is not just the doctrine of liberals: it is also upheld by greedy employers who want to renew an exploitable labour-pool. Access policies – especially of the selective kind we have now but also those unregulated except by the market – can leech talent from the developing world via a 'brain drain'. Immigration controls foment racism – but so does immigration, if it exceeds a variable but always critical threshold. History has few lessons but one of them is that minorities get victimised when their numbers are seen to increase.

These arguments should make us hesitate to be dogmatic in favour of uncontrolled migration. But they are not sufficient to explain modern Britain's hostility to migrants, which greatly exceeds rationally intelligible limits. The real cause of xenophobic anxieties was revealed in David Blunkett's infamous gaffe about the potential 'swamping' of public services. On the face of it, this disclosed nervousness about the scale and distribution of the 'resources' that ministers always recall and often mention when they contemplate the escalating cost of a decent society. Underlying this apparently economic anxiety is a deeper cultural anxiety: people worry not just about the strain on resources but also about the attenuation of traditions – about Britain becoming a 'foreign' country, to recall another politician's equally alarmist phrase. I suspect – though this is a difficult proposition to test – that most British xenophobes worry more about the potential self-alienation of British culture than about Britain becoming 'coffee-coloured', if I may quote one last soundbite from the great tradition of British politicians' anti-immigration gaffes.

Now this is an irrational fear but not altogether an ignoble one. It is irrational because all cultures change all the time and the heroics of culture conservation are usually no more likely to succeed than those of species conservation or landscape conservation or the conservation of monumental buildings that have outlived their usefulness. Yet the conservationist aim is noble in all these cases. I weep for lost culture – dying religious traditions, vanished languages, unfashionable cuisines and clothes, bygone pastimes, decayed manners and discarded rites and customs – as I do for endangered animals, demolished mansions and despoiled countryside. I find it, however, odd – even outrageous – that the British blame immigrants for their present rate of cultural loss. There is no real doubt where the blame lies: with the British themselves – and more so with those Britons who were born British, with longstanding British ancestry, than with those recently ascribed to Britain.

In my lifetime, the British, among whom I have lived happily and, on the whole, admiringly, have changed unrecognisably. All the characteristics that defined Britishness when I was born – and for many generations past – have dwindled or disappeared. We are well rid of some of its tics: insularity, haughtiness, snobbishness, obsessive self-repression. But much of the old Britishness was admirable. It was rooted in romantic attachment to an idealised 'pleasant land', hedgerow-riven or heath-blasted and full of idio-syncratic species and varieties. Since then, the most ruthless, efficient, machine-intensive agriculture in Europe has raped the land. Meanwhile, trash-capitalism has made British cities drearily uniform. The famous reserve has crumbled, to be succeeded by extremes of amicability and aggression: the British abroad exhibit bare bellies, obese bums and bad manners. The stiff upper lip has gone wobbly: it slackened feebly in the mawkish reaction to the death of Diana, Princess of Wales. A new emotional candour has dissipated the pluck and coolness in crisis once felt along that reeling, rolling road from Plymouth Hoe, via Clifton Close, to the playing fields of count-less imitations of Eton. The old austerity has sold out to consumerism and trash-capitalism. Irony is in danger. Self-deprecation, which was once a gloriously British form of irony, has succumbed to feelgood-counselling. There is no more room for the deification of the amateur. The Corinthian spirit has departed from Wembley and Westminster.

Of the traditional oddities of British morality, none seems to have survived, except the power of sex scandals. Britishness was once engagingly dissident: now the obituary columns mark the passing of the last great eccentrics. Service and selflessness, which were formerly the training and totem of the establishment, have succumbed to toadyism and cronyism. The business-school ethos reigns even in the public schools. The British now persecute their old anomalies: imperial measures, historic counties, heredi-tary legislators, hunting with hounds. Cool Britannia has replaced sangfroid, warm feelings have replaced warm beer. Cool Britannia is frosty about her past. Celebrity status has overtaken respectability as the standard of esteem.

An 'underclass' has replaced the 'British worker' – the blessing and bane of a former age. Embourgeoisement has swallowed the traditional working class, to which not even the deputy prime minister will admit he belongs. Class configurations are rejigged, politics irremediably professionalised. Even the cooking has 'gone foreign'.

So Britain really has become a 'foreign country' – foreign to its former self. Yet none of this has had anything to do with the effects of immigration. Immigrants are vectors of change, which sometimes seems to threaten indigenous culture; but you can't immunise culture by excluding immigrants. On the contrary, the balance of evidence suggests that immigrants help keep Britain British. Food feeds identity and British food survives thanks largely to Italian-owned cafés. Sport is characteristic British culture: many of Britain's best athletes are black, while her cricket and soccer depend on Asians and Swedes. The British abandon their historic religions – but immigrants from the old empire help keep up Anglicanism and peculiarly British forms of radical Protestantism. Vast sections of British society have abjured tolerance – the best of Britain's traditional virtues – but most immigrants, sensing the threat, cling to it faithfully.

All the vanished and vanishing elements of British identity – good and bad alike – have been freely sacrificed by the British. The only really important help from outside has come from America, and the influence of American popular culture, which British people have received and relished with uncritical zeal.

Instead of targeting immigrants, people who want to 'keep Britain British' should work at their own Britishness. It's not a matter of being white: there's plenty of white trash in other countries. It's not a matter of how you talk English: few of the British have ever spoken it well. It's not a matter of observing the Tebbit test or the Blunkett test – these are trivial and defensive. It's nothing as vulgar as declaring allegiance: there have been many thoroughly British traitors. It's positively celebrating and maintaining the most characteristic traditions the British have inherited from the past: eating the food and playing the games – if you like – but, more importantly, practising the tolerance, relishing the eccentricity, resisting conformism and retrieving the romance. ❏

Felipe Fernández-Armesto is the author of Civilisations *(Macmillan) and teaches history at Oxford University and Queen Mary and Westfield College, London*

MIGRATION BY NUMBERS

JASON POLLARD & ANDREW SMITH

The UN estimated in 2000 that 175 million people, 3 per cent of the world's 6.1 billion people, lived outside of their country of origin.

Some 2.3 billion of the world's 3 billion workers live in developing countries.

Some 75 per cent of migrants from Africa have some college education.

The 0.1 per cent of India's population living in the US earned 10 per cent of India's GDP in 2001.

Of the world's migrants, 32 per cent (56 million) work in Europe, 29 per cent (50 million) in Asia, 23 per cent (41 million) in North America and 9 per cent (16 million) in Africa.

In 1976, only 7 per cent of UN nations had policies aimed at restricting immigration. In 2000, 40 per cent had them.

A 1994 report estimated that France required a net inflow of up to 100,000 foreign workers a year in order to fill gaps in the French labour market caused by its ageing population. In the US, 16 per cent of the population are over 60. By 2050, this will have risen to 27 per cent.

Since 1992, 800,000 out of an original population of 4 million has emigrated from Armenia.

Some 12 million people of Lebanese origin live outside Lebanon, more than in Lebanon itself. Companies owned by Lebanese émigrés generate around 60 per cent of the GDP of Côte d'Ivoire.

There are an estimated 6.4 million Filipinos employed abroad, of whom the US employs 2.1 million.

Jamaica sees 22,000 migrants leave the country each year to generate an annual US$967 million a year in remittances.

Malaysia has a total foreign workforce of 1.2 million people of whom 450,000 are in the country illegally.

There are an estimated 900,000, mainly Burmese, migrant workers in Thailand. There are 1.3 million unemployed Thais. Burmese migrant workers remitted US$300 million in 2001.

The British government's work permit scheme allowed 104,000 foreigners to fill jobs in 2001.

Britain made 118,195 asylum decisions in 2001. Nine per cent of applicants were given leave to stay in the country.

There are 120 million internal migrants in China.

In 1994, one county in rural China received US$138 million in a year from family members abroad, more than the US$115 million value of locally produced goods.

Some 45 per cent of China's population is under 26. 150 million rural Chinese are unemployed.

Of 220,000 Chinese youth who have gone abroad to study, only 75,000 have returned.

Some 700,000 people have been forced to move from their homes around Chernobyl, the Aral Sea area and the Semipalatinsk nuclear test site due to environmental or nuclear contamination.

There are 270 areas in Russia deemed unfit for human habitation.

Some 33 per cent of transit migrants through Turkey planned to use traffickers to reach their final destination.

At any one time there are an estimated 200,000 illegal migrants in Moscow, 60,000 of whom are believed to be ethnic Chinese and 40,000 South Asians.

There were a total of 4.04 million asylum application decisions worldwide between 1990 and 2000. In 2001, approximately 923,000 people applied for asylum worldwide.

The US war against the Taliban in Afghanistan added 511,000 to the country's internally displaced population (IDP), bringing the total to 1.1 million, the largest IDP population in the world. The second largest rise in IDPs was in Colombia, up 190,500 to 720,000.

Some 7.7 million of those under the care of the UN High Commission for Refugees (UNHCR) are under the age of 18.

The largest non-European community within the EU is its 1.2 million Moroccans.

By 2005, 15 per cent of the US workforce will be immigrants.

In January 2001, 6,078 unaccompanied children arrived in Britain claiming asylum. There are 80,000 refugee children in Britain.

Sources: AFP, American Museum of Natural History, webfamilytree.com, AP, *The Cambridge Survey of World Migration*, Council of Europe, *Daily Telegraph*, *The Economist*, *Far Eastern Economic Review*, *Financial Times, fiscal effects*, *Los Angeles Times*, *Migration News*, *New York Times*, OECD, Refugee Council, Reuters, Dr Martin Richards, Save the Children, *South China Morning Post*, *The Straits Times*, *Xinhua*, UK Home Office 2002 *The Migrant Population in the UK*, UK Trades Union Congress, US State Department *Annual US Country Reports on Human Rights Practices for 2001*, *Wall Street Journal*, *Washington Post*

A WEALTH OF EXPERIENCE

BOB SUTCLIFFE

THE DEMOCRATISATION OF
MIGRATION WILL TAKE US ALL
A LONG WAY TOWARDS A FAIRER
AND MORE INTEGRATED WORLD

While virtually all human beings are in some sense descended from long-distance migrants, today scarcely 2 per cent of them are migrants themselves – people who live in a country they were not born in. Is this a little or a lot? It may be quite little compared with the epochs before economic change and the invention of frontiers virtually brought nomadic lifestyles to an end. But it is quite a lot compared with the decades between the start of World War I and the end of World War II, during which nations generally closed their borders. Migration and population statistics suggest that there has been a continuous increase in the international movement of people during the last 40 years; erratically, and often in the face of governments' reluctance, borders have been opening or are being prised open.

Since international migration flows are not random, the migrant 2 per cent come disproportionately from some countries and go disproportionately to others. There is a built-in, and insufficiently examined, assumption in thinking about international migration: that it is the opposite of water, it flows (economically) uphill from poor countries to rich countries. As a result the most studied flows are those to the rich countries: to the traditional immigration countries, the US, Canada and Australia, and to Western Europe, until recently a major area of emigration. But there are also important flows into the faster developing South-East Asian countries and to oil-producing countries in the Gulf as well as numerous intra-regional cross-border flows of both workers and refugees.

It very difficult to compare the importance of immigration in different recipient or host countries since their statistics are not based on common definitions. The US, Canada, Australia and New Zealand log the proportions of their populations who were born in a foreign country – immigrants by definition. In the US, those born elsewhere form more than 10 per cent of the population, in Canada over 17 per cent and in Australia 24 per cent. Most European countries, however, provide figures based not on place of

Bamako, Mali: a migrant worker returns to his village by train.
Credit: © Patrick Zachmann / Magnum Photos

birth but on current nationality. In Europe in the year 2000 the percentage of foreign residents ranged from around two in Portugal and Spain, three in Ireland, four in the UK, five in Sweden, six in France, nine in Germany to nearly 20 in Switzerland. But some of these were not born abroad and others who have immigrated and then become naturalised are not included. Therefore, in countries with a high rate of naturalisation there can be a large gap between the numbers of foreign nationals and the numbers born elsewhere. It is possible to illustrate the difference in the case of France, a country with an intermediate rate of naturalisation of about 4.5 per cent of the foreign population per year. Unusually, it publishes figures for both categories: in 1999, 5.6 per cent of residents in France had foreign nationality but as many as 10 per cent had been born elsewhere. The gap between the two figures is likely to be less than this in Germany, Spain and the UK, countries with relatively low rates of naturalisation of less than 3 per cent, and more in the Netherlands and Sweden, with comparatively high rates of naturalisation of more than 7 per cent. In nearly all developed countries, as new immigrants enter, these percentages continue to rise, but only gradually, as they have done consistently now for several decades. (All these figures are from SOPEMI, *Trends in International Migration*, 2002 edition, OECD 2003.)

If politicians and their mentors were less hypocritical, however, international migration would be much higher than it is. Even in relation to trade and investment neo-liberal ideologies have been very selectively applied, but in relation to migration they are totally ignored. While in the case of goods and capital it is the international frontiers that have been demonised, in the case of migration it is the people who cross them. Economic migrants are reviled and governments justify restrictions on asylum applicants by accusing them of being economic migrants in disguise. Yet, despite multiple restrictions, migration has become more globalised. After World War II, when many borders were legally far more open than they are now, Western European countries received large numbers of migrants from their colonies or ex-colonies. Up to the mid-1960s, migration into the US was based on racist quota systems reflecting the ethnic national structure of the existing white populations (never the African-American or other non-European); and migrants to Australia were all white. In 1962, the UK partially closed its doors to Asian, African and Caribbean immigrants, but in the US and Australia racist rules were relaxed or abolished and the nature of immigration changed profoundly. In the US, today's immigration is from virtually everywhere except Western Europe, and Australia's is becoming similar. In this way, immigration from rich to richer countries has been partly replaced by immigration from poor to rich countries. Migrant populations today match the ethnic and social composition of world population somewhat more closely than they did 50 years ago.

International migration thus exemplifies a somewhat different kind of globalisation from that of trade or investment: the huge majority of international trade and investment is still conducted between the rich countries of the OECD; but of all the foreigners and immigrants in those countries only 45 per cent come from other OECD countries, including Mexico and South Korea; more than half are from the rest of the world (SOPEMI 2003, p42).

This may now be changing. Despite the demonisation of economic migrants, nearly all rich country governments are now engaged in a major

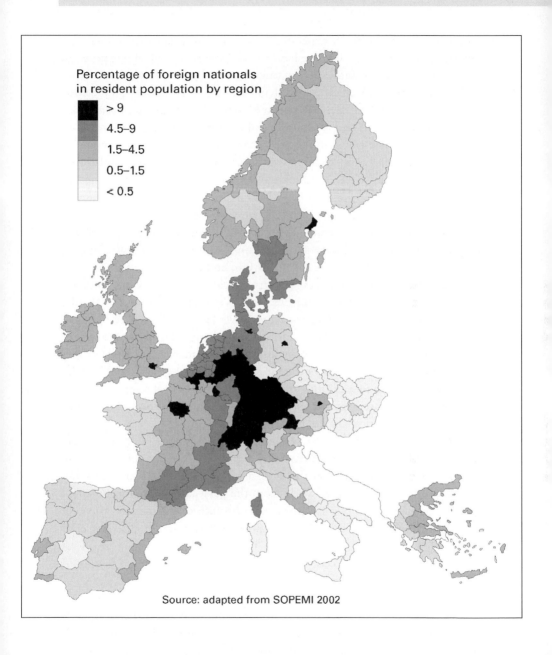

Percentage of foreign nationals
in resident population by region

> 9

4.5–9

1.5–4.5

0.5–1.5

< 0.5

Source: adapted from SOPEMI 2002

competitive drive to attract explicitly economic migrants to work in activities where skilled labour shortage hampers economic growth and exports. In both rich and poor countries, recruitment campaigns are carried out, especially for nurses and other medical personnel, information technology workers and teachers. Rules have been liberalised to facilitate international transfers of managerial and technically skilled workers between branches of multinational corporations; and foreign students are encouraged to come to study – Britain has by far the highest number in relation to its population – and then to stay and work. And many countries offer almost instant settlement to immigrants who arrive with more than a certain minimum of money to invest.

All this has begun to produce a new shift in the national composition of immigration. While in Europe most asylum applicants now come from the Middle East and Africa, in the UK from Iraq and Afghanistan according to the latest Home Office statistics, a high proportion of legal work migrants come from other developed countries. This is especially true in the UK: the five countries with the highest migration flows to the UK in 2000 were the US, Australia, India, South Africa and New Zealand. The UK is also exceptional in that over 85 per cent of its immigrants come from countries that have English as their official language, or one of them (SOPEMI 2003, pp33, 35). The vilification of economic migration is evidently not a principle but a tactic devised for use against the unwanted, relatively poor and unskilled immigrants from Africa and the Middle East.

International migration is an amalgam of many heterogeneous phenomena. The business executive transferred to an overseas branch of an international company, met at the airport by a limo and driven to his/her fancy apartment, is in another world from the persecuted and poor emigrant from an African country who must pass through transit camps, travel at night in small dangerous boats to reach a destination where his/her presence is illegal, or of the asylum applicant, perhaps forcibly detained, or at least forbidden to work and forced to live on inadequate government handouts, and with a very high chance of having his/her application refused.

There are many experiences of migration between these extremes. A growing number of statistics tell something of the story of the economic life of immigrants in Europe – immigrants again defined as resident non-nationals and not including asylum applicants. The rate of participation of male immigrants in the labour force is, with the exception of a few communities, higher than the host populations, partly because their age structure is more concentrated in the middle of the age distribution. Women who immigrate usually have a lower rate of labour force participation, including in Britain where, exceptionally, women are the majority of foreign nationals. But in Spain, Ireland, Italy and Greece they have a higher participation rate than the national population. Immigrants' unemployment levels, while similar to the national average in the US and Canada, are generally higher in Europe; in Britain, for example, the unemployment rate among foreign workers is 70 per cent higher than the national figure (SOPEMI 2003, pp43–4, 60, 68).

The allocation of immigrant workers between economic sectors is not strikingly different from that of the workforce as a whole, although in most countries there is a somewhat disproportionate concentration of foreigners in particular sectors: in the US it is in retail and wholesale trade; in Spain, Greece and Italy in domestic service, in the UK and Scandinavian countries in health and education. Immigrant workers in nearly all countries are more likely to have temporary jobs than workers as a whole but they are no more likely to have part-time jobs or second jobs (SOPEMI 2003, pp63–4). Information about wages is very scant. But in the rather special case of Britain it is likely that wages are closely tied to the education levels of immigrants, about which there is considerable information. Thirty per cent of immigrants have received no more than basic secondary education, compared with 18 per cent for the whole population. Yet at the same time 41 per cent are graduates of tertiary institutions, compared with only 28 per cent for the population as a whole. Foreign residents, then, are collectively both less educated and more educated than the national average. Such a bipolar structure of education is no doubt associated with a bipolar structure of jobs and wages. It implies that there are a sizeable number of immigrants receiving both less than and more than national average pay levels. This is an increasingly common result of a pattern of immigration that embraces flows from just about every type of country and at the same time gives special encouragement to the immigration of highly skilled workers (SOPEMI 2003, p45).

The general assumption of an unambiguous, one-way relationship between poverty and international migration leads to various expectations: that the poorer the country, the more incentive there will be to emigrate; that migration is likely to be from poorer to richer countries; that more development and wealth will reduce emigration; and that migration from poor to rich countries will tend to promote more international equality.

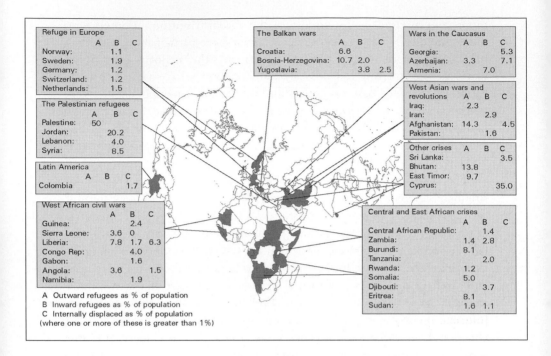

Refuge in Europe

	A	B	C
Norway:	1.1		
Sweden:	1.9		
Germany:	1.2		
Switzerland:	1.2		
Netherlands:	1.5		

The Palestinian refugees

	A	B	C
Palestine:	50		
Jordan:		20.2	
Lebanon:		4.0	
Syria:		8.5	

Latin America

	A	B	C
Colombia			1.7

West African civil wars

	A	B	C
Guinea:		2.4	
Sierra Leone:	3.6	0	
Liberia:	7.8	1.7	6.3
Congo Rep:		4.0	
Gabon:		1.6	
Angola:	3.6		1.5
Namibia:		1.9	

The Balkan wars

	A	B	C
Croatia:	6.6		
Bosnia-Herzegovina:	10.7	2.0	
Yugoslavia:		3.8	2.5

Wars in the Caucasus

	A	B	C
Georgia:			5.3
Azerbaijan:	3.3		7.1
Armenia:		7.0	

West Asian wars and revolutions

	A	B	C
Iraq:	2.3		
Iran:		2.9	
Afghanistan:	14.3		4.5
Pakistan:		1.6	

Other crises

	A	B	C
Sri Lanka:			3.5
Bhutan:	13.8		
East Timor:	9.7		
Cyprus:			35.0

Central and East African crises

	A	B	C
Central African Republic:		1.4	
Zambia:		1.4	2.8
Burundi:	8.1		
Tanzania:		2.0	
Rwanda:		1.2	
Somalia:	5.0		
Djibouti:			3.7
Eritrea:	8.1		
Sudan:		1.6	1.1

A Outward refugees as % of population
B Inward refugees as % of population
C Internally displaced as % of population
(where one or more of these is greater than 1%)

These are not all completely false; but greater knowledge of actual migration flows makes them look oversimplified.

One thing that is certainly true is that even a poorly paid migrant worker in a rich country can contribute significantly to the welfare of an even poorer family in his/her country of origin. Some migration is definitely equalising in this way. World Bank figures suggest that in 2000, at a minimum, US$63 billion was sent home by migrant workers. This total is considerably more than all the official aid given by all the rich governments of the world to poorer countries and multilateral development agencies. Twenty countries received more than US$1 billion each. India was first with US$11 billion, followed by Mexico, Turkey and Egypt. These migrants' funds were equivalent to more than 10 per cent of exports for 26 countries; for a few such as Eritrea, Cape Verde, Albania, Jordan, Yemen, El Salvador and Nicaragua they add up to more than one-third of exports. In Jordan, these remittances are worth more than one-fifth of the national income, and in a further 32 countries they amount to more than 2 per cent (World Bank, *World Development Indicators 2002*, CD-Rom edition).

These remittances help the economies of poor countries: they provide scarce foreign exchange, they can increase the level of demand for locally produced goods, and they are often spent on health and education. More directly they make an indispensable contribution to millions of families' survival in dozens of countries. That does not mean that they always go to the poorest families, though they are probably more equitably distributed than most official development aid.

But emigrants seldom come from the very poorest countries or the very poorest families and social classes. Emigration in the first instance can be costly and emigrants often need quite large sums to finance the journey and installation costs. Considerably more will be needed if they do not have recognised papers, work permits and so on.

Moreover, developed countries are increasingly pursuing immigration policies that polarise rather than equalise. They facilitate the migration of skilled and highly paid workers and managers but they are strewing more and more obstacles in the path of needier immigrants. The more illegal a migrant is the greater are not only the economic costs of financing the journey, but also the dangers of not surviving the journey or of being cheated, exploited, indentured or even enslaved by 'traffickers' and un-scrupulous employers. These ills, often presented as the results of immigra-tion itself, are in fact the consequences of its illegality for poor, oppressed and isolated people. Illegality and the threat of denunciation to the authori-ties, followed by detention or deportation, reduce the bargaining power of illegal workers, and so indirectly of all workers. In the short term, therefore, the removal of immigration restrictions would be one of the most positive steps that developed countries could take to increase social justice and decrease world inequality.

Even if immigrants have the right to be where they are, they frequently lack other elementary civic and political rights such as the right to vote. For this and related reasons migration, even when legal, can reduce the level of democracy and thereby intensify inequalities. A priority for a more demo-cratic and egalitarian approach to migration therefore would be to accelerate the acquisition of political rights, including naturalisation, by foreign resi-dents.

The formidable size of political opposition to increasing the rights of immigrants leads some supporters of greater equality to urge a large increase of development aid to poorer countries to increase incomes and jobs and so reduce the urge to emigrate. But this argument, however well intentioned, implicitly accepts the prejudice against immigration; and in any case it also once again assumes an oversimplified relationship between poverty and migration. In fact, faster development usually seems to stimulate rather than to reduce immigration, since it provides more people with the means with which to finance migration and multiplies the economic and social ties with developed countries that facilitate migration. Arguments for more generous development aid should be sought elsewhere.

Decisions to migrate are not taken by the mythical individuals of economic theory. Much migration is a cause and a consequence of the burgeoning of millions of multinational families, as well as multinational communities of many kinds, ethnic, linguistic and so on. This transformation, which so revolts cultural conservatives who wish to maintain the purity of national and local cultures, undermines another aspect of the oversimplified view of migration flows – the idea that people do not really want to migrate but would always be happier to stay in their 'own' place if only they had more money. But millions of people now have more than one 'own' place, and these places may be thousands of miles apart. Faster and cheaper transportation and communication mean that emigration no longer entails, as it so often did in the nineteenth century, a permanent separation from family, friends and culture and entry into a completely new life; it is more and more an aspect of two-way international mobility. This is the main reason why dual citizenship is such an important right for many people.

A dominant issue in discussions about migration and world inequality has always been the 'brain drain', the idea that migration from poor to rich countries involves a permanent loss of valuable human resources. World salary differentials combined with the present drive to import skilled labour may sometimes make it very difficult for some poor countries to afford their own skilled workers. Often there are domestic reasons for the under-use of skills in poor countries. Two-way migrants who develop their personal skills can put them to use in their country of origin when they return.

The popularity of the brain drain argument is greater than the evidence warrants; perhaps this is partly because, like the aid argument, it provides an apparently pro-development cover for arguments opposing migration.

A growing anti-immigration coalition in politics, the media, academia and think-tanks is based on the idea that migration is pathological and blames migrants for an awful lot – for diluting national cultures, for damaging the labour markets and overburdening the social services of the recipient countries, for failing to make their due contribution to the development of their countries of origin, for crime, for terrorism, for environmental damage and much else. When they ask for jobs they are denounced for greed; when they ask for asylum they are condemned as bogus. The developed recipient countries, the coalition argues, are full and immigration must stop. These arguments employ systematically exaggerated estimates and projections of the number of immigrants and empirical arguments of very dubious validity. The answer to them is not to minimise the numbers: that implicitly accepts the assumption that migration is bad; and it conceals the inevitable conclusion that more democratic, egalitarian and just immigration, asylum and nationality laws would undoubtedly lead to more immigration and not less. Nor is the answer to counter tendentious arguments about the bad effects of migration with equally tendentious arguments about its good effects. Migration is a heterogeneous phenomenon with evidently contradictory effects. But on balance, and despite the ordeals endured by many immigrants, its growth is a benign development. A radical democratisation of its rules, however, would allow it to contribute a great deal more to a fairer and more integrated world. ❑

Bob Sutcliffe is an economist specialising in development and immigration, who teaches at the University of the Basque Country in Bilbao

DIRE STRAITS

AFVIC

According to the Moroccan Association des amis et familles des victimes de l'immigration clandestine (Association of friends and families of victims of clandestine immigration; AFVIC), 100,000–110,000 people a year try to cross the Strait of Gibraltar and the dangerous waters between Morocco and the Spanish Canary Islands to reach Europe. Last year, AFVIC conducted a survey of 600 Moroccans aged under 30 to discover what motivated their desire to move away. Their findings show that plans to leave emerge in childhood and become an obsession by young adulthood. Although 85 per cent of primary schoolchildren are optimistic about the future, this drops to 6 per cent among young people without regular incomes; the corresponding figures are 21 per cent at *lycée* level and 25 per cent in universities. Some 71 per cent of young people without steady incomes believe their living conditions are inadequate and only 8 per cent of them believe their circumstances will improve; by contrast, 87 per cent of primary schoolchildren believe things will get better.

Uncertainties increase as adulthood approaches; the desire to migrate grows accordingly. All those interviewed want to visit Europe and believe their lives would be better there. Of the *lycée* students, 82 per cent expressed a desire to move to Europe, compared with 94 per cent of young people without stable incomes and only 19 per cent of those with steady jobs; 62 per cent of the employed describe themselves as willing to risk relocating without a visa, as illegal immigrants. ❏

Translated from Le Monde diplomatique *by Gulliver Cragg*

Tarifa, Spain, 2000: travelling towards Europe. Sub-Saharan Africans aboard a patera

All photographs by Michel Lozano

Above: Tarifa: waiting for the police van

Opposite: Playa de Los Lances, Spain: a patera
with over 30 people on board has capsized

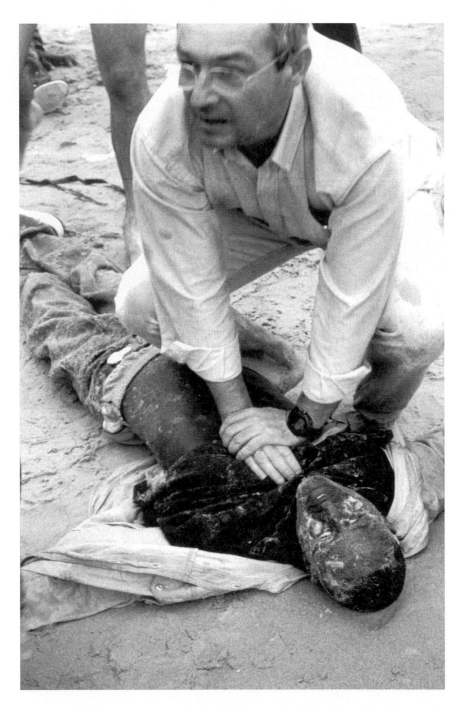

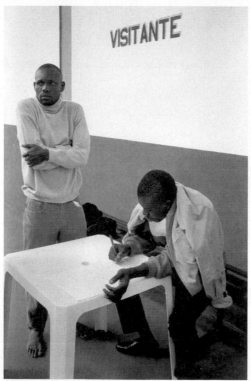

Above: Bolonia Beach, Spain: caught by the National Guard

Left: Tarifa: waiting for the National Guard, who will take photographs, statements and fingerprints

Right: the 'clandestine' immigrant's hands are marked. Letters specify where they were captured; numbers represent the order in which they were caught

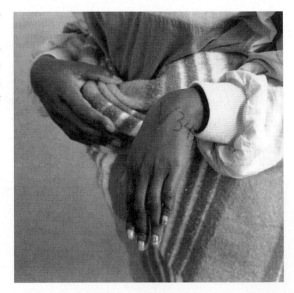

Below: Campo del Rio Oro, Melilla, Spain: a migrant brings meat to the camp that he found in the rubbish

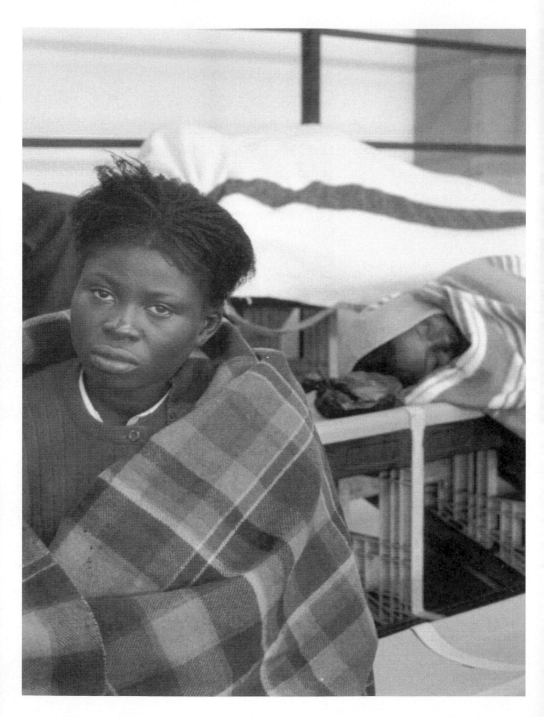

At Campo del Rio Oro, Melilla, Spain

Opposite: in Tarifa the cells are full of North Africans, so sub-Saharan Africans are taken to one of the town's gymnasiums

CROSSING THE LINE

ROBIN COHEN

ONE CONSEQUENCE OF GLOBALISATION IS
THE GROWTH OF A MORE COSMOPOLITAN
APPROACH TO LIFE: A BENIGN SUBVERSION
OF NATIONALISM OF ALL KINDS

We funnelled out of a flight from New York towards the immigration desks at Heathrow. At the time, the channels were labelled 'UK and Commonwealth', 'European Economic Community' and 'Other'. 'But where should I go?' demanded a perfectly groomed American woman with expensive hand luggage. 'Other,' replied my wife, rather tartly. The woman jerked back, astounded at the thought of being so categorised.

While the American's reaction was openly and innocently indignant, we all experience a sense of quiet unease or anxiety as we approach an immigration officer in an unfamiliar country. Many officers are no doubt perfectly charming people who don their slippers and stroke their cats when they get home from work. Others behave like cardboard Hitlers. Often underpaid and working unsocial hours, immigration officers derive their occupational power from being the 'frontier guards' of national identities. The turnstiles they protect are symbolic gateways to belonging and acceptance. If the light is green we are wanted and feel relieved. By contrast, being stopped or deported can be interpreted as what Lévi-Strauss called 'anthropemy' (from the Greek *emein*, to vomit), the ejection of dangerous individuals from the social body.

The passport we carry is normally the key to determining a 'stop' or 'go' at a frontier. William the Conqueror is said to have invented the document in the wake of his successful invasion of southern England. Concluding that it was all too easy for someone to emulate him, William nominated five exclusive ports of entry (the Cinque Ports of Hastings, Romney, Dover, Hythe and Sandwich). The process of passing through these points gave birth to the word 'passport'. Though eleventh-century in their origin, passports were not widespread until 1914, when they became one way of separating out the combatants in the confused circumstances of war-torn continental Europe.

Galice, Spain: tourism, the new migration.
Credit: Martin Parr / Magnum Photos

Nationalists have always needed strong frontier controls and stony-faced sentinels because identities are much more fragmented and overlapping than their fantasies or historical reconstructions allow. For the pure nationalist a process of ethno-genesis has taken place (often in the pre-historical past and with divine or biblical sanction). In this reconstruction, a particular 'race' is meant to inhabit a particular space, to the exclusion of all others. Even the most naive cursory appreciation of the history of migration (reinforced now by the evidence of the Human Genome Project) demonstrates a more plausible alternative proposition. Humankind has a common origin in Africa and intermingling, plurality and segmentation based on non-biological markers characterise its subsequent dispersion and settlement patterns.

The idea that nations are socially, not somatically, constructed reached its apogee in Benedict Anderson's oft-cited book *Imagined Communities* (1983). In fact Anderson, or perhaps more precisely the epigones who casually referred to his book, rather over-egged the constructionist custard. Incommensurate languages, religions, histories, political institutions and, as Anderson himself emphasised, appeals to a common culture through the medium of print, *have* created distinct societies. Often, too, there are phenotypical differences. One does not have to be a Nazi to observe that most Finns look different from most Malians. By recognising the weight of ethnonationalism and the heritage of ethnocentricity, we are better able to gauge the strength of cultural, economic and linguistic imperialism, as well as the political and military hegemony of the USA – forces often borne by incremental technological means and trading ties. By contrast, we can also better describe the major bearers of the new pluralism – namely migrants who generate an enhanced social diversity and complexity and who provide major challenges to the national identities of all societies, particularly Western industrialised ones.

Despite more guards, more laws and more restrictions, the symbolic and real boundaries that divide societies are eroding. This is a result of ideas, images, money, music, electronic messages, sport, fashion and religions that can move without people, or without many people – forms, if you like, of virtual migration. But nothing is as disturbing to national societies as the movement of people. It is perhaps useful to think here about population mobility in general, including tourists – though tourists are not normally considered as migrants. From 1950 to 1990 the volume of tourist arrivals across the world increased by 17 times. There was a modest fall in 2001 as a consequence of the fear of flying following the terrorist attacks in New York on 11 September 2001, but 'arrivals' are now up again, reaching 715 million in 2002. It is important to recognise the sheer size of the movement: it is as if every member of the entire population of Britain each had 12 holidays a year. But as salient as the numbers is the increasing exoticism of the destinations, particularly to the tropical world, which leads to major cultural and social effects. Well-intentioned but mulish visitors demand familiar goods, services and forms of entertainment, stipulations that serve to cover isolated societies like a cultural oil slick. More and more people are drawn into the web of tourism as participants, service agents or objects of a tourist gaze. Few societies can remain unaffected by the scale and intensity of such cultural contacts.

Nor should we forget other kinds of mobility, such as people on religious pilgrimages (millions go to Mecca or Lourdes each year) or the movement of troops during war, or the prelude to war (think of current US military deployments). The impact of such forms of mobility is often overlooked; because the predominant focus of political sensitivity and social unease are is, without question, migrants who are thought to be potential settlers. Despite the disquiet surrounding such migrants, numbers alone do not provide irrefutable evidence of a necessarily major impact. Take the example of the USA. While the proportion of the foreign-born population reached a 90-year high in 2000 at 10 per cent (26.4 million people), it was considerably short of the 14.7 per cent record achieved in 1910. (The low was 4.3 per cent in 1970.) However, the turn of a century has seen a huge qualitative change in the reception of immigrants. In 1910, the USA was committed to an ideology and often a practice of Americanisation. Just two years earlier Israel Zangwill's Broadway hit musical, *The Melting Pot,* had opened and played to packed houses. The pogrom orphan of the play declaimed:

> America is God's Crucible, the great Melting Pot where all the races of Europe are melting and re-forming! Here you stand, good folk, think I, when I see them at Ellis Island, here you stand in your fifty groups with your fifty languages and histories, and your fifty blood hatreds and rivalries, but you won't be long like that, brothers, for these are the fires of God you've come to – these are the fires of God. A fig for your feuds and vendettas! Germans and Frenchmen, Irishmen and Englishmen, Jews and Russians – into the Crucible with you all. God is making the American.

The melting pot never entirely worked, but even Zangwill's rhetoric now looks hopelessly dated. Governments have all but abandoned policies of assimilation in favour of 'integration', or more nebulous goals such as 'multiculturalism', 'pluralism' or 'rainbow nationhood'. They have abandoned assimilation partly because key local actors are xenophobes or outright racists. Many who have been citizens for a long while and, sometimes more fiercely, many who have recently acquired a secure legal status determinedly pull up the ladder behind them. With increased global inequalities, violent political conflict and often the complete collapse of livelihoods, attaining work and residential rights in favoured societies can be a matter of life and death. Consequently, illegal and refugee migrants advance their claims with similar determination. The stage is thus set for ethnic tension between the self-declared indigenes and the desperate new-comers. To be sure, the number of undocumented and irregular migrants is exaggerated by the popular media and is rarely comparable to the number of tourists and other migrants, namely those allowed entry by family links, common descent, permits, visas and work programmes. However, the unpredictability of illegal migrant flows and the sense that governments and frontier guards are losing control of the borders fuel nativist fears. To the familiar taunts that outsiders take jobs, houses and women away are now added the charges that they bring crime, terrorism and contagious disease with them.

The collapse of programmes and policies that imply cultural absorption also stems from a general scepticism regarding all forms of social policy. Many political elites have largely abandoned social interventions in the cynical belief that the poor will always be with us, criminal conduct and corruption are (to a degree) acceptable, certain minority groups are unedu-cable and immigrants are not dissolvable – either in melting pots or any other receptacles. For such elites, social relations themselves have been reduced to reified commodities – to be bought and sold, like everything else, in the marketplace. Poor locals and marginalised outsiders who are the victims of the evacuation of the state from its sites of social responsibility will have a long wait for relief from their poverty and isolation. Although there are small signs of positive movement in a few social democratic regimes, it will still take some time before naive neo-Thatcherites recognise the utter futility of relying on the marketplace to solve social, political and cultural problems.

We must not, however, assume that immigrants do not 'fit in' only because they are not allowed to by angry racists or indifferent ruling classes. Retaining an old identity in a new setting, or manufacturing a syncretic compromise between old and new, is often a matter of choice. Migrants are more than ever prone to articulate complex affiliations, meaningful attach-ments and dual or multiple allegiances to issues, people, places and traditions that lie beyond the boundaries of the resident nation state. This holds true especially of members of ethnic diasporas and other transnational communi-ties, including faith communities. For diasporas in the traditional sense of that word, this is not at all surprising. Groups such as the Jews, Armenians,

Africans, Irish and Palestinians were 'victim diasporas' dispersed by force. They ended up where they were more by accident than intent. The traumatic events that triggered their movement were so encompassing that such populations remained psychologically unsettled. They characteristically looked backwards, or manifested a dual loyalty to their places of settlement and also to their places, often creatively fabulated, of origin. Indeed, this propensity to link 'home' and 'away' often got them into hot water at the hands of monochromatic nationalists.

What has changed is that many more groups than the traditional diasporas are now attracted to a diasporic consciousness and a cosmopolitan lifestyle. People move to trade, to study, to travel, for family visits, to practise a skill or profession, to earn hard currency, to experience an alternative culture and way of life, and for other reasons too. They either are not permitted or do not intend to settle permanently, adopt an exclusive citizenship, abandon their own language, culture or religion or cut off the possibility of return to a familiar place. In short, they are transnational by intent, adaptation or compulsion. From time to time social researchers have questioned the extent of transnationalism of the migrants. Leading sociologists in the USA, for example, have found that new migrants are accomplished in 'switching' between a transnational mode when with their families and 'home' communities, and standard US idiom when seeking jobs, university admission or social acceptance by neighbours of dissimilar backgrounds.

While accepting that many social actors display versatility in managing their various affinities, this does not obviate the profound legal and political changes of moving from a singular to a complex identity. Take the litmus test of dual citizenship. From less than 10 per cent, the proportion of countries that legally accepted dual citizenship rose to 50 per cent by 1998. In that year, Mexico (notably) permitted its citizens in the USA, comprising some 4–5 million people, to retain both US and Mexican nationalities. They were encouraged, for example, to vote in Mexican elections and they affected the outcome of the last election. By the same token, the USA, which had historically been highly negative about such arrangements, tacitly accepted dual nationality and, perhaps even more crucially, abandoned its hitherto unshakeable monolingual stance by recognising Spanish in a number of key states. The outcome of such a shift away from the goal of cultural absorption can be stated in a more exaggerated form. If full loyalty to a state cannot be assumed, the recruitment of a citizen army, one of the key elements of nation-state power that dates from the French Revolution, has to be abandoned. Increasingly, states are modifying and abandoning conscript armies because citizens are likely to include members of the enemy's country or their descendants. It is thus no coincidence that, with rare exceptions, states will more and more come to rely on technologically driven warfare and a professional, paid army.

As the Mexican example also illustrates, the attitudes of those governments that export migrants has shifted radically. In the nineteenth century, indentured workers from India, Japan and China were recruited by Europeans to work in tropical plantations. This period is often regarded in those countries with shame, as demonstrating their weakness in the face of European power. Now the descendants of such communities (in Brazil, Peru, the USA and elsewhere), together with new emigrants, are celebrated and lionised in their counties of origin. The NRIs (Non-Resident Indians) provide an excellent example. They are a conduit for Indian goods and influence flowing out and a source of remittances and investment income flowing back. In 1970, remittance income to India was US$80 million; by 1993, the sum had increased to US$3 billion. Returnees and investments placed by NRIs have developed the burgeoning and successful Indian software industry. The government of India has made large-scale investments in training Indian IT professionals for work abroad. What was decried as 'brain drain' in the 1970s and 1980s is now constructed as 'brain gain' as skilled exported professionals place contracts at home with Indian companies and close the virtuous circle. Some rich and wonderfully unexpected cultural products also arise from this new acceptance in the originating countries of their communities abroad. One case concerns two Scottish Pakistanis who developed a TV soap called *Des Pardes (Foreign Homeland)*, filmed in Britain, but aimed at audiences of 2–3 billion viewers in the Indian subcontinent and beyond. While cultural flows are still overwhelmingly sourced from a limited number of countries, as this example illustrates flows can go both ways, indeed in multiple directions. As diversity is enhanced, social actors become self-aware that they are transgressing national frontiers and identities become broader.

Much, if not all, of my argument has so far focused on the benign effects of transnationalism or cosmopolitanism. If old-fashioned nation states, based on the idea of either racial uniformity or cultural absorption, are failing, so what? The benefits of enhanced trade, the return flow of income, the movement of fertile ideas and the enhancement of cultural choices and opportunities may greatly outweigh the benefits of retaining an undisturbed national heritage. Better a chapati and a curry than a cold chop in a cold climate. However, there are two crucial counter-reactions to our emerging cosmopolitan, criss-crossed world, neither of which is benign. The first is a direct form of reaction, witnessed most notably in the emergence of many nation states from the ruins of the Soviet empire and Yugoslavian federation. Here the appeals to ethnogenesis are as enticing as ever, whether in the Caucasus, the Balkans or the Baltic. Georgia for the Georgians, Bosnia for the Bosnians and never mind the ethnic and religious minorities who have been living there for centuries. One of the early theorists of nationalism, Lord Acton, linked the emergence of nationalism to the growth of liberalism and democracy. What would he think now of those thuggish conjurors of Balkan nationalism with their fake army uniforms, bulging bellies and menacing handguns? What of the long lines of refugees, the orphanages, the camps, the burning of neighbours' houses, and that chilling practice, ethnic cleansing?

The second malign reaction to our embryonic cosmopolitanism concerns that increasingly clumsy, bloated and dangerous Gulliver, the USA. Enter 9/11 or, as us we Lilliputians say, 11 September 2001. As I currently work in Africa, I need parenthetically to represent discussions here. We suffer from the scourges of Aids (unabating) and ethnic violence (fortunately diminishing). While 3,000 New Yorkers died, we died in our tens of thousands. At the same moment that seven astronauts burned to their deaths, 40 people died in a bus crash in Ghana. It is a poor argument, and definitely one I do not make, that what happened in the USA was of relative insignificance. However, it is important to understand our sense of incredulity when we see armies mobilised, Afghanistan pounded and a perilous world war against terrorism unleashed when Gulliver has been injured. The fatuous evocations of biblical eyes and teeth, that tone of moral righteousness by President Bush, the diminished civil rights for travellers or residents in the USA who are 'Arab-looking' or Muslim – all this looks quite hypocritically one-sided from where we stand. The conservative Sikh community, resident in California since 1907, were compelled to pay for TV and newspaper advertisements showing Sikhs and Afghans with their differing turbans. This is a good guy, this is the bad one, pointed the red arrows. Perhaps the very Orwellian name of a Department for Homeland Security says it all. Shoes off at the airports, surveillance and interrogation of the enemy within and an apparent war without end abroad.

I have nearly managed to get through this whole article without

ROBIN COHEN

'He doth bestride the narrow world like a Colossus . . .'
Credit: RG Mossa, Garden City Publishing, 1930

mentioning the word 'globalisation' once, preferring to see the challenges to uniform national identities and impermeable frontiers as manifestations of transnationalism and cosmopolitanism. The distinction is not generally accepted, but what I wanted to infer is that powerful nation states and big corporations often lead the key forms of globalisation. By contrast, cosmopolitanism implies a more subtle form of subversion of the nation state led by a multitude of social actors, notably migrants, who have no grand scheme in mind but, through their choices, conduct and movements, can effect profound long-term changes. As Steven Vertovec and I argued in a recent book on cosmopolitanism, one reason why the word has acquired fresh appeal is because the term (a) transcends the nation-state model based either on uniformity or cultural absorption; (b) is able to mediate actions and ideals oriented both to the universal and the particular, the global and the local; (c) is culturally anti-essentialist; and (d) is capable of representing variously complex repertoires of allegiance, identity and interest. In these ways, cosmopolitanism seems to offer a mode of managing cultural and political multiplicity and now extends far beyond its historical reference to rootless, disengaged members of the leisured classes, literati or 'bohemian' outsiders. Instead, though through the agency of travellers and migrants, transnationalism or cosmopolitanism may presage our post-national future. ❏

Robin Cohen *is Dean of Humanities, University of Cape Town, while on long leave from his Professorship of Sociology at the University of Warwick. His books on migration include* Frontiers of Identity: the British and the Others *(1994) and* Global Diasporas: An Introduction *(first published in 1997, with subsequent editions and translations)*

COMMON ENTRANCE EXAMS

The following table charts nationality and citizenship requirements in selected countries around the world. With the exception of the EU, the preferred destination for most migrants, the countries represented are those in which the UNHCR (United Nations High Commission for Refugees) has declared a 'complex', that is to say man-made, emergency. Attitudes to cross-border movement are described against the background of domestic law and criteria for settlement. Each entry indicates the number of people involved and their recognised status.

The post-1945 world has been largely defined by the international legal instruments and treaties passed within the United Nations. The international legal framework defining refugee status and determining the validity of claims to enter the territory of another state has delegitimised and politicised a fundamental human desire – to move.

Modern attitudes towards migration have altered as our understanding of sovereignty, citizenship and nationality becomes increasingly rigid and legalistic. The shift is demonstrated in the UK, for instance, by the erosion of the longstanding common law principle that all who gave allegiance to the Crown had a right to remain within its jurisdiction. All states now define citizenship in terms other than simple allegiance: Sudan seeks to protect the moral integrity of its citizens by adding moral criteria to its naturalisation rules; others, in particular Norway, require the fulfilment of practical measures, such as the payment of outstanding paternity payments, as a precondition of citizenship.

The criteria for citizenship are sometimes applied selectively to include, as in the majority of Gulf States, patriarchal lineage alone. When this occurs, as in Saudi Arabia, the result is the denial of work and education rights to offspring of Saudi females and foreign males. Kuwait further limits citizenship to settled Kuwaitis, excluding the Bedou who lose the right to live and work in the country of their birth if they cross international borders. In fact, limitation on residency rights is increasingly widespread as industrial economies from Western Europe to Asia seek to protect their workforces. Malaysia has recently introduced a time limit on the stay of foreign-born labour and EU member states impose quotas on foreign labour.

The reasons for movement are legion: the flight from famine, war and persecution are the most evident. The 'economic' migrant, an increasingly common phenomenon, is moving on for the oldest reason in the history of humanity: the search for a better life. Given that the older industrial societies will be forced more and more to seek labour from abroad to replace their ageing workforce – in 2050, Europe will have an average age of 53 compared with only 36 in the USA and, according to a recent UN study, will need 159 million migrant workers to maintain the present ratio of workers to retired people – the rules governing the status of economic migration are likely to change to reflect the new situation. ❑

Jason Pollard

Note on Symbols

🌍	Signatory to the Universal Declaration on Human Rights
👤 51	Signatory to the 1951 Convention on the Status of Refugees
👤 67	Signatory to the 1967 Protocol on the Status of Refugees
✔	Indicates that a state is a party to a convention
✗	Indicates that a state is not a party to a convention
ᴾᵘ	Citizenship Law
👪	Number of refugees recognised by the UNHCR (unless otherwise indicated)
📖	Rules on naturalisation law
✋	Policy towards refugees
IDP	Internally Displaced People

EUROPEAN UNION SCHENGEN AREA

AUSTRIA
🌍 👤 51 ✔ 👤 67 ✔

ᴾᵘ Citizenship Law, 1965
📖 Naturalisation after 10yrs residence and by marriage after 5yrs. Citizenship is automatic on taking a professorship at an Austrian university.
👪 85,800
✋ Asylum discouraged: Russian, Armenian, Turkish, Azerbaijani, Macedonian, Yugoslavian and Nigerian asylum seekers lose their right to state accommodation after failure of 1st application. The UNHCR has 'expressed concern' over a ruling that bars all asylum seekers from countries negotiating entry into the EU from accommodation shelters.
NB At the end of 2002 Austria was subject to 36,441 asylum applications. Of these 15,187 represented Eastern Europeans claiming political asylum.

BELGIUM
🌍 👤 51 ✔ 👤 67 ✔

ᴾᵘ Nationality Code 1984, amended 1992
📖 Citizenship conferred by at least one Belgian parent or if a child is born in Belgium to non-citizens who were also born in Belgium.
👪 59,200
✋ Policy of forced repatriation for Roma. Belgium censured by European Court of Human Rights for the deportation of dozens of Slovak Gypsies seeking political asylum.

NB 18,805 asylum applications made in 2002.

DENMARK
🌐 ♂ 51 ✔ ♀ 67 ✔

🔒 Danish Nationality Law
📖 Citizenship automatic only for children born in Denmark to unknown parents; 7yr residency requirement in all other cases.
👪 77,442
✋ Embassy officials state that Danish Nationality law 'is very complicated' and suggest contacting the Danish Embassy with any questions, particularly concerning dual citizenship.

FINLAND
🌐 ♂ 51 ✔ ♀ 67 ✔

🔒 Citizenship Act of 1968, amended in 1984
📖 Continual residence in Finland for 5yrs, no offences committed, and with means of support.
👪 15,933 (plus 100,000 foreign workers)
✋ Of all Scandinavian states, Finland takes the smallest number of asylum seekers and has the lowest number of successful applications. Criticised by Sweden as too strict and overloading neighbouring countries. Finland blames its 'harsh climate and difficult language'.

FRANCE
🌐 ♂ 51 ✔ ♀ 67 ✔

🔒 French Nationality Code
📖 Citizen if born in France, if one earns a degree from a French university and lives in France for 2yrs, or serves in the Foreign Legion.
👪 190,936 (plus a further 300,000 estimated illegal workers)
✋ 50+ industries are denied to foreign workers.

GERMANY
🌐 ♂ 51 ✔ ♀ 67 ✔

🔒 Either by descent from parents (*jus sanguinis*) or, after 1 January 2000, by birth within Germany (*jus soli*).
📖 At discretion of naturalisation service following 8yrs minimum residence.
👪 1,310,544 (plus *c*2m Turkish foreign workers)
✋ Increasingly restrictive. Recent bill proposing liberalisation of laws allowing foreign workers blocked in the upper house by recently elected conservative majority.

GREECE
🌐 ♂ 51 ✔ ♀ 67 ✔

🔒 Citizenship Code, amended 1968 and 1984
📖 n/a
👪 9,164 (plus 500,000 illegal immigrants)
✋ Reports of abuse towards refugees and Roma asylum seekers by security agencies.

IRELAND
🌐 ♂ 51 ✔ ♀ 67 ✔

🔒 Irish Nationality and Citizenship Act of 1956
📖 Minimum residency of 4yrs out of 8.
👪 22,534
✋ Stricter criteria applied to asylum seekers following recent declaration that less than 10% of immigration applications were justified. Recent overturning of a 1990 decision that asylum seekers who have a child in Ireland automatically gain residency.

ITALY
🌐 ♂ 51 ✔ ♀ 67 ✔

🔒 Law on Nationality amended 5 February 1992
📖 3yrs residency if familial ties to Italy, 4yrs for nationals of the EU, 5yrs refugees.
👪 27,900 (plus 1.3m registered foreign workers and *c*500,000 illegal workers)
✋ Changes in law proposed to declare an immigrant illegal immediately on rejection of an asylum application.

NETHERLANDS
🌐 ♂ 51 ✔ ♀ 67 ✔

🔒 Nationality Act of 1984
📖 Minimum 5yrs residence and ability to speak Dutch. Residency reduced to 3yrs if married to a Dutch national.
👪 129,100 (plus 460,000 migrant workers from ex-colonies)
✋ Increasingly strict application of law led to 43% drop in successful asylum applications in 2002. Legal requirement for citizenship to sit an exam and have 1,000 hours of Dutch lessons.
NB Due to the changes in Dutch asylum policy the Netherlands have fallen from 6th to 11th largest net recipient of refugees, with 18,667 applications in 2002. There are 40,000 places for 460,000 migrant workers.

NORWAY

⊕ ♂ 51 ✔ ♂ 67 ✔

Nationality Act of 8 December 1950

Citizenship granted upon fulfilment of 7yrs residence, with not more than NOK20,000 owed in child maintenance payments. Residence period for individuals married to Norwegian nationals is computed according to a formula that adds the time married to the length of residency.

65,386

Norway has some of the most generous laws towards asylum seekers. Applicants may take holidays in the country they claim oppressed them without proceedings against them.

PORTUGAL

⊕ ♂ 51 ✔ ♂ 67 ✔

Citizenship Law #37/81, dated 1981

Citizenship acquired after 6yrs residency if from a Portuguese speaking country, otherwise 10yrs. Working knowledge of Portuguese required.

625 (plus 400,000 migrant workers)

Immigration policy dictated by requirements for skilled labour. Government has previously declared an amnesty for illegal immigrants with work contracts.

SPAIN

⊕ ♂ 51 ✔ ♂ 67 ✔

Articles 17–26 of the 'Codigo Civil' modified by Laws 18/1990 and 29/1995

Minimum 10yrs residency requirement if no connection to Spain. Former nationals of Portugal, the Philippines and certain South American countries need only reside for 2yrs.

15,879 (plus 1.4m legal foreign workers)

Naturalisation for refugees is discouraged. Changes to Spanish asylum policy will deny asylum seekers the right to naturalisation even after 10yrs residency.

SWEDEN

⊕ ♂ 51 ✔ ♂ 67 ✔

Swedish Nationality Law

Among the conditions for naturalisation one must have led 'a respectable life'.

200,411

Since Sweden entered the Schengen area there have been recorded instances of the police entrapping illegal immigrants with bogus job interviews.

UNITED KINGDOM

⊕ ♂ 51 ✔ ♂ 67 ✔

British Nationality Act, 1984

Naturalisation after 5yrs residence. 6 categories of citizen are recognised, each with different criteria for citizenship: British Dependent Territories Citizens; British Overseas Citizens; British Subjects; British Protected Persons; Commonwealth Citizens; Citizens of the Republic of Ireland.

264,550 (including pending applications)

In February 2003, 7 more countries added to the list of those considered safe for minority groups. Introduction of targets to reduce asylum applications by 50% by September 2003.

NB The UK received 80,530 applications in 2002.

WEST AFRICA

BURKINA FASO

⊕ ♂ 51 ✔ ♂ 67 ✔

n/k

Naturalisation after 10yrs residency, reduced to 2yrs if some service performed for the state.

707 (plus 250 pending applications)

Burkina Faso has a policy of cooperation with the UNHCR to deal with the 38% rise in asylum applications due to civil war in neighbouring Côte d'Ivoire since September 2002.

CÔTE D'IVOIRE

⊕ ♂ 51 ✔ ♂ 67 ✔

n/k

Naturalisation on completion of 5yr residency, making a significant investment in the country or rendering it a special service.

128,563 (plus 3 million Burkinabe workers)

Refugee policy complicated by accusations that rebel groups fighting against President Laurent Gbagbo's regime have recruited fighters from within refugee camps, resulting in systematic razing of refugees' homes in shanty towns and personal attacks, especially on Côte d'Ivoire's Burkinabe population.

NB Since September 2002 up to 20,000 Liberian refugees have fled back to Liberia, together with a further 30,000 Ivorians.

GUINEA

⊕ 🚹 51 ✔ 🚹 67 ✔

🏠 n/k
📖 n/k
🚻 189,000
✋ Policy of cooperation with UN agencies in the area. Despite pressures on domestic economy, has kept its borders open to civilians fleeing conflict in neighbouring countries.

LIBERIA

⊕ 🚹 51 ✔ 🚹 67 ✔

🏠 Based on the Liberian Constitution
📖 The Constitution states: 'In order to preserve, foster, and maintain the positive Liberian culture, values and character, only persons who are Negroes or of Negro descent shall qualify by birth or by naturalisation to be citizens of Liberia.'
🚻 54,760 (plus an additional 196,116 IDPs registered by the UNHCR)
✋ The Liberian government works with aid agencies through the Liberian Refugee, Repatriation and Resettlement Commission. Since civil war began in 1999 the

government has been unable to guarantee the security of refugees in border areas or aid workers supporting them.

SIERRA LEONE

⊕ 🚹 51 ✔ 🚹 67 ✔

🏠 Law of Citizenship, 1961
📖 Citizenship is automatic for 'Persons of African Negro descent, born in Sierra Leone on or before 26 April 1961'.
🚻 10,501 (plus *c*25,000 additional Liberians in 2003)
✋ The UNCHR has responsibility for several camps housing Liberian refugees fleeing fighting in the neighbouring country. The Sierra Leonean government is actively assisting the repatriation of 11,000 of its own citizens currently in Liberia following its own civil war.
NB There are a total of 92,330 returned refugees in Sierra Leone.

THE GREAT LAKES

BURUNDI

⊕ 🚹 51 ✔ 🚹 67 ✔

🏠 Nationality Code of 10 August 1971
📖 Naturalisation after 15yrs residency
🚻 35,890
✋ A net exporter of refugees, Burundi has no obvious policy on refugees claiming asylum within its territory.
NB At the end of 2001 Burundi had 125,775 people of concern to the UNHCR, including

89,885 returnees, internally displaced and resettled Burundians.

DEMOCRATIC REPUBLIC OF CONGO

⊕ 🚹 51 ✔ 🚹 67 ✔

🏠 The Civil Code/The Special Law on Nationality
📖 5yr residency requirement.
🚻 362,012
✋ DRC is a net exporter of refugees.

RWANDA

⊕ 🚹 51 ✔ 🚹 67 ✔

🏠 Code of Rwandese Nationality, 28 September 1963
📖 Naturalisation is possible through marriage alone.
🚻 36,502
✋ Rwanda is a net exporter of refugees; however, recently a delegation has been sent to neighbouring Tanzania to work out a strategy to repatriate Rwandan refugees living there.
NB The UNHCR has overseen the return of 26,656 refugees up to June 2002.

UGANDA

⊕ 🚹 51 ✔ 🚹 67 ✔

🏠 Constitution declares every person considered a citizen at independence is a citizen of independent Uganda.
📖 Citizenship granted to those with at least one Ugandan parent or grandparent.
🚻 200,363
✋ Ugandan/UNHCR policy recognises refugee status only in designated

camps. Some of the 50,000 refugees outside camps have reported abuse and persecution by law enforcement agencies.

UNITED REPUBLIC OF TANZANIA
⊕ ♦ 51 ✔ ♦ 67 ✔

🏳 Citizenship Act No 6 of October 1995

📖 Citizenship via naturalisation following 5yrs residency. Citizenship granted otherwise if at least one parent was born in Tanzania.

👪 689,483

✋ Policy of repatriation driven by threat of social instability if conditions at camps deteriorate. As a part of this repatriation policy, Rwanda has been declared safe enough for returning refugees.

HORN OF AFRICA

ERITREA
⊕ ♦ 51 ✗ ♦ 67 ✗

🏳 The Proclamation on citizenship

📖 Continual residency requirement of 10yrs before 1974 or any 20yrs if many trips abroad were made.

👪 2,272

✋ Eritrea is a net exporter of refugees. 333,107 Eritreans currently live in neighbouring countries.

ETHIOPIA
⊕ ♦ 51 ✔ ♦ 67 ✔

🏳 n/a

📖 n/a

👪 152,554

✋ Policy of segregation in order to avoid tribal tension in areas of settlement. Periodic relocations of tribes hostile to each other, especially Sudanese Dinkas and Anuaks.

NB Ethiopia is a net importer of refugees, with 58,903 Ethiopians claiming refugee status in other countries.

SOMALIA
⊕ ♦ 51 ✔ ♦ 67 ✔

🏳 n/a

📖 n/a

👪 589 (total population of concern of 51,982)

✋ Somalia is a failed state with no effective administration to form policy. It is a net exporter of refugees.

SUDAN
⊕ ♦ 51 ✔ ♦ 67 ✔

🏳 Law of Sudanese Nationality 22, amended 1972

📖 Naturalisation requirements include a good moral character, an ability to speak Arabic and 10yrs residency.

👪 349,209

✋ Policy of segregation and containment. Most aid in Sudan flows through the umbrella group Operation Lifeline Sudan. In 2002 agreement was reached between government and rebel groups to allow unimpeded access to populations of concern.

NB With 498,868 Sudanese having fled the country due to civil war, Sudan is a net exporter of refugees. 324,546 of Sudan's refugee population are Eritreans living in makeshift camps in the north of the country.

ASIA

AFGHANISTAN
⊕ ♦ 51 ✗ ♦ 67 ✗

🏳 Contained in the Official Gazette of the Ministry of Justice for the Republic of Afghanistan dated 19 March 1992

📖 Requirement of 5yrs continuous residency.

👪 1,226,098 IDPs

✋ Refugee policy is determined by Afghanistan's own citizens returning from other countries. A net exporter of refugees, Afghanistan in 2002 had over 26,000 returnees.

BANGLADESH
⊕ ♦ 51 ✗ ♦ 67 ✗

🏳 Citizenship Order dated 1972

📖 Citizenship granted upon investment of US$5m in an industrial or commercial project or on transfer of US$1m into a financial institution. Permanent residency may be granted upon a non-withdrawable investment of US$75,000.

👪 22,194

🏳 In 1999 Bangladesh launched a drive to identify at least 100,000 illegal foreign workers employed mostly in garment factories, construction, hospitals and guest houses.

CHINA

🌐 👤 51 ✔ 👤 67 ✔

📕 The Nationality Law of the People's Republic of China, 10 September 1980

📖 In addition to having relatives in China, one has to demonstrate 'legitimate reasons' for wishing to obtain Chinese citizenship.

👪 295,326

✋ China operates a policy of forced repatriation of all asylum seekers regardless of their claims. UNHCR refused access to asylum seekers to determine the strength of their claims. All claims treated as 'economic'. China routinely in breach of the 1951 convention on the status of refugees.

DEMOCRATIC PEOPLE'S REPUBLIC OF KOREA

🌐 👤 51 ✘ 👤 67 ✘

📕 Nationality Law of 9 October 1963

📖 Powers to grant citizenship reside solely in the Presidium of the Supreme People's Assembly.

👪 n/a

✋ North Korea is a net exporter of refugees.

NB The majority of the 23m population of North Korea are of concern to the UN and the WFP since existing food supplies are insufficient to provide even basic nutrition.

INDIA

🌐 👤 51 ✘ 👤 67 ✘

📕 Citizenship Act of 1955

📖 5yrs residency requirement.

👪 169,756

✋ India is not a signatory to the 1951 Refugee Convention nor does it have any domestic legislation dealing specifically with refugees. Alternative policy of *non-refoulement* where it will not deport illegal immigrants if there is a danger of torture in the country of origin.

NB India has previously deported Maoist rebels to Nepal in violation of *non-refoulement* principles and a 1950 treaty with Nepal. Despite the variety of states, peoples and languages in India, the law recognises only Indian citizenship.

IRAN (ISLAMIC REPUBLIC OF)

🌐 👤 51 ✔ 👤 67 ✔

📕 Iranian Civil Code

📖 One condition for naturalisation is that the applicant has not escaped from military service in the country of origin.

👪 1,868,000 (UNHCR official), *c*2.4m second-generation Afghans and 1.4m Iraqi Kurds

✋ Unofficial repatriation policy. Afghans encouraged to leave through denial of full participation in Iranian society; Afghan children not allowed to enrol in current school year.

JAPAN

🌐 👤 51 ✔ 👤 67 ✔

📕 Nationality Act of 4 May 1950

📖 n/a

👪 3,528

✋ Japan operates a 'closed door' policy to refugees and asylum seekers. Applications only recognised if made within 60 days. Power to grant refugee status to asylum seekers resides with the justice minister alone. At the end of 2002 only 10% of applicants were granted refugee status.

MALAYSIA

🌐 👤 51 ✘ 👤 67 ✘

📕 Citizenship laws based on the Constitution of Malaysia

📖 Citizenship through naturalisation is not encouraged.

👪 50,718 (plus foreign workforce of 1.2m and *c*450,000 illegal immigrants)

✋ Malaysia has been criticised for arresting potential asylum seekers. Illegal migrant workers are also punished with six strokes of a cane plus prison sentences.

MIDDLE EAST

IRAQ

🌐 👤 51 ✘ 👤 67 ✘

📕 n/a

📖 n/a

👪 130,503

✋ The ability of Iraq to co-operate with aid agencies is determined by the terms of the aid available under the oil-for-food programme.

NB Of Iraq's refugee population 90,000 are Palestinian, 23,680 Iranian.

ISRAEL/PALESTINE
🌐 ♂ 51 ✔ ♂ 67 ✔

- Citizenship Law of 1952 amended in 1968
- Citizenship restricted to Jews recognised by religious authorities, and pre-1948 Arabs and their descendants.
- 4,731 (plus 183,000 illegal foreign workers)
- Israel is in violation of the 1951 Convention for refusing to grant refugee status to Ethiopian and Eritrean asylum seekers. Since the intifada, Israel has a pressing need for migrant labour to replace Palestinian workers.

JORDAN
🌐 ♂ 51 ✘ ♂ 67 ✘

- Citizenship Act of 1954
- Naturalisation following 15yrs residency.
- 6,364 (UNHCR official); c400,000 2nd/3rd generation Palestinians
- Despite granting Palestinians displaced in 1948–67 full citizenship rights, Jordan still remains committed to their repatriation to former homes in Palestine. Recent calls for this are dictated by economic and social pressures. Recently refused to plan for possible influx of Iraqi refugees in event of US attack until necessary funds received from international agencies.

LEBANON
🌐 ♂ 51 ✘ ♂ 67 ✘

- n/a
- Naturalisation requires a decree from the Lebanese Council of Ministers.
- 6,495 (UNHCR official); c350,000 2nd/3rd generation Palestinians
- Policy of forced repatriation where Lebanon is third-party country. Failure to discriminate between political and economic refugees. Official policy is to work for the full repatriation of Palestinians.

SAUDI ARABIA
🌐 ♂ 51 ✘ ♂ 67 ✘

- Article 42 Basic Law of Government (1992)
- Article 42 declares that 'the state grants political asylum when public interest requires it'. For other (unspecified) individuals, naturalisation conditions include 5yrs residency.
- 245,502 (plus c3m foreign workers)
- Saudi refugee and migrant policy complicated by 'Saudi-isation', which denies foreigners the right to work in certain industries.

NB The Saudi government's failure to grant citizenship through female parentage is a violation of the Convention against the Discrimination of Women (CEDAW), of which Saudi Arabia is a signatory.

SYRIAN ARAB REPUBLIC
🌐 ♂ 51 ✘ ♂ 67 ✘

- n/a
- Naturalisation granted following marriage to a Syrian citizen and a 10yr residency requirement.
- 3,956
- The Syrian refugee population is aided through the United Nations Relief and Agency (UNRWA). Syria has cooperated with the UN since the first influx of refugees after the Arab–Israeli conflict of 1948.

TURKEY
🌐 ♂ 51 ✔ ♂ 67 ✘

- Articles 1, 2, 3 and 4 of Turkish nationality law
- Minimum of 5yrs residence with 'intent to remain', familiarity with the Turkish language plus a means for self-support.
- 7,687 (plus 72,905 registered foreign workers)
- Turkey has been accused of barring many of the 1m Kurdish IDPs from returning to their villages. Turkey limits refugee status to successful European applicants only.

NB The Red Crescent Organisation estimates that in the event of an Iraqi war Turkey would have to deal with 1m refugees.

EASTERN EUROPE / CIS

ALBANIA
 51 ✔ 67 ✔

🏷 Parliament is currently debating the criterion for granting citizenship; however, as with all Albanian law, the basis will be the constitution itself.
📖 n/a
👪 363
✋ Albanian authorities have been criticised by human rights organisations for failing to uphold the rule of law, trafficking in human beings, and widespread violations of children's rights. In particular, Albania continues to be a major point of transit and origin in the regional web of trafficking in human beings.

BELARUS
🌐 51 ✔ 67 ✔

🏷 Laws of Citizenship, 18 October 1991
📖 Naturalisation after 7yrs residency and a sufficient means of support.
👪 584
✋ Refugee policy and co-operation with aid agencies was effected by a presidential decree in the latest elections. All donor monies go through the presidential office and bank account to ensure they are not used for 'political' purposes.
NB Officially, the UNHCR has accorded refugee status to only 584 refugees, but a total of 34,567 people are 'of concern' to the UN. These include persons still displaced fol-

lowing contamination by the Chernobyl explosion in 1986.

BOSNIA AND HERZEGOVINA
🌐 51 ✔ 67 ✔

🏷 n/a
📖 n/a
👪 32,745
✋ Together with Croatia and Serbia, Bosnia-Herzogovina has established a tripartite plan to repatriate all refugees in the region, and is a co-operative partner with the EU in dealing with refugees.
NB Including refugees, IDPs and returnees, Bosnia has a total population 'of concern' of 570,221.

BULGARIA
🌐 51 ✔ 67 ✔

🏷 Law on Bulgarian Citizenship, November 1998
📖 Naturalisation after 5yrs legal residence in the country.
👪 4,508
✋ Bulgaria's 2002 Refugee and Asylum Bill has established the State Agency for Refugees and recognises 4 classes of claim: asylum, refugee status, humanitarian status and temporary protection. The law grants asylum to people who are persecuted for their beliefs or activity in defence of internationally recognised rights and freedoms.
NB As a part of its application to join the EU Bulgaria is cooperating in international initiatives to become a final destination for refugees, rather

than a transit point into Western Europe.

CROATIA
🌐 51 ✔ 67 ✔

🏷 Law of Croatian Citizenship, June 1991
📖 One condition determining naturalisation is an attachment to the legal system and culture of Croatia.
👪 21,875
✋ Croatia is a partner in the EU-sponsored Programme for Regional Action accepted as the basis of a tripartite agreement between former Yugoslavia, Bosnia-Herzogovina and Croatia to solve the outstanding issue of the 1.4m refugees in the region.
NB Croatia is a net exporter of refugees with 245,263 of its own citizens claiming asylum abroad. In addition to UNHCR refugees, there are an additional 46,077 IDPs, returnees and returned IDPs.

CZECH REPUBLIC
🌐 51 ✔ 67 ✔

🏷 Acquisition and Loss of Citizenship Act (January 1993), amended by Law 272 (October 1993), Law 140 (June 1995) and Law 139 (April 1996)
📖 5yr residency requirement, unless an individual was a citizen of Czechoslovakia or the Czech and Slovak Federal Republic on 31 December 1992, which grants an automatic right of citizenship of the Czech Republic.
👪 12,805

In February 2002 an amendment to Czech asylum law made it more difficult for illegal immigrants to seek asylum in third countries. There has since been a drop in asylum applications to the Czech Republic.

NB Only those persecuted on the basis of race, political opinion or religion are eligible for asylum. Romas who have been victims of racist attacks do not qualify, as they have not been subject to 'state persecution'.

HUNGARY
🌍 ♂ 51 ✔ ♂ 67 ✔

Law No 55 dated 1 June 1993

Minimum of 8yrs residency.

👪 956

The UNHCR has declared that Hungary has reached a 'level of maturity' in its attitude towards refugees. Previous attitudes were marked by xenophobia which led several Roma to be granted refugee status in third countries. There was a 22% rise in applications in 2002.

POLAND
🌍 ♂ 51 ✔ ♂ 67 ✔

Citizenship Act of 15 February 1962

Naturalisation on renunciation of former citizenship and 5yrs legal residency.

👪 1,311

Poland has been criticised for violating the 1991 UN Refugee Convention on Poland for refusing access to 150

Chechens on the Polish–Belarusan border.

NB A 2002 poll commissioned by the UNHCR revealed that 37% of Poles believe that refugees should be allowed to remain 'for a longer period of time', 21% that they should be sent back, 3% that they should be 'left to their own fate' and 13% expressed no opinion.

REPUBLIC OF MOLDOVA
🌍 ♂ 51 ✔ ♂ 67 ✔

1990 Law of Citizenship

All who resided in the territory of Moldova before 23 June 1990, and have a viable means of support, may obtain citizenship automatically upon request.

👪 1,275

🖐 n/a

ROMANIA
🌍 ♂ 51 ✔ ♂ 67 ✔

Law 21 dated 1991

To qualify for citizenship via naturalisation one must first pass a test on Romanian culture and history.

👪 1,805

New Romanian legislation on the status of refugees ensures compatibility between Romanian asylum rules and those of EU member states in order to eliminate Romania's attraction as a route into Europe.

NB Romania is a net exporter of refugees, especially Roma fleeing state and social persecution. There are 6,055

Romanians (officially) granted refugee status abroad, with up to 400,000 claiming or awaiting decisions. Romania generates the second highest number of refugees for a developed country.

RUSSIA
🌍 ♂ 51 ✔ ♂ 67 ✔

Law on Citizenship dated 6 February 1992

Minimum criteria for naturalisation include 5yrs permanent residence, or 3yrs continuous residence immediately prior to filing an application. For recognised refugees the criteria are halved.

👪 17,970 (plus 3m illegal immigrants)

Russia recognises a need for foreign workers and has established an annual quota of 583,000 for 2003. A new law is designed to make it easier and quicker to deport illegal immigrants within 72 hours of their arrest.

NB Russia has a total population 'of concern', including IDPs, of 1,139,842. 700,000 of these are internal migrants affected by environmental pollution in Chernobyl and around Russia's nuclear test sites.

SERBIA AND MONTENEGRO
🌍 ♂ 51 ✔ ♂ 67 ✔

n/a

n/a

👪 400,304

Serbia operates a policy of segregation, keeping refugees and asylum seekers in collective centres. Serbia has agreed to solve the regional refugee situation in cooperation with Bosnia-Herzegovina and Croatia.

NB Serbia has a total population 'of concern' of 777,104, of which 263,600 are IDPs.

SLOVAKIA
☺ ♂ 51 ✔ ♂ 67 ✔

↳ Law No 40, dated 19 January 1993
▯ One condition for naturalisation is that the individual has not been pronounced guilty of a deliberate crime within the last 5yrs.
👫 3,623
✋ Due to the fact that most asylum seekers move to third countries before their applications are processed, Slovakia has the fewest number of approved asylum claims despite having the highest number of initial claims.

NB Out of nearly 10,000 applications for asylum in 2002, only 20 claims were approved.

SLOVENIA
☺ ♂ 51 ✔ ♂ 67 ✔

↳ Citizenship Act of 25 June 1991
▯ In addition to being up to date with tax payments, one must pass a Slovenian-language examination.
👫 7,171
✋ In 2002 changes were proposed to the Asylum Act allowing the interior minister to deport asylum seekers before the completion of an application

by the country's Administrative Courts. The changes in the act are also intended to bring Slovenia's domestic asylum law into line with EU law in order to deter third country applications.

THE AMERICAS

MEXICO
☺ ♂ 51 ✔ ♂ 67 ✔

↳ Federal Constitution as amended 20 March 1998
▯ One of the grounds for naturalisation is that an individual has contributed distinctively to Mexico.
👫 15,467
✋ Mexico was one of the last states in the Americas to ratify the 1951 Convention and the 1967 Protocol, only doing so in 2000. Since then Mexico has officially ended the repatriation of Guatemalan refugees, and has been praised by the UNHCR for the work it has done towards resolving its refugee problem.

NB Mexico's main concern is with its own citizens currently in the US. Mexico has previously criticised US policy towards illegal Mexican immigrants as not helping to 'maintain a positive climate' between the two nations.

UNITED STATES OF AMERICA
☺ ♂ 51 ✘ ♂ 67 ✔

↳ Title 8 of US Code 1401 –1409
▯ Naturalisation conditions include minimum 5yr residency, a demonstrated ability to read and write English, good moral character, familiarity with the history and culture of the country, attachment to the principles of the US Constitution, and renunciation of former citizenship.
👫 911,730 (plus c3.5m 'unauthorised' Mexican immigrants)
✋ Since the 11 September 2001 attacks the INS (Immigration and Naturalisation Service) has initiated a policy of registration of certain nationalities, including Iranians, Saudi Arabians and Iraqis. Security concerns are leading refugee policy, with the INS now merged with the new Department of Homeland Security.

NB The total figure for refugees includes 395,877 awaiting decisions in the US. In 2000 the US census recorded a Hispanic population of 35m, projected to rise to 70m by 2020, which will be the largest Hispanic population in the world after Mexico.

GULF STATES

BAHRAIN
☺ ♂ 51 ✘ ♂ 67 ✘

↳ Nationality Law of 16 September 1963

Continuous residency since 16 September 1963, for at least 25yrs, or 15yrs if person is of Arab descent. Individual must be of good character, have a good command of Arabic, and have an estate registered in his or her name in Bahrain. In addition the applicant must have acquired permission from the ruler of Bahrain.

21 (plus 200,000 foreign workers)

Bahrain has some of the toughest naturalisation laws in the world. Immigration policy is directed towards illegal workers rather than refugees.

OMAN

51 ✘ 67 ✘

n/a

Naturalisation is only available to women through marriage to an Omani, or to men through special decree. The child of an Omani mother and a foreign male is not granted citizenship, but instead is given an internal passport and considered a resident alien.

0 (plus 250,000 illegal foreign workers)

Migration and asylum both discouraged. Oman does not recognise refugee status under 1951 Convention and holds periodic amnesties for illegal foreign workers to leave without penalty.

NB 23 asylum seekers were awaiting decisions by the UNHCR at the end of 2001.

KUWAIT

51 ✘ 67 ✘

Citizenship laws based upon the Constitution of Kuwait

Naturalisation can only be granted through a specific act of government.

1,255 (plus 138,000 other people 'of concern' to the UNHCR)

Immigration policy is particularly strict towards the Bedou, who are denied the right to return to Kuwait if they travel abroad. A Bedou born in Kuwait does not have Kuwaiti citizenship.

QATAR

51 ✘ 67 ✘

Law No 2 of 1961, amended by Law No 19 of 1963 and Law No 17 of 1966

Citizenship is automatic for a person who resided in Qatar prior to 1930. Other applicants must have 20yrs lawful residency or, if of Arab descent, 15yrs.

79

There is no basis in Qatari law for recognising refugees. All 79 of Qatar's refugees are recognised by the UNHCR only.

UNITED ARAB EMIRATES

51 ✘ 67 ✘

Nationality Law No 17, dated 1 January 1972, amended by Law No 10, dated 1975.

To qualify for citizenship non-Arabs must reside in the country for at least 30yrs, 20yrs of them occurring after 1 January 1972.

917

The UAE is not a signatory to any of the international legal instruments on refugees and therefore relies on the UNHCR to provide relief and resettlement in a third country outside of the Middle East.

YEMEN

51 ✔ 67 ✔

Citizenship Law No 2, dated 1975

Yemen recognises a need for foreign skilled migrants. Muslims with specialist skills must fulfil a 10yr residency requirement, non-Muslims 5yrs. Both sets of applicants must have a viable means of support, be healthy, have behaved properly, and know the language.

72,039

Out of all the Gulf States, Yemen alone has the legal framework required to recognise migrants as refugees as it alone is a signatory to the UN Convention. ❏

Sources: Asahi Shimbun, Associated Press, Asia Intelligence Wire, UNHCR, US State Department, Human Rights Watch, Comtex News Network, AFP, Radio Uganda, BBC Monitoring, Guardian, Financial Times, Economic Times, Xinhua, Hungarian Radio, PAP News Agency – Warsaw, TASR Website, The Times, Gulf News, US State Department

*Compiled by **Jason Pollard***

THE PRICE OF RETURN

VERA RICH

WHEN THE SOVIET EMPIRE FELL,
AND COMMUNISM BIT THE DUST
IN ITS SATELLITE STATES, IT SET
OFF THE BIGGEST MOVEMENT OF
PEOPLE SINCE WORLD WAR II

The demise of the Soviet Union bequeathed its successor states some tricky demographic problems. These were largely the result of four factors:

• forced relocations over the past two centuries, whether of individual political exiles or (under Stalin) of whole social or ethnic groups;

• the influx of Russians into non-Russian areas as administrators, industrial managers, etc;

• Red Army conscripts, who normally did their military service outside their home republic, staying on after completion of their service. Career soldiers, on retirement, were settled in the area of their final posting. To 'pay' for their education, university graduates were obliged to work for several years wherever the relevant ministry sent them – and frequently stayed on permanently;

• the boundaries of the constituent Union Republics of the USSR, which were in many cases deliberately drawn to cut across ethnic divisions, for fear that an ethnically homogenous republic might be tempted to defy the central authorities in Moscow.

The net result was that a significant percentage of the 15 ethnic groups that had given their names to a Union Republic lived outside the boundaries of that republic – ranging from 4.7 per cent Lithuanians to a massive 28.5 per cent Armenians. When the Soviet Union collapsed, these people found themselves ethnic minorities in what were now independent states, a situation that ethnic Russians, who had until then been the 'elder brothers' of the Soviet Union's 'minorities', found especially traumatic.

There were also several small ethnic groups whose ethnic homeland lay outside the Soviet Union; many of these now tried to return. Apart from the special case of Israel, which had for more than two decades been actively encouraging the 'return' and settlement of Jews from the USSR, these would-be returnees put an unexpected strain on the 'homeland' social services and job markets. Returning Greeks found themselves settled in Thrace, where, the Greek government hoped, they would dilute the local Bulgarian and Turkish minorities. The last Soviet census in 1989 recorded 1.1 million 'Poles' – of whom only just over one-third claimed to speak Polish. In addition, after 1991, many new claimants to Polish descent began to emerge, citing ancestors deported to Siberia or Central Asia after one of the nineteenth-century risings. The price of artefacts that could bolster such claims soared on the flea markets of Central Asia: a broken rosary, a tattered volume of Polish poetry. Poland's government – struggling with its own problems of post-socialist reconstruction – played for time. Claims for 'repatriation' were processed on a one-by-one basis. The Catholic Church launched a fund to build churches in Kazakhstan, to encourage the 60,000 Poles there to stay put. In the event, Poles repatriated from Central Asia turned out to be mainly those whom Poland could most easily absorb – young and middle-aged people with professional training.

In most cases, the governments of the former Soviet republics in the Commonwealth of Independent States (CIS) have shown little interest in repatriating their ethnic kin. An exception is Kazakhstan which in recent years has encouraged the immigration of ethnic Kazakhs from both the CIS and beyond. But this was a special case: political deportations and the relocation of young people in the 1960s to develop the 'Virgin Lands' had left the Kazakhs a minority in their own republic. This state-sponsored gathering, plus the departure of almost a third of the country's ethnic Russians, restored the Kazakhs to a 53.4 per cent majority by 1999.

Some exiles of the Stalin period have managed to repatriate themselves in the face of official discouragement or worse. The most notable case was the Crimean Tatars, deported en masse to Central Asia as a punishment for alleged collaboration with the Nazis; they began their return to Crimea in the late 1980s in defiance of all Soviet regulations on residence, and in spite of the repeated destruction of their shanty-built homes by local officials. As a result, the figure for Tatars in Crimea has risen from some 47,000 in 1989 to 248,200 in 2001. This influx caused problems with the mainly Russian

Slav residents. There have recently been a number of incidents when the Moscow-ruled wing of the Ukrainian Orthodox Church has erected roadside crosses and the Tatars have simply destroyed them or protested to the local authorities.

The Russian government made no major attempt to repatriate the 25.3 million ethnic Russians from the territories of the former USSR, what it now terms the 'near abroad'. It used them instead as political capital – a means to intervene in the politics of its neighbours ostensibly in the defence of its co-ethnics' rights. Nevertheless, there has been a slow drift home, a net immigration of ethnic Russians to Russia over the period 1991–2001 of 3.7 million, particularly from Central Asia and the Caucasus. Residents of the xenophobic Russian heartland have, however, been less than welcoming, attacking these incomers verbally and, on occasion, physically on the grounds that they had acquired the undesirable characteristics of the non-Slavs among whom they had been living.

The same hostility has faced ethnic Russians from the non-Slav areas of the Russian Federation, in particular those fleeing north from the Chechen war.

The antipathy is even worse against non-Russians wishing to settle in Russia – whether from the 'near abroad' or from non-Slav republics of the Russian Federation. One particularly hard-hit group is the Meskhetian Turks. During the civil war in Tajikistan in the early 1990s, an estimated 50,000–70,000 fled from that country to Russia, where the majority were able to claim citizenship. However, some 13,000–16,000 living in Russia's Krasnodar province have encountered hostility and discrimination from the local authorities. According to Amnesty International, some 10,000 of them still remain without the necessary registration papers – and they could be evicted at a moment's notice from the homes they have built and the land they till.

However, for most residents of the CIS, the goal of migration is the 'affluent' West. Some arrive legally as students, tourists or as temporary workers, and attempt to prolong their stay either legally – as asylum seekers, highly qualified immigrants, etc – or by disappearing into the black economy on the expiry of their visas. Others are illegal from the beginning,

Tatar Muslims at a memorial commemorating the deportation of their people to various sectors of the USSR 50 years ago. Credit: AFP

VERA RICH

in particular the estimated half-million young women recruited for the global sex industry.

Estimates of their numbers vary widely and are, for obvious reasons, impossible to check. Thus although Russia's official total for emigrants from 1991–2000 is given as 1.1 million (of whom 57 per cent are said to have gone to Germany, 26 per cent to Israel and 11 per cent to the United States), one journalist working for the London-based *New Russian* newspaper guessed there are now up to 250,000 'new Russians and Russophones' in the UK alone. The launch and survival of such newspapers, both Russian and Ukrainian, suggests a sizeable market.

But illegal migration is not easy, even to continental Europe. Under EU pressure on its aspiring members and partners, border controls are tightening on the outer frontier of the CIS. Ukraine, for example, is joining the Eurodac fingerprinting system and has this year allotted 2.5 million hryvnyas (US$470,000) to migrant and refugee problems. It is, for instance, offering its own illegal immigrants refugee status and travel documents to proceed further if any country will take them. It is also building two new refugee centres in Kiev and Kharkiv in addition to the partially completed centre at Odessa.

However, illegal migration agents continue to flourish, though the local media now report only the more spectacular captures, involving non-CIS citizens – Pakistanis, Chinese, etc. But anecdotal evidence suggests that some agents have an arrangement with the border guards: the clients (who have paid in advance) are captured, and the guards and agents split the fees. Some, indeed, seem prepared to send their clients to a permanent destination: a UK official who had to identify the bodies of two British citizens drowned in the River Sozh in Belarus said the morgue also contained some 15 or so dark-skinned bodies also apparently dredged from the river.

Even so, the floundering economies of the CIS continue to fuel the flow, augmented, according to the latest reports from Ukraine, by a new wave from the south, triggered by fear of the knock-on effects of war in Iraq. Altogether a figure of some 12 to 15 million people displaced as a result of the Soviet collapse may not be too wide of the mark. ❏

Vera Rich is a freelance journalist and writer specialising in the former communist world

THE NEW SLAVE TRADE

IRENA MARYNIAK

Human trafficking is one of the most lucrative businesses in the world. UN estimates suggest that the 4 million people moved across international borders by traffickers each year generate profits of up to US$7 billion, subsequently laundered and fed into other activities including drugs and arms smuggling.

More than 700,000 of those trafficked are women and children sold into prostitution or forced labour. Sex slaves working in Europe account for about two-thirds of this figure. Many are East European women and girls from impoverished rural areas, who had hoped to flee unemployment, family restrictions and conflict at home for a better life abroad. Victims are recruited by boyfriends, family members and trusted female friends, or through seemingly reputable employment, travel or marriage agencies. Some are as young as 13. They may be offered jobs in fashion, tourism, housekeeping, catering or entertainment in Western Europe, with promises of travel documents, transport, comfortable accommodation, even education. Occasionally they are kidnapped. About 20 per cent may be aware of the possibility of becoming involved in sex-related work but none expects to be enslaved.

The collapse of the Berlin Wall and simpler exit procedures have increased freedom of movement in Eastern Europe, but factors such as inadequate education, idealised notions of life in the West, legislation favourable to the commercial sex industry in many countries, and particularly the feminisation of poverty have created excellent conditions for trafficking. In parts of Russia women represent 70–95 per cent of the unemployed. Throughout the former communist bloc public childcare centres have been closed, social security structures dismantled, pensions reduced. This has left women carrying the burden of care and breadwinning, with less access than ever to the labour sector. Opportunities for careers or political participation have been blunted; women are poorly paid, the first to be dismissed, and may have to offer sex to their bosses to stay in a job. 'Central Eastern Europe is comparable to Latin America or the Philippines in terms of women's desperation,' says Gyorgyi Toth, director of NANE, a Hungarian NGO that campaigns against domestic violence.

At home, and in the informal sector of charring and sexual services to which so many women are relegated, physical abuse is widely accepted. For women from Ukraine, Russia, Moldova, Romania, Belarus or Bulgaria there seems to be little to lose and everything to gain in risking a job abroad or simply away from family pressures. Their notional destination may be a Western European country or a big city closer to home, but once in the hands of the trafficking network, the victims lose any power to decide for themselves. They are coerced by violence, rape, food deprivation and drugs: the procedure is called 'seasoning'. They are forced to give up passports and money, and stay locked in their accommodation until allowed out by their pimps to work as prostitutes. They may find themselves shunted via Albania or former Yugoslavia to almost any country in Western or Northern Europe, Turkey, Israel, the US or the United Arab Emirates. During the course of a journey from Moldova to Kosovo, for example, a woman may be bought and sold up to six times. In the country of destination designated for her by the traffickers, she will be obliged to repay 'debts' consisting of the cost of her documents and transport, or her purchase price, which can range from US$700 to US$2,500. She will have no protection from STDs or Aids, and will receive medical care on an emergency basis only, especially if her symptoms threaten to affect her 'performance'.

Sex trafficking is denied and trivialised by the authorities and media in many regions, and the women see police not as a potential source of help but of harassment. Prosecution of offenders and assistance to victims are not high priorities, and corruption is rife. The international community has offered few preventive initiatives and little assistance to victims, although some EU funding has gone to East European NGOs and the International Organisation for Migration has run awareness campaigns in a number of countries. The Special Trafficking Operation Programme (STOP), launched in 2001 by the UN in Bosnia, led to revelations about the involvement of the International Police Task Force and the Stabilisation Force (SFOR) in sex trafficking, and to an increase in prosecutions. But it also helped to push the business underground. Police raids simply encourage gangs to change their routes and relocate.

For the victims there is no effective escape. One way to get out is to recruit others, but women who do find their way home are often dragged back into the prostitution network by blackmail and threats against themselves and their families. It is a brutal fact that as public awareness rises the trafficking business becomes ever more violent and dangerous.

Teplice, Czech Republic: a policeman questions a prostitute on the road from Dresden to Prague. Credit: Piet den Blanken / Panos Pictures

'MARINELLA', ROMANIAN

Back home I had no income. My grandmother had her pension, my mother got child benefit for three children, and the alimony. My brother's best friend was an exchange dealer, he'd been visiting our house for years. He'd eaten with us, he'd sat with my father and brother at the same table.

His name is Ion. I don't know his other name, in our town they all call him Manet ('handle'). I said to him, 'Manet, if you're taking me away to make a whore of me, don't do it, brother. Don't take me away from my child.' And he said, 'If I didn't know your family and your brother, maybe I'd do it, but as it is, I won't.' So I went, telling myself that in a month I'd be sending money to my mother.

My brother's girlfriend went too. He said he was taking us to Italy, and that once we were there he'd take me to a pizzeria to do the dishes, and her to a bar (because she could speak Italian) to work as a sort of bartender. I had a passport, but my brother's girlfriend didn't and he took us over to

Serbia by boat. I asked why weren't we going through customs, I was afraid of water. I argued with him for at least an hour. Eventually they talked me into doing it and he said I'd cross the next border with the passport. So I crossed over into Macedonia with my passport and the others went through a forest.

There were three girls and four boys – two of them said they also wanted to get to Italy – and we all left for Skopje. We stayed in an apartment, the boys went off, and we moved to another place where there were 40 girls staying. I thought they were all living there.

The girls all wanted to get to Italy to work as photo models, as cooks or in hotels. They had been promised large sums of money. When I heard from the Russian and Moldovan girls that we were going to be sold and become prostitutes, I couldn't believe my ears. I tried to kill myself. For one and a half months I couldn't call home. I have a little girl . . . no, no . . . I can't find the words, I didn't think I'd ever get home.

A week later, some guys came over and looked at us, but we still didn't know we were being sold. A few days later somebody took me and two other girls to an Albanian's house in Macedonia, near the border with Albania.

There were 200 girls living in the villa. We were held there until we could be sold for a higher price. The girls were Russian, Romanian; many of them had run away, been captured and returned by police in Bulgaria, and sold back.

Four of us would share a hamburger, there was a packet of cigarettes for eight girls. That was all the food we had in a day. He beat us. We'd ask for water, and got 20 litres in plastic bottles. That had to be enough for the day. We had to wash, we couldn't stay like that, and if we wanted to use the lavatory, it was only allowed at certain times. We were starved.

None of the girls had passports, but I was left with my identity card. They even took our clothes away. In Albania I was beaten. Once I ate nothing for four days. Before I was taken away, I hadn't gone out for a week. My eyebrow arch was broken, he'd hit me with a pistol on the head, and said he'd shoot me. The Albanian's mistress was a Moldovan, she could speak Romanian and she was our boss. And she hit us whenever there was something she didn't like. I was afraid. Maybe I wouldn't have given in, but then I saw they meant what they said. They killed a girl in front of me and buried her behind the house. She was only 17.

The owner's mistress was distantly related to her. The girl had shouted at her and said she'd tell the owner's wife about their relationship. So the mistress went and complained to the owner, who was drunk. He came and trampled her, he held on to the wall and kept jumping on her, and then he lifted her up and threw her against the wall. I think that was when everything broke inside her because the wall was all splashed with blood. She was lying there moaning, with blood gushing from her eyes, her ears, everywhere, her mouth, her nose, and then he took out his pistol and shot her dead and dragged her outside. He ordered us to clean the floor, the wall was going to be whitewashed later. Five or six days after that, we were sold.

For three days I wasn't able to raise a cigarette to my mouth, I was trembling all over, I was having nightmares about her, I can see it in my mind right now. He wasn't a human being.

In all the bars where I worked, the girls were beaten and starved. If they wouldn't dance or go with a customer, they got nothing to eat. In Gostivar there was a cop from the airport . . . I asked him to help me, I gave him my address, I gave him everything, and he went to the owner and told him I wanted to escape and report him to the police . . . I didn't trust anyone any more. The policemen from Gostivar came – in uniform and in plain clothes – they had girlfriends, *falice* they called them. When a more serious inspection was to take place, they'd tell the owner and he'd hide us . . . Important men came from Skopje – the police used to announce their arrival . . . senators . . . They knew about our situation and our life there, but they didn't care.

A nephew of his took me away in secret and said he'd take me home. He said he loved me, but he sold me . . . me and another girl. He sold her too, in Albania, but to a different person. Our former owner wanted to sell us for a very high price and nobody would buy us. This guy said we had a hard life, we were suffering, he'd take us home . . .

I fell ill, otherwise he wouldn't have let me go. There was snow, I ran out and stood barefoot in the snow, in my dress, and fell seriously ill, and needed medical treatment. I had a haemorrhage, they took me to hospital and they couldn't stop it unless I stayed in. The owner didn't want to leave me there. But he knew a police raid was due that night and the girls were to be rounded up. So he gave us up – me and two other girls. ❏

Edited excerpts from interview by International Organisation for Migration (IOM), Romania. Translated by IOM, Romania

'RUKA', KOSOVO ALBANIAN, 16

I was out walking with a friend from the village one day, when we were invited out for coffee by a third friend. He offered to drive us to the café-bar so we wouldn't have to walk in the dust. But when we got into the car, this guy drove off at high speed and took out a gun threatening to kill me if I tried to escape. I couldn't believe my friend was part of this nightmare.

He drove to Kacanik and forced me into a motel. When we'd got a room, he made me drink something and I can't remember what happened after that . . . When I woke up, I saw these four Kosovar guys. They were drunk, laughing at me. Two of them had guns . . . They raped me several times, for several hours, abusing and beating me when I tried to say anything . . .

When it was dark, they brought me to a private house in Ferizaj. There were four men there, one from Albania and three young Kosovars from Ferizaj. They kept me in the house for more than a month . . . They raped me every day, night and day . . . Most of the time I was lying on the floor, I couldn't stand. There wasn't enough food and I was hungry. I didn't know if it was day or night . . . They kept shouting and threatening me with their guns. I couldn't talk for the fear and confusion, I couldn't even cry.

After a while one of the guys took me away by car to Albania. They brought me to another motel and left me there. In this motel they gave me to two Albanian brothers. They kept me there for another month. They and two other, older men raped me several times.

One night I was taken away to another city. They put me in a speedboat full of desperate people and sent me to Italy . . . The weather was so bad, we had not eaten for so long . . . I thought we'd die but I didn't care. When we got to Italy we arrived on an abandoned beach and walked through deserted places in the dark . . . I was still in the hands of the Albanian brothers.

The next day we arrived in a small village where we met a woman, the girlfriend of one of the brothers. They locked me in an apartment. The next day they told me I had to work for them – on the street. I refused, began shouting . . . They beat me a lot, they told me that if I refused they'd kill me and my family back in Kosovo . . . I was so afraid, I was in Italy illegally, I couldn't ask for help, I didn't know what to do. They were checking my every move.

For two years they made me work on the streets as a prostitute. The Albanian brothers followed me every time. During the day I was locked

Riga, Latvia: a young girl washes her hands after a night's work.
Credit: Jörgen Hildebrandt / Panos Pictures

in an apartment with other girls, during the night they sent me to work on the street . . .

One night they brought a very young woman to the house, very young. She had the same desperate look in her eyes, and they began to abuse her in front of me. I saw a knife on the table . . . I was so desperate, I couldn't bear to see it all again . . . I saw darkness . . . I took the knife and wanted to stop this nightmare . . .

The police came and took me away. The Albanians made a statement against me. They said I was a prostitute, that I was making trouble, I was dangerous, I had no documents . . . They wanted to get rid of me.

I stayed in the jail for a while and when the police released me they deported me to Albania.

In Albania 'Ruka' was sheltered by the International Organisation for Migration (IOM) and helped to return to her family in Kosovo.

My parents wept when they saw me . . . I wept too . . . for the happiness of being alive and home, but also for all that I couldn't say to them.

I wanted to lead a normal life, to forget what happened, to go back to school. My parents didn't let me, they told me not to go out, it was better to stay home. One day my father got drunk and began to blame me for what happened. He said that he couldn't go out any more . . . he beat me . . .

After that, my parents wouldn't let me leave the house. I remembered the time the traffickers had kept me locked up and sometimes I couldn't see the difference. I felt as though my life didn't belong to me any more . . . that they were destroying my life again. ❏

Edited excerpts from interview by IOM, Kosovo
Translated by IOM, Kosovo

AUTOBURG

GAZMEND KAPLLANI

'THIS PSEUDO-POET IMITATING REACTIONARY ART HAS TRIED TO INTRODUCE POISONOUS PLANTS TO THE PURE GARDEN OF OUR LITERATURE AND SO DESTROY ITS ATMOSPHERE' — FILE 12102, TIRANA 1980

Visar Zhiti is one of Albania's best-known poets. The quotation above comes from the indictment that condemned him to ten years' hard labour in the terrible prison of Spaç; he has included it in his latest work, *The Roads of Hell: A Story I Wish Wasn't True.*

I'm walking with Visar down the main avenue of Tirana, the Boulevard of the Martyrs of the Nation, which begins at the statue of the national hero Skanderbeg and ends at the university. It was here that the big May Day marches used to take place, where enormous crowds proclaimed their passion for the leader and the party. On our right is the former headquarters of the Party's Central Committee. Behind it lies the Leaders' Block, the district where Enver Hoxha used to live. Entrance was once strictly forbidden; now it's become a sort of West End of Tirana, known simply as 'the Block'. On our left is the Rogner Hotel, symbol of post-totalitarian Albania, the meeting place for foreign businessmen and ambassadors and Albanian politicians, businessmen and gangsters. (The distinctions between the last three groups can sometimes be difficult to discern.) In front of the hotel, two well-dressed middle-aged ladies are trying to determine the exact time when Leka Zog, son of Albania's former king, is arriving to set up house in a nearby villa.

'The autoburg was the prison bus,' says Visar. 'From the outside it looked like an ordinary bus; when I got inside I was shocked to see that in fact there were no windows. They were painted on to fool people. For me that sums up Albania in those days.' A Chinese couple walk past – maybe tourists, maybe immigrants doing good business in Tirana. 'I remember two people in prison who were there because of Mao Tse Dong. One was there because he'd cursed him, the other because he'd praised him. The first was arrested when Albania was having its great love affair with China, the second after the divorce. They used to say to each other, "One of us is

superfluous." In the mines they pushed the same wagon, for the ghost
of Mao Tse Dong.'

When Hoxha's regime collapsed in 1990, everything seemed to go into
reverse. The country you couldn't leave became the departure point for a
biblical exodus to the West. The country where watching television could
land you in prison became the country with more satellite dishes than
Italy. Dreaming of consumer culture, the Albanians were transformed into
worshippers of capitalism; ignorance, political corruption and the fantasy of
a quick escape from poverty cost 70 per cent of the population their savings
in the disastrous pyramid-selling financial scam (*Index* 4/97). Then came
the uprising and the dissolution of the state. Hundred of thousands of
weapons were stolen, gangs with or without political connections turned
Albania into a jungle, and within a few months about 2,000 people had
been killed. 'We passed from the prison of repression to the prison of
anarchy,' says Visar. 'But today we are finding ourselves, and that gives
me hope.'

Now a semblance of order has been restored in Albania. New
motorways are being built. Tourists are beginning to arrive – at least,
in Tirana and the south.

'BLOOD IS NEVER WASTED'
The Kanun of the mountains

After 9pm the streets of Shkodra are empty, and the capital of the Albanian
north resembles an occupied town. The Kanun and the blood law have
become one of the north's worst nightmares. 'The Kanun,' explains
Professor Lulzim Lelçaj of Shkodra University, 'was used in the Middle
Ages to regulate violence. The Council of Elders decided the terms of a
vendetta.' But now there is no Council of Elders. 'Every time the state
disappears, the Kanun resurfaces to take its place.'

This old, unwritten code, which once regulated life in the mountains,
was abolished by force under communism; in the chaos of 1991, it rose
again. As Emin Spahia of the Apostles of Peace explains: 'A murder victim's
relatives try to take their blood back from anyone who has the same
surname as the killer. As a result, hundreds of families are forced to live
for years shut up within the four walls of their houses.' According to his
organisation, there are about 520 families in the region of Shkodra alone
who cannot leave their homes.

Dukagjin Mountains, Albania, 'the right to bear arms': Kanun code gained popularity in the 1990s. Credit: Rhodri Jones / Panos Pictures

Françesk, a former small businessman in the village of Bushat, has been shut in for five years now with his brothers and their families – a total of 19 people, nine of them children. The vendetta began when 'strangers' asked him to give them his 13-year-old niece to take to Greece. 'I told the police, who did nothing. After many threats they shot me on my doorstep.' In the fight, one of Françesk's attackers was fatally wounded, by accident, by a member of his own gang. But since that day Françesk and his relatives have hardly left the house. 'I dared to go out once last year. I took my young daughter with me. In Baçallek [a neighbourhood in Shkodra] they fired at us. They hit my daughter with three bullets and me with eight or nine . . .' His daughter Arieta is 11 now; she can barely read or write. 'I wish I could go to school, but I can't because we're shut in. My friends are happy, they're free, but we . . .' she says, and her eyes fill with tears.

Vendettas and the lack of security are among the reasons why so many Albanians leave the country. 'Since 1997, when this thing happened to me, more than 300 people from our village have left with their families,' says Françesk, who spends his nights on guard with his gun in his hand. According to the Kanun, attacks at home are not permissible, and women and children under 14 are immune. But it is not so much the Kanun at work here as organised crime and the total absence of the state. 'People claim that they're applying the Kanun,' says Professor Lelçaj. 'But how can you apply something you know nothing about?'

Frederik, 25, knows nothing about the Kanun either. He left for Greece at 14; in Athens, he learned that they had murdered his father. 'I was 16. After seven or eight years I went back to Albania.' The first thing his relatives did was to point out his father's killer. The pressure to submit to the blood law was intolerable. 'I started losing my family. My friends wouldn't go out with me. They considered me unworthy. Every day I saw the murderer in front of me . . . if they'd put him in prison, he would have survived and I wouldn't have become a murderer myself.' How does he feel now? 'I shouldn't have listened to them. I should have gone back to Greece. But now it's too late for everything. Much too late.'

OMONOIA SQUARE

Northerners often end up in Tirana, whose population has increased from 250,000 to 1 million since 1991. Many of the young go on to the West; those left behind and unemployed gather from six every morning in 'Omonoia Square', nicknamed after the square in Athens where Albanian migrants gathered to find work when they first went to Greece in the early 1990s. Edi has come from Shkodra. Two years ago he was working in Greece, but he never managed to become legal. 'Unemployment is the same everywhere,' he says. As we are talking, a man leans out of a white Mercedes and spits some angry words at the crowd. 'There's a lot of racism here,' says Edi. 'Worse than in Italy or Greece. They call us *malok* all the time.' *Malok* (mountain man) is used as a derogatory term for northerners.

The mass exodus has left Albania with an ageing population. But without the US$650 million the migrants send home each year, those who are left behind could not survive – let alone finance the building mania that is now sweeping the south. The price of a visa on the black market varies. The cheapest is a Greek visa, for US$1,000; the most expensive an American one, for US$12,000. But the Western dream is not paid for just in cash.

CEMETERY

'You left a terror without end and were sent to a terrible end'
(Cemetery of the Otranto Dead, Vlora)

On the night of 28 March 1997, when Albania has become a living hell in the uprising that followed the collapse of the pyramids, the Italian warship *Sibylla* sank the Albanian ship *Katerti i Radës* in the Strait of Otranto. Eighty-seven people drowned; 34 survived. The Cemetery of the Otranto Dead in Vlora holds the remains of only 54; the rest were never found. Virion and Krenar Xhavara have come to lay flowers on the graves of their families. Virion lost his wife and three young children; Krenar his wife and baby.

VIRION: On the ship we had raised two white flags to show that we were people in need . . . At one point we took the children up to the bridge. There were about 40 children, aged from one to 12 or 13. The children were waving to the Italian ship, the way children do.

KRENAR: When it began to get dark the ship took up a position behind us. We thought it was going to escort us . . . Instead, it got up tremendous speed and rammed us twice.

VIRION: We men on the bridge fell into the sea. The ship took the women and children who were inside down with it. We heard howls, we were finding the drowned in front of us . . .

The Xhavara brothers' only wish is for those responsible to be identified. But up to now they have met absolute indifference from the Albanian and Italian authorities. Still, life is full of coincidences. Krenar has remarried and is trying to rebuild his life. The day we met, his wife had given birth to a healthy baby boy. 'What I wish for him is to live in a country where the young don't emigrate any more, where they don't leave their bones in the seas and on the mountains.'

DANCING IN THE DARK

Organised crime is thriving in Albania – a profitable cocktail of migrant trafficking, drugs and prostitution. Without high-level political cover, it would not be nearly so successful. Yet the rush to leave Albania is slowing down. Composer Altin Shehu lived for 11 years in Greece before deciding to come home: 'I realised that whatever I do in Greece I'll be a foreigner. In the summer of 1999 I gave a concert, but very few people came. The police were rounding up thousands of Albanian immigrants indiscriminately: on the buses, the trains, the streets, everywhere . . . That's when I decided to leave.'

But when he came back he felt foreign in Albania, too. 'It's as if I've emigrated for a second time, but this time to a country where I speak the language and no one asks for my "green card".' Gradually, his work is gaining recognition. 'In Greece, I became a better person and a better musician. I'm trying to bring the best of what I learned back here. I think of Greece as my second home. When I say that, sometimes people look at me strangely. But the Greeks don't know Albania. They should come and have a look some time – it would be good for both of us.'

Sabina has also just come back, after finishing a law degree in Italy. Why? 'Because after ploughing through a mountain of books I don't feel like cleaning houses for uneducated rich people,' she says, and bursts out laughing. I show her Visar's new book and ask her if her generation is interested in the past. 'Of course. But the dictatorship we have now is called poverty, corruption and mafia.'

It's past midnight on a Saturday; the pub is filled with young people. 'We've had enough of extremes,' says Sabina. 'All we want is a normal life.' The whole pub is throbbing to Bruce Springsteen: 'You can't start a fire without a spark / This gun's for hire / Even if we're just dancing in the dark.' ❑

Gazmend Kapllani is a journalist working in Greece and Albania. He is a producer for Greek Public Radio and writes for Ta Nea, *Greece's largest daily newspaper, and* Koha Jone, *the main newspaper of Albania*

Translated by Maria Margaronis

FANTASTICAL LANDSCAPES

ANGUS MACQUEEN

NESTLING IN THE GENTLY ROLLING HILLS OF
REMOTE NORTH-WEST ROMANIA IS A MAGICAL
LAND THAT TIME FORGOT. BUT NOW THE
YOUNGER GENERATION WANT OUT

Driving into the Maramures, the world feels totally familiar, not from reality but from the world of our imaginations. This is the set for a Thomas Hardy film or an ambitious costume drama, with extras on their horses and carts bouncing along barely treated roads, men scything in the fields and families threshing their wheat in water-driven machines made in the nineteenth century. The villages are dominated by the spires of wooden churches dating back to the Middle Ages. Inside are frescoes painted directly on to the wood depicting a world of devils and witches. Drive through on a Sunday, and the roads are packed with groups of young men and young women promenading in their Sunday best like groups of peacocks in some obscure mating ritual. The women, boasting bright flowery skirts and scarves, along with white blouses and white court shoes, demurely wander up and down the road eyeing up the men who sport embroidered woollen waistcoats and a range of very strange hats.

Stay longer and you realise that these villages are one of the very few farming areas in the former Soviet empire in which the basic culture of the people has not been destroyed or at least fatally undermined by commu-

*Maramures, Romania, images
of Hell: frescoes adorn the
walls of a wooden church.
Courtesy: October Films*

nism. Anyone who has spent time in that part of the world has found a countryside that has lost nearly all sense of its individual and communal past. Most villages are now dominated by the old and the weak, whose farming skills are lost in some alcoholic haze.

Not so the Maramures. For reasons best known to himself, Nicolae Ceauşescu, Romania's last dictator, who wanted to urbanise or 'systematise' villages, thought the people of the Maramures were the perfect peasants. As a result, there was almost no collectivisation in the area and the villagers, give or take the odd party meeting, seem simply to have got on with their lives as they had for centuries. For all its boasts of turning Romania into a future utopia, the communist regime preserved much in aspic, providing the Western visitor with a utopia in the past. The sheer scale of the economic failure of the giant state-owned factories and bureaucratic infra-structure meant that very little investment was put into the countryside: peasants were there to feed the towns.

The ugly concrete electricity pylons tell of some modernity and this village, Budesti, got a phone system a couple of years ago. Many peasants went off to the local towns and mines to work in equally Victorian condi-tions. That income took them and their families beyond the pure subsis-tence farming in the valley. But until the fall of the Berlin Wall in 1989, for most peasants the only contact with the outside world came via the army, years of conscription for masters they barely knew, which turned the men into cannon fodder, border guards and sometimes secret policemen.

And then came 'democracy'.

The Oprisc family are the threshers of Budesti. For generations they have threshed the village's corn. Their fantastical machine was built in 1857 when an emperor ruled this part of the world from Vienna. The thresher stands to one side of the street that makes up the village; on summer evenings its whirring water-driven wheels turn the Oprisc house into the heart of the village, as families line up their carts loaded with the harvest.

Each family knows how the system works, with the men forking the sheaves of wheat down on to the threshing floor before they are passed gently up to the women on the top of the thresher who open them and feed them in. Children sweep up the remains: every little bit is kept. At the end of this elegant dance, Ghiorghie or his wife Irina bring out the scales and take their 10 per cent. Budesti remains in part a barter economy and Ghiorghie later uses the bags of corn in his cellar to buy logs for his new

Oral tradition: Ghiorghie Oprisc.
Courtesy: October Films

wooden roof and a pig at the weekly market.

Thirty years ago, Ghiorghie married well. His wife Irina brought with her orchards and good fields, and the Oprisc family are now among the richest in the village. Under the communists they kept their heads down so as not to be accused of being rich peasants; now they can show off more. Recently, they set up a new still to make brandy and are thinking of opening a village bar. Ghiorghie has also built a new house for his two sons, Ghitsa and Laurenciu.

Ghiorghie is the repository of village music and stories, a tradition of songs, dances and storytelling that is famous across the whole country. The culture of the Maramures has been studied by anthropologists and musicologists all over the world. Ghiorghie has faithfully passed on these traditions to his children as part of their inheritance, just as he soon intends to hand on the farm. Both sons are fine musicians; the older was part of a folk group that is regularly filmed and shown on Romanian television.

And there's the rub: while the sons have taken on the music, they are rejecting the life. Where once there was little choice but to take on the ploughing and the scything every year, the end of communism opened up horizons as well as political systems. For the first time, along with films and soap operas, there was news of the outside world – a remote world that spoke of freedom and opportunities. This world challenged people not to be afraid.

In the local town that outside world manifested itself in Twix and Mars bars, foreign cars and McDonald's. At the same time, the local factories and mines closed down, removing overnight almost all sources of local employment. The harsh realities of capitalism and competition removed at a stroke the peasants' ability to supplement their income from subsistence farming.

But now they knew about jobs abroad and took advantage of their vague political status of having lived in an oppressive system to claim the right to leave. In the mid-1990s, the first networks to get people abroad illegally were set up and the first money started to arrive back home, money that built new concrete houses and gave families plumbing and central heating and washing machines.

The irony for Ghiorghie is that one of the networks involved the very music he had taught his children. Soon Ghitsa and his group were invited to the United States and he decided to stay. That was in 1996. Ghitsa is still there. He occasionally plays his fiddle in a local restaurant in Atlanta but like so many immigrants he is fighting to become a businessman. At least that is what his father says. Or understands.

He and Irina do little but dream of Ghitsa's return. Meanwhile, their louche younger son Laurenciu does little but dream of going to join his brother and wants nothing to do with the farm. Using some cash that Ghitsa has sent from the US, Laurenciu has moved out of the village to the local town where he has dabbled in various shady business deals. His parents have had to dig him out of a couple.

As in any of those Hardy novels, the son is not grateful. While his mother and father fret at what is going to happen to the farm when they get old and die, Laurenciu schemes to get abroad. He tries everything from setting up his own music group to trying to buy papers on the black market. At the same time, he brings further shame on his parents by moving in with a married woman in the town, a break in tradition that is almost too much for them to bear.

They refuse to meet the woman, describing her as a witch who has cast a spell on their son. They despair for themselves and their children going off into a world they simply do not understand. At one point, Ghiorghie talks of trying to get to the US to bring his beloved Ghitsa back. As so often, the child who has gone is the perfect one and will surely save them. Ghiorghie barely understands what he is proposing, let alone the likely reality of his son's reaction when he gets there. Irina's face is a picture of uncertainty and fear. She has lost one child, maybe a second, and now her husband is planning to travel into that distant world. But despite phone calls to Atlanta, the idea is never followed through.

Instead, Irina begins seriously to look in local orphanages for a child to bring up, someone to look after them in their old age and the farm when they are gone. They know that everything they have lived for is at stake.

In Budesti the Christmas of 2000 is marked by there not being enough young men left in the village to perform the traditional all-male nativity play set to a traditional poetic text. The future has arrived.

'An age away': spring ploughing. Courtesy: October Films

What has happened to the Opriscs is happening to every family in the village and in the region — to families all over Eastern Europe. Their sons and daughters are our illegal immigrants.

Laurenciu, his brother and thousands of others like them are bogeymen on two fronts: in the course of one generation they are destroying their parents' world and becoming our hated illegal immigrants. Yet they are doing exactly what our forebears did, making economic decisions driven by the realities of the world around them. Now, instead of making their way to the local town, they are travelling to the nearest source of real jobs.

When and if they return to the village (and many do), these migrants want the three-storey concrete house that, unlike wooden buildings, will not have to be constantly rerooled and rebuilt. They want the sofas, the washing machines, the hi-fis and the big televisions they have seen in houses in the West. They want the cars as well. And illegal immigration is just about the only route available to satisfy those desires.

They will do almost anything to get here. Ion and Maria, two poorer peasants who work as hired hands for Irina and Ghiorghie, have borrowed huge sums to get out. Their relatives made it, and the only messages coming back are dollar signs. While they know it is difficult, little is said about the loneliness and the danger facing them abroad.

Ion was shocked to realise that the moment he got to the West, under a train, he had become a criminal in the eyes of the state and of many people around him. 'Romanians are criminals, that is what everyone thinks,' murmers Ion in muted horror when he returns home as a deportee. These economic migrants are cast into a legal minefield whose logic few of them understand.

What they do learn fast are the rules of the street. They know they are not political asylum seekers, but in Britain are encouraged to ask for it. In France, they know that if they apply for asylum at the local police station they will either be arrested and deported on the spot, or simply chucked on to the streets. In Britain, they know jobs are easier to come by and the pay is better than in France, where employment laws are much stricter and attack the employer not the immigrant. Equally, they know that in France, without the right identity document, they can be picked up at any moment.

Such are the vagaries of life for men and women brought up an age away. They know it will be tough in the West but, like those men and women who invaded the slums of industrial towns in the nineteenth century to make a living and transform their lives, this new generation of migrants has both the energy and the drive to survive. And, just as 150 years ago, our cities need them. ❏

Angus Macqueen's three-part series The Last Peasants *was shown on Channel 4 in the UK on 9, 16 and 23 March 2003*

A CAMP IN AFRICA

CAROLINE MOOREHEAD

AFRICANS MAKE UP 40 PER CENT
OF THE WORLD'S REFUGEES, OVER
3 MILLION LIVING IN CAMPS, MOST
OF THEM VICTIMS OF WAR AND THE
MILITARISATION OF THEIR HOMELANDS

One thousand kilometres to the east of Conakry, Guinea's seaside capital, deep in the forest region that runs in a thick green band along the borders of Côte d'Ivoire, Sierra Leone and Liberia, lies the small market town of Lola. Few of Lola's buildings rise above a single storey, and most of its houses are made of mud bricks and thatch. Very occasionally a bus comes to Lola, along the red earth tracks that cross the forest, and a few lorries bring people and their goods for the weekly market under the mango trees; but there is seldom much electricity and the telephone rarely works. Lola is a quiet, tranquil place, in which little happens. The rainy season, when the earth turns into red mud and the potholes become barely passable, lasts almost eight months.

Lola may have little to offer outsiders, but its position is strategic. Situated at the crossroads of one of Africa's busiest refugee flows, it lies a little less than 50km from Liberia to the South and 30km from Côte d'Ivoire to the East, both countries currently poised to slide further into civil war. Guinea's forest lands are accustomed to refugees: they have been coming across these borders for many years, fleeing the region's savagery and war. As one of the most forgotten countries in a neglected continent, Guinea would not be in the news today were it not for the fact that, at one of the most crucial moments in the United Nations' 55-year history, it finds itself president of the Security Council. As for Lola, some time in the 1980s, a vast hangar was built in the middle of the town. No one quite remembers what this was intended for, nor why, some years ago, it was given the name of Centre d'Accueil pour les Jeunes, for there can be no more unlikely youth centre than this cavernous building, almost completely dark inside, its ceiling rising far up into dusty blackness. Today, however, the Centre d'Accueil has found its purpose: it has become a transit centre for refugees, those escaping renewed fighting in Liberia, and those fleeing ethnic and xenophobic troubles in Côte d'Ivoire, where politicians from Abidjan are fanning the divisions between the Muslim north and the Christian south.

What is taking place in Lola is an operation that shows up the international refugee agencies at their best. It is an impressive spectacle, a coordinated and efficient process masterminded by the UN's High Commission for Refugees and executed with the help of the major international agencies, and it is likely to please funders for which Guinea, wavering in its commitment to war in Iraq, might prove a worthy country for increased aid. None of the things that afflict long-term refugee situations – the camps stagnating in depression and apathy, the bickering over limited resources, the prevarications of politicians and the racism of asylum policies – is at play here. The fact that, for this possibly brief moment at least, the crisis is contained, the numbers manageable and the arrivals calm gives Lola an orderly air. That this could alter at any minute, should the LURD (Liberians United for Reconciliation and Democracy) rebels intensify their operations in nearby Nimba County, or Côte d'Ivoire's own rebels step up their campaigns, adds a feeling of alertness and anticipation.

Fallah, who arrived towards the end of January from Danane, 30km inside Côte d'Ivoire, is a lively, handsome woman in her 30s with two young sons. Her manner is excited and she is eager to talk. She was working for a farmer in his cassava fields, she explains, using her wages to buy cocoa which she sold in the market, when rebels began advancing on Danane in December. After she started hearing shots at night in the surrounding forest, and learned that the rebels were looking for boys to take as soldiers, she packed all she could carry into a basket to put on her head, and set out with her sons for the border. Fallah has no husband. She laughs at the very thought of it. With her, from Danane, went Maja, who is a little younger, and the mother of two small girls, one just 18 months old. Maja does not have a husband either, and the two women have evidently become good friends.

The journey from Danane to the river that marks the boundary with Guinea took them four days, living off bananas and sweet potatoes found along the way. As they walked, encouraging the children as they went, they met Peter, a farmer with a wife and four children, Sekou, travelling with his elderly mother, and a small party of traders, men carrying heavy bundles of clothes to sell, tied around the middle with string. The track to the frontier was crowded.

Though coming from Côte d'Ivoire, not one of these people is Ivorian, a fact that gives their odyssey a particular edge, and says much about the ebb and flow of refugees along Guinea's forest region. Fallah and Maja are both Liberians, who settled in Côte d'Ivoire in the mid-1990s, having been driven from their villages in Nimba County by LURD's predecessors, the ULIMO rebels. Peter and his family come from Niger, drawn down into Côte d'Ivoire many years ago after ethnic differences with their neighbours. Sekou and his mother are Nigerians and have been exiles all their lives – she has crossed backwards and forwards over Africa's frontiers since she was a girl. The traders are all Guineans, long-term residents of Côte d'Ivoire, who have now decided that home is a safer land to be in these times of endless conflict. For all these people, exile is a familiar place: they have inhabited it for much of their lives. Inside Lola's vast hangar – shelter from the rains for 1,002 people, of whom almost half, 444, are children – the space has been marked out into a mosaic of patches of private territory, outlined by bags, bundles, rolled-up mattresses, water containers, the luggage of wandering people. They sit quietly on the floor, in the dim light.

Over 3 million Africans live in camps today, in a lasting and intractable state of limbo, in which they are sequestered, concentrated and out of harm's way, the better to serve a convergence of interests between host governments, international agencies and, to some extent at least, the refugees themselves. Camps at least appear safe; they contain others as vulnerable and dependent. But camps are also fundamentally destructive of people, places of poverty, powerlessness and lack of freedom. Africans make up 40 per cent of the world's refugees.

Lola, for its current occupants, is a staging post, a pause while plans are made to move them on, to proper camps far removed from these permeable borders where the Guinean government feels that they are too vulnerable to incursions of fighters keen to recruit refugees for their endless wars. Three years ago, soldiers crossed into the forest region from Liberia and hundreds of Guinean refugees – and one member of UNHCR's staff – died in the fighting. The president, Lansana Conté, long hospitable to the refugees who have flowed around this part of West Africa for many decades, has now decided that they must reside in camps. Lola is just one step in an operation of military proportions and complexity. The 50,000 or so remaining Sierra Leoneans are due to be repatriated, now that there is a fragile peace at home. Their places can be taken by new arrivals from Liberia and Côte d'Ivoire, alongside the 120,000 Liberians and 3,000 Ivorians already in camps around the country. Can those now in Lola hang on until the Sierra Leoneans leave, via a bridge being hastily constructed by German funding before the rains close the roads? Like captains at sea, scanning the horizon for approaching trouble, those who work with Guinea's refugees watch and wait.

Behind the stories of Lola's new arrivals, narratives recounted with verve and much humour, lies a backdrop of sadness and loss. Few among them have not seen friends or relations killed or wounded, have not escaped massacres or watched their houses burn down, do not worry about people left behind, or grieve for their abandoned homes and livelihoods. Some of the most painful of these stories involve children. According to the International Rescue Committee, which runs the schools in the camps as well as a whole range of programmes with families, between 5 and 7 per cent of children lose their parents during flight, for many different reasons. Alone, frightened, hungry, many stop along the way to safety, finding refuge with local people in exchange for work, so that a whole generation of child workers is growing up along these West African borders. A number of them, with the help of the International Committee of the Red Cross, are reunited with their parents: of the 7,000 unaccompanied children identified by ICRC in 2002, over 1,600 are now back with their parents.

What no one knows is how many never make it to safety. When in January Fallah and Maja reached the river that separated Côte d'Ivoire from Guinea, they found a group of children sitting on the bank, too afraid to cross. Though not deep, the water flows swiftly in these parts. Some they were able to help across. But then, looking back from the Guinean side, they saw a little girl, perhaps five or six years old, hesitate, before plunging into the river. For a while it seemed as if she would be able to keep her footing on the stony river bed. But then she suddenly slipped and disappeared below the water. They watched her body, in its bright yellow T-shirt, swept away by the current, bobbing brightly in the water, until it disappeared from sight. ❏

Caroline Moorehead has recently returned from Guinea, which she visited as part of her research for a book on refugees

IN DETENTION

THOMAS CHAZA

I fled to Britain from my home country, Zimbabwe, after suffering persecution for my political views. I came to the UK in October 2001 as a visitor, on the bad advice of a friend. The immigration authorities at Gatwick airport didn't believe that only a visit was intended, so they served me with deportation papers. I contacted a solicitor, who told me not to say a word to the authorities about coming to seek asylum. That same evening I was transferred to Tinsley House, an immigration detention centre. After a week, the solicitor demanded £850 from me. When I told him I did not have that kind of money he threatened to abandon my case so that I would be deported. I contacted a different solicitor, who entered my asylum claim. I was taken to Oakington for 'fast track' processing; my claim was refused.

I decided to appeal and was taken to Harmondsworth where I was to wait for my court hearing dates. After three weeks I was transferred to Lindholme Detention Centre, which was no different from a real prison. On arrival, I was made to strip naked and they searched me and my bag in the most humiliating and degrading manner. Detainees were not allowed to wear their own clothing. The prison gear made my skin feel itchy from the first time I put it on. Some prison officers were very abusive and the food was terrible. We were locked up most of the time and they counted us four times a day. If you wanted to write a letter, you were not allowed to seal the envelope and if you received one you would get it already opened.

When I was at Lindholme my solicitor said he could no longer represent me since I was now miles away from him. I managed to get a new solicitor the week I was supposed to go for my hearings. My dates were then shifted to two months later since the new solicitor said he needed to have a look at my story. I could not sleep at all at night, but lay awake thinking about how I got myself into that horrific place. I thought of escaping, of sneaking into the community and settling illegally. It became obvious to me that asylum seekers are often detained for no reason that they can understand, to deter would-be asylum seekers from coming to Britain to seek protection.

I finally went for my full hearing in the seventh month of detention, and was granted refugee status. ❏

Thomas Chaza *is a pseudonym*

COME ONE COME ALL

PATRICK WILCKEN

UNLIKE MOST DEVELOPED COUNTRIES,
ISRAEL SEES IMMIGRATION AS
THE CURE TO ITS MOST PRESSING
PROBLEM, EVEN THOUGH IT CANNOT
ALWAYS CONTROL THE SIDE EFFECTS

In an era of heightened anxieties about immigration from poorer parts of the world into wealthier, Westernised countries, Israel stands as the great exception. While UK Prime Minister Tony Blair plays to the electorate with promises of halving the number of asylum seekers in Britain by September 2003, his Israeli counterpart, Ariel Sharon, has talked openly of his goal of attracting 'another million' immigrants in the next decade, to match the million, mainly from the former Soviet Union, who have been absorbed into Israel through the 1990s. The paltry benefits that refugees entering the UK are due are constantly under threat from governments trying to combat the popular perception of Britain as a 'soft touch' for immigrants. Jewish couples arriving in Israel, in contrast, can expect a handout of around US$6,000 a couple, help with finding a job, mortgage assistance and tax exemption on cars (halving their price), as well as the state-funded absorption process that includes free intensive courses in Hebrew.

In the West, the past few decades have seen a progressive clampdown on immigration; in Israel it has been the reverse. There, falling, not rising, levels of immigration are a cause for concern. The recent decline (down by one-third in 2002), due to the continuing Israeli–Palestinian violence and the country's economic woes, is producing an immigration 'crisis' of a type that would be welcomed by Western governments. Under the new circumstances, Sharon has toned down his rhetoric, speaking now of attracting just half a million immigrants over the next ten years – still a huge number when you consider the population of Israel is only 6 million, one-tenth the size of the UK's.

Of course, compared with other parts of the developed world, immigration is thought of very differently in Israel. The drive to recruit is ideological – the 'Right of Return' law under which Jews worldwide can settle in Israel and claim Israeli citizenship is a central plank of the Zionist project;

Aliyah (the move to Israel) a Jewish rite of passage. But there are also hard demographic calculations involved, the inverse of those being made elsewhere. The combined population of Israel and the occupied territories is finely balanced. Just over 50 per cent of the 9 million total west of the Jordan river are Jewish Israeli, but with a higher birth rate in the Arab communities this is set to change. While the UK tabloids and even the odd Labour minister talk of being 'swamped' by the influx of immigrants, Israeli politicians see immigration as a bulwark against the rising Arab tide.

So far, the strategy seems to be working, aided by the fall of the Berlin Wall and subsequent mass immigration as the Soviet Union unravelled. At first the USA was the favoured destination for Russian Jews but changes in regulations, requiring immigrants to apply for visas in Moscow and face a Washington-imposed quota system, tipped the balance in favour of Israel. From 1989 to 1992, a staggering 300,000 entered Israel from the former Soviet Union, increasing the population by 5 per cent at a stroke. Migrants poured in from the vast swathe of the disintegrating Soviet empire, from Kazakhstan, Russia itself, Belarus and the Ukraine. Known in Israel collectively as 'Russians', they settled mainly in the coastal plain around Tel Aviv. By the end of the decade, almost 1 million had set up in Israel, making the Russian community by far the biggest ethnic group in the country. The majority were at least college-educated, many had degrees, some doctorates. Most were forced at first to work as cab drivers, cleaners and barmen, but were soon entering the professions. With three television stations, over 20 daily newspapers as well as representation in the Knesset, by the end of the 1990s the Russian-speaking community had carved out a niche in their new country. One in six Israelis is now 'Russian' and their impact on Israeli society has been, and will continue to be, enormous.

A short drive down from Jerusalem to the Mediterranean coast lies the town of Ashdod, nestled between Tel Aviv and the northern boundary of the Gaza Strip. After the cool air of the semi-arid hills around Jerusalem, the central plains are hot and fertile. The road to Ashdod runs through fruit orchards and agricultural plots. Large greenhouses flash by, growing export quantities of tomatoes, herbs and flowers, before farmland gives way to the leafy suburbs on the town's outskirts. Up ahead, rows of freshly built apartment blocks stretch out and, off in the distance, construction work goes on apace. Ashdod's roads are broad and palm-lined, the town well planned, its population 130,000 and rising. In the market area of Shchunat Yud, shopfront signs are in Russian. Rows of salamis hang in Russian delicatessens –

Jerusalem, 1999: Minister of Trade and Industry Natan Sharansky marches with Red Army veterans. Credit: André Brutmann / Rex Features

which also, controversially, sell pork – and travel agents advertise flights to Moscow, Kiev and Minsk. In the centre of town, near the municipal buildings, stands a new arts centre housing a ballet school with spacious dance studios.

The deputy mayor of Ashdod, Shimon Katznelson, was one of the early immigrants from the former Soviet Union to reach Israel. He left Kiev in 1970, at a time when those managing to get out of the Eastern bloc knew that they were on a one-way ticket with little prospect of return. A balding man in his 50s, he now presides over a city that is one-third Russian-speaking. Katznelson tells me that Ashdod 'Russians' are from all over, but that the bulk are Ukrainian. They came 'to be together', in what they saw as their 'home', although many are clearly economic migrants, fleeing from the worsening situation in the former Soviet Union to what has every appearance of a Mediterranean boom town. On the political spectrum, they are 'to the right' or 'to the right of right', says Katznelson, maybe because of security fears or perhaps, the deputy mayor remarks drily, because of their long, bitter experience under regimes 'to the left of left'.

It was not always so. Russians have played king-makers through the 1990s — as a crucial block of swing voters they have supported Yitzhak Rabin, Binyamin Netanyahu and Ehud Barak, before turning to Ariel Sharon, moving rightwards with the wider Israeli electorate. Under the old voting system, in which they could cast one vote for a party and another for prime minister, they also supported Russian sectarian parties — Avigdor Lieberman's ultra-rightist National Union and former Soviet dissident Natan Sharansky's right-of-centre Yisrael B'Aliya. In January's election, though, when a single-ballot electoral system was introduced, the likes of Sharansky and Lieberman went head to head with Sharon and their vote collapsed. Yisrael B'Aliya emerged from the elections with just two seats in the Knesset and was forced to merge with Likud.

Israel's burgeoning Russian community has taken to Sharon, although many would have preferred to see Netanyahu on the Likud ticket. The son of Russian immigrants, Sharon has been careful to cultivate the Russian vote, campaigning in towns like Ashdod and even going to Moscow for a photo opportunity with Vladimir Putin. Sharon fulfils many Russians' desire for a strong man at the top with uncompromising rhetoric and a military background. Newly arrived immigrants often know little of the history of the Israeli–Palestinian conflict, wanting only a secure environment for themselves and their families. Their stance is pragmatically nationalist and they see Sharon as the best defender against what they perceive as unjusti-fied Palestinian claims. It is a situation much like that in Russia itself, where voters have rallied behind Putin for his hard-line approach to the Chechen rebels.

The move away from sectarian immigrant parties is also a sign that the newcomers are beginning to integrate into Israeli society, albeit in distinc-tive enclaves such as Ashdod, and are looking beyond their narrow interests. 'Today marks the end of a chapter in the immigration process into Israeli society,' as Natan Sharansky himself admitted after his disastrous election showing, 'and we are beginning a new chapter in which leaders of the immigrant community are a voice and a partner in the largest national camp party.'

The process has been a difficult one. Not everyone in Israel is happy about the sudden wave of immigration over the past decade. Orthodox Jews in particular are concerned about the number of non-Jews who are being allowed into Israel. There have been renewed calls to change the Law of Return which, in 1970, was amended to include the descendants of Jewish

MISSION IMPOSSIBLE

Three times a week, Myriam, Sigal and the other members of the association they run visit the local prison to meet the men and women of Israel's new lumpenproletariat, incarcerated for being in the country illegally. The members of Hotline for Migrant Workers, one of the few Israeli organisations dedicated to defending foreign workers, also take 150 phone calls a month from prisoners and their families wanting to know and protect their rights.

After the 5 January suicide bombing that killed and wounded several migrant workers in a working-class district of Tel Aviv, the volunteers gave support to the families, visited the wounded and collected phone cards so that the migrants could contact relations back home. For its part, the Israeli government had to promise those of the wounded without the right papers that they would not be thrown out of the country if they went to hospital for treatment.

Around 180,000 people – almost two-thirds of the 300,000 foreign workers in Israel – are without visas and live in fear of a police raid. 'Over the last few months, the authorities have tightened regulations and a xenophobic campaign is presenting foreign workers as a plague responsible for all evil: crime, drugs, prostitution,' laments the hotline's Myriam Darmoni-Sharvit.

Elections or no elections, no political grouping other than the Communist Party pays the slightest attention to these second-class citizens – they may make up 5 per cent of the country's population but foreign workers can't vote. In August 2002, Ariel Sharon's government announced its decision to expel 50,000 people between now and the end of 2003. He presents his latest policy as a 'national mission'.

Since then, arrests have multiplied and now run at around 500 every month. New detention centres have opened and, in 2002, a record 6,000 people were repatriated. Paradoxically, the government continues to bring in tens of thousands of new foreign workers every year. Whole sectors of the economy – in particular agriculture, construction and care for the elderly and handicapped – have been deserted by the Israelis and now rely on this unskilled, undemanding workforce.

Despite soaring unemployment, Israeli construction companies are 15,000 workers short; a recent offer of work stipulating that employees should be Israeli was a failure. In any case, employers prefer to take on 'fresh flesh', says Sigal Rozen, director of the charity. The new arrivals accept lower salaries, are totally in the dark about their rights and are not organised. 'Thais are prepared to work in agriculture for the equivalent of US$500 a month when the minimum wage is US$700,' adds Myriam. As for illegal workers, their status saves their employers from having to pay social security. 'That explains the government's refusal to listen to one of our demands, which is to legalise those people who are here rather than bring in new ones,' she continues.

Recruitment of these workers, who come from the Philippines, Thailand, China, Moldova, Romania, South America and Africa, started in the early 1990s. Over the years, they have replaced Palestinian workers. Before the intifada, 200,000 Palestinans were working in Israel; today, there are no more than a few thousand. Migrant workers enter the country with a visa linked to a particular employer valid for two, three or five years. If they change jobs, for whatever reason, they lose their residence permits and are automatically driven underground. This is how Albert, a 40-year-old Filipino, ended up in prison. 'My employer, who was old and sick, died and I lost my work visa.'

Despite their precarious situation, foreign workers make Israel their home: many have been there for more than ten years. Various communities, African, South American and Asian, often supported by Christian churches, have organised themselves. Their members start families here. Children born in Israel are simply declared 'living infants' and have no official papers. At 18, they are as likely as their parents to be sent back to 'their' country. ❑

Stephanie Le Bars *is a journalist with* Le Monde
Translated by GC

grandparents, their spouses and the spouses of Jews, extending rights to those persecuted by Nazi Germany in the 1930s and 40s. The changes opened a gulf between those who qualify as Jewish under religious law (whose mothers are Jewish) and those who are allowed in under the looser 'grandfather clause' of the Law of Return. Non-Jewish Russians are seen by Orthodox Jews as a threat. 'By the end of 2010,' warns Eli Yishai, chairman of the Orthodox Shas Party, 'the state of Israel will lose its Jewish identity,' bringing 'more stores that sell pork'. Isolated incidents of anti-Semitism – swastikas appearing on walls and the desecration of Jewish cemeteries – have been blamed on Russian immigrants. With as many as one-quarter of Russians now in Israel considered non-Jews by Israel's chief rabbis, some feel that the continuing immigration is undermining the *raison d'être* of the State of Israel.

The presence of growing numbers of secular Russians is also throwing up anomalies. Russians, like all Israelis (except, ironically, Orthodox Jews), must do military service, a duty they take up with alacrity, many staying on to forge army careers. One battalion even became known as the 'Red Army' before the Israeli Defence Forces (IDF) introduced a policy of dispersing Russian draftees among the brigades. Russians now make up over 20 per cent of draftees in the IDF, often serving in the most dangerous posts in the occupied territories and later graduating into elite sniper units. Many have died in the conflict, yet, under strict religious law, some Russians cannot even be buried alongside the Jews they were supposedly fighting for. The issue was graphically illustrated in June 2001 when three teenage Russians killed in a Tel Aviv suicide bombing were refused burial in a Jewish cemetery, creating an uproar within the Russian community.

Away from the debate about Jewishness and amending the Law of Return, there are immigration worries more familiar to Western Europe. With the Gaza Strip now essentially sealed off and movement in the West Bank often curtailed by curfews, jobs that would have gone to Palestinians are being filled by guest workers from as far afield as Thailand and China. The system has been widely abused, with Sharon ordering the expulsion of 50,000 illegals in July last year. Immigrants from the former Soviet Union have also fallen under suspicion. In a recent case, a Ukrainian woman discovered carrying false papers was traced back to the office of a Russian lawyer in Tel Aviv. A police raid uncovered a workshop churning out fake government seals for border crossings, visas, Israeli driving licences and work papers. The extent of illegal immigration from the former Soviet Union is unknown, but reports such as this one cause disquiet in some quarters, a displaced anxiety about the whole Russian venture.

Despite the calls from religious leaders, there is little prospect of a bar on secular Russian immigration. More Russians are in fact being sought by Jewish Agency emissaries. According to a recent study, around 600,000 Jews and Jewish descendants eligible under the Law of Return remain in the former Soviet Union. A further 300,000 are in the USA, many of whom have close relatives in Israel, and they are also being actively recruited. New sources are being tapped. Argentine Jews are arriving in the wake of the country's economic collapse – the town of Ashdod now boasts a 3,500-strong community. There has also been an upsurge of French Jews making the move, even at this most inauspicious time. And Sharon has recently agreed to airlift 20,000 Ethiopians with Jewish roots who have been clamouring to be resettled in Israel since the main Ethiopian migration in the mid-1980s. With an estimated 7.8 million Jews living outside Israel, the potential for further demographic engineering in the Middle East is far from exhausted.

My cab driver on the way back from Ashdod is from Moldova and came to Israel with his family a few years back. When we reach Jerusalem, I stop off at the Putin Bar in the Russian compound. There, surrounded by black-and-white pictures of the president – Putin as a boy, as a teenager, as a handsome young man and as a statesman – we find a table in a small room packed with young Russians drinking Russian beer, downing shots of vodka and smoking Russian cigarettes. It could be Moscow or St Petersburg but it's not. Whatever happens from now on, Israeli society has already been fundamentally altered by the aftershocks of the end of the Cold War. ❏

Patrick Wilcken's book, Empire Adrift, *will be published by Bloomsbury in July 2003*

ON THE MOVE AT LAST

JASPER BECKER

WHEN THE WORLD'S MOST POPULOUS
NATION SETS ITS PEOPLE ON THE
ROAD, MILLIONS CAN LITERALLY
TURN UP ON YOUR DOORSTEP

Walk into any station and there they are: China's huddled masses, squatting or sleeping next to their bundled belongings, yearning to settle in the big cities. Some, a few, are indeed migrating but most work for a while and then go home. Walk around any of the building sites in Beijing, Shanghai or any of the other cities that are being rebuilt and expanded at a furious rate and you soon spot the crude dormitory shacks where the peasant workers live.

Tens of millions are on the move in China but the scale of this internal migration is not as great as it might seem. The state's grip has loosened but the controls over the population are still very tight.

China's Ministry of Public Security has been sufficiently alarmed about the 'blind flow' of 120 million peasants streaming to the cities to impose a whole new set of controls on what it calls the 'floating population'. Although this creates the image that at any given moment 120 million people are wandering about China like so many Dick Whittingtons, it is China's restrictions on the basic rights of its citizens that remain more significant.

The vast majority of the Chinese, that is its 1 billion peasants, still do not enjoy the basic right – enshrined both in the UN charter and the Chinese constitution – to choose where they live in their country. Under the country's household registration system they are tied to the land like medieval serfs and only a relatively small number are temporarily allowed to work in the cities. Some are construction workers, sent home when the job is over; many others are young girls making toys, clothing and shoes in the sweatshop factories of Guangdong Province and other coastal cities.

Although the numbers seem huge by the standards of any other country – some ten million migrant workers in Guangdong, for example – the vast majority of Chinese never leave their home county. The preponderance of rural–urban migration consists of peasants moving to work in local market

Shenzen, special economic zone, 2002: living on the job in a migrants' dormitory.
Credit: AFP / Catherine Touzard

towns, formerly called commune headquarters and now known as townships.

Yet something very fundamental is changing in China, and for the better. For the first time since the household registration system was introduced in the 1950s, the Chinese government is now making a genuine effort to phase it out, thereby removing a root cause of much social injustice and inequality in China.

To see how significant this is, one has to go back in history. The state's power to determine where an individual lives has a long tradition in China, dating back to the totalitarian dictatorship established by the Qin dynasty over 2,000 years ago under China's first emperor. Under the *baojia* system, villagers were put in groups of ten households and held responsible for each other's adherence to the state's edicts. Only after the collapse of the imperial system in 1911 were the villagers allowed to move around the country at will.

After 1949, Chairman Mao's government copied the Soviet Union's internal pass system and divided the population into rural and urban *hukous*, or household registrations, and quickly made any internal travel impossible through the rationing of tickets. Urban and rural *hukous* conferred very different rights and status. Residency was hereditary, passing through the mother, and could not be changed. Naturally it was better to be an urban resident, for then one enjoyed the full benefits of a cradle-to-grave social welfare system and, above all, the best food rations. Even when urban residents were sent to work in the countryside, they still enjoyed a different status from their peasant neighbours, including guaranteed food rations.

The residency system did not mean that people stayed put. The state moved unprecedented numbers around the country, often at the whim of Chairman Mao. In all, 170 million were moved around the country, including soldiers and prisoners sent to colonise borderlands, Red Guards and some 20 million 'educated youth' emptied out of the cities, as well as peasants, cadres and intellectuals. Many families were broken up, with husbands and wives forced to live far apart. Around 16 million were sent from the coastal cities into the interior to construct Mao's 'Third Line', designed to scatter a military-industrial complex in remote locations to enable his regime to survive a Soviet nuclear attack.

Among the other victims were over ten million peasants who were forcibly evicted to make way for the 80,000 reservoirs built during the massive dam-building drive. Since 1949, 45 million people have been moved to make way for these and other infrastructure projects.

Massive internal migration has therefore been as much a feature of Communist rule as it was in the Soviet Union, where Stalin transported whole nations thousands of miles. Even his vast network of gulag prison camps is dwarfed by the scale of what happened in China.

Yet while the Soviet economy was designed to accelerate the urbanisation and proletarian nature of rural Russia, Mao's policies actually reversed the urbanisation of China, especially during the Cultural Revolution.

The urban population declined and, when Mao died in 1976, China had the lowest urban–rural ratio in the world, with just 15 per cent considered urban compared with an average of 50 per cent in most developing countries. Next to nothing was spent on the urban infrastructure or housing for decades and this caused huge problems when Mao's successor, Deng Xiaoping, allowed people to leave their internal exile and go home.

Tens of millions of young and old flooded back into cities but there were no jobs or housing waiting for them. In the 1980s, families that had been split for decades were reunited but forced to live in overcrowded, squalid and shabbily built housing. Although China's population nearly doubled in 30 years, not a single new city was built until Shenzhen was quickly thrown up across the border from Hong Kong.

This desperate state of affairs was tackled only in the 1990s, when a real start was made on developing the cities. However, China stuck to a policy of discouraging the expansion of big cities in favour of developing small rural towns to absorb peasants leaving agriculture. So although China's urban population has doubled to over 30 per cent of the total, most of the increase was in small towns that were really just commune headquarters. From 1986 to 1996, the official count of cities rose from 295 to 666, although 400 of these had populations of fewer than 200,000.

Intrinsic to these policies is the strict enforcement of the *hukou* system whereby the authorities at all levels do their utmost to prevent the rural population from moving into the cities, swamping both the overstretched facilities and the labour market. To enforce this, the police carry out spot checks of the population, going from house to house checking identity papers or picking people up off the streets. Transgressors are then forcibly expelled and punished with months or even years in re-education camps. The punishments are meted out not by courts but by an administrative decision. Even so, as many as ten million did manage to find a way of migrating to big cities in the 1980s.

Many more followed when, in the 1990s, most Chinese cities began a series of construction projects requiring lots of extra rural labour. A similar phenomenon took place during the 1958 Great Leap Forward when 19 million peasant workers and their families were brought to the cities to take part in a temporary frenzy of construction, only to be sent home when the economy collapsed.

As more and more rural workers arrived in the cities, the police who are responsible for enforcing the *hukou* system uttered dire warnings that social chaos would follow. When, in 1995, Beijing reported it had 3 million migrants, the local police announced a series of counter-measures: forced evictions of migrant villagers, tough enforcement of family planning, closure of unofficial migrant schools, new taxes on employing migrants and new identity documents. The measures coincided with a nationwide, draconian 'strike hard campaign' to round up and execute large numbers of criminals – mostly young peasant males.

From a peasant point of view, the *hukou* system works like apartheid: peasants do the dirtiest, hardest jobs and are barred from access to schools, hospitals, nurseries and public housing; they enjoy almost no legal rights whatsoever. Almost all the central government's budget is spent on providing for the urban population.

Many peasant workers are paid only at the whim of their employers and have little recourse to the courts. Those who employ peasants are not bound to enforce the health and safety regulations; under social insurance legislation, drawn up for state industries, the deaths or injuries of peasants are not recorded in national statistics. Those peasants who find jobs in the cities can be expelled, without appeal, at a moment's notice because they have no legal right to live there.

However, major changes are afoot. Big cities are now operating what is effectively a selective migration policy, by issuing residence permits to those who invest a sufficient amount in property or who possess special skills needed in the local economy. New identity documents issued in 1996 also abolished the distinction between agricultural and non-agricultural *hukous* for residents of municipalities such as Beijing which include large swathes of rural areas; half of Beijing's population actually comprises peasants living in villages. Cities such as Shanghai or Beijing have also had to attract new migrants because the effect of the one-child policy is an ageing and, in some cases, a shrinking population. Shanghai has had to close many primary schools because there are no longer any young pupils.

Nor is it any longer economically possible to employ the rural population in agriculture. The surplus rural workforce is estimated at 150 million to 180 million workers. Another 100 million have already left agriculture – 36 million work in construction and about ten million have left their home provinces to find factory work in places such as the Pearl River delta. Their remittances often underpin the prosperity of large parts of rural China.

This year, new decrees have been issued to remove some of the discrimination towards rural migrants, to ensure that they are paid properly and that their children can attend schools. New health and safety regulations have been introduced to ensure that the same standards are applied across the board, and a rudimentary social insurance system for rural workers is being tried out.

In short, the state is coming round to recognising the legal right of peasants to work in cities, thus opening the door to permitting citizens the basic right to live and work where they please without discrimination. ❏

Jasper Becker is the Independent*'s Beijing correspondent and author of* The Chinese *(John Murray, 2000; ppb 2003)*

POWERS OF TRANSFORMATION
SALIL TRIPATHI

LEICESTER CITY COUNCIL ONCE TOOK OUT
ADVERTISEMENTS IN THE UGANDAN PRESS
IN AN ATTEMPT TO DETER THE COUNTRY'S
DISPOSSESSED ASIANS FROM SETTLING IN
THEIR TOWN. STILL THEY CAME. THE CITY
SIMPLY HAS NOT BEEN THE SAME SINCE

Picture yourself on a grey morning in an alien land, with the sky overcast and the rain falling silently, as you emerge bleary-eyed, holding a suitcase in one hand, a precious British passport in the other hand. You have left behind a warm, tropical city called Kampala, with its lush countryside and brilliant sun. You have also left behind everything your family had owned after building a business over two generations. It isn't easy being robbed of all possessions and kicked out of one country and landing up on another shore, the passport being the sole, tenuous link.

The British officials are sour, letting you in reluctantly. They give you ham sandwiches, not aware that you might be a Muslim, or a chaste vegetarian Hindu or Jain. And they tell you not to go to Leicester. 'There are no jobs there, no houses either. We cannot help you if you go to Leicester.' Jafar Kapasi was one of some 30,000 Asians who left Uganda for London's Stansted airport in November 1972. He had £55 with him in his pocket, the sum total of his remaining wealth, but he also had fierce determination. Uganda had been his home; India was where his parents came from, and the British passport was going to be the key with which he would unlock his potential and create a new, even better life for his children than the one he had enjoyed in Uganda.

His nightmare had begun with a coup that brought General Idi Amin to power in Uganda. Amin saw Indians as parasites prospering while Africans toiled; he called them 'bloodsuckers'. In August 1972, Amin informed Indians they had 90 days to leave the country. There were over 80,000 of them and surely the general must have been joking, many thought in their clubs and gymkhanas over tea and *kanda-na-bhajias* (onion bhajis).

To be sure, Indians did keep to themselves. Few married Africans and many were cunning traders of the kind that emerge in Paul Theroux's early novel, *Fong and the Indians*. As Amin's deadline neared, their treatment worsened; some sold their property at distress prices, others found their businesses confiscated.

Kapasi and his family left their home, daring roadblocks to get to Entebbe airport. Abandoning everything but what they could fit into a van, they trundled towards Kampala, being looted by Ugandan soldiers at every stop. They managed to get to the airport alive only because an officer who used to shop at their store helped them.

Kapasi refuses to forget what he went through, but says: 'I was determined to get back the high standard of living that we had lost. It provided me with the motivation to succeed.'

It is important for such experiences not to be forgotten because nostalgia can perform its familiar trick of allowing us to remember the past but not the pain. For example, last year, as Britain celebrated the 30th anniversary of the arrival of British Asians in the UK, a collective amnesia seemed to grip the country.

Edward Heath's Conservative government got the credit for opening the door for the British Asians when nobody else would accept them. But declassified Cabinet papers show that Britain tried hard to fob them off elsewhere. India was a natural option, but it was the first to refuse. It was burdened by refugees from the previous year's war over Bangladesh and it correctly reminded Britain that the Ugandan Asians had British passports. Heath then even considered sending them to the Falkland Islands but in the end accepted them in Britain.

Leicester officials were alarmed when they heard that Asians wanted to come to their then declining city. The city council placed advertisements in Ugandan newspapers, warning: 'In your own interests and those of your family you should accept the advice of the Uganda Settlement Board and not come to Leicester.' Bloody foreigners, Leicester's leaders must have thought, presaging arguments about 'bogus asylum seekers' today.

In 1974, with Labour back in power, these worries found an echo at the highest levels after President Jomo Kenyatta passed a law requiring foreigners in Kenya to have work permits. Anticipating another influx, Home Secretary James Callaghan changed laws, effectively ending the freedom of entry of Asian, but not white, settlers from East Africa, spuriously claiming that the distinction it was drawing up between two classes of British national was geographical, not racial. Those who could trace British-born ancestors were exempt, effectively excluding all but white applicants.

Callaghan protested at the time: 'I repudiate emphatically the suggestion that it is racialist in origin or in conception or in the manner in which it is being carried out.' But recounting a recently declassified memo in the *New Statesman*, Mark Lattimer reveals Callaghan's private view: 'It is sometimes argued that we can take a less serious view of the scale of immigration and settlement in this country because it could be more than offset by total emigration. This view overlooks the important point that emigration is largely by white persons . . . while immigration and settlement are largely by coloured persons. The exchange thus aggravates rather than alleviates the problem.' Today's tabloid newspapers would approve of such a message; they'd find a pithier way of saying it.

Callaghan's legislative changes came on top of the thunderous 'rivers of blood' speech Enoch Powell made in Birmingham in the late 1960s, warning Britain that bloody civil warfare lay ahead if immigration was not stopped. What was deemed a fringe view was now becoming a government policy. Graffiti like 'wogs go home' and abbreviations like 'KBW' (Keep Britain White) sprouted everywhere. Columnist Yasmin Alibhai-Brown arrived from Uganda as a child; she recalls 'people standing at airports with placards telling us to "get back to where you came from".'

Today, Kapasi can afford to laugh at this as a bad dream. Much has changed in his life. Not only is he a leading financial consultant, he is also a proud recipient of the Order of the British Empire award from the Queen, runs local charities and is regarded as a community leader.

His community has grown, in size and wealth. Indians from East Africa such as Manubhai Madhvani and Jasminder Singh figure highly in the *Sunday Times* annual ratings of Britain's richest people. According to an analysis by *Garavi Gujarat*, a leading Gujarati publication in Britain, some 65 per cent of British Indians earn more than £30,000 a year. The average British Indian earns £460 a week, compared to British Pakistanis (£270), Afro-Caribbeans (£260) and whites (£334).

To understand Indian wealth in Leicester, step out of Kapasi's office and turn right, heading for Belgrave Road, once marked for demolition but transformed by the Asian business presence into what is now known as Leicester's Golden Mile. The Diwali celebrations in Leicester, heralding the Hindu new year, are believed to be the biggest outside India. Today, more jewellery is sold, it is said, in Belgrave Road than anywhere else in Europe. TF Cash and Carry is a no-nonsense 7,000-square-foot shop selling every-thing from incense, idols and Indian music to cooking vessels made of stainless steel. There are vast sari shops and busy vegetarian restaurants, a lively handicrafts store and the tasteful art gallery of Maz Mashru, an internationally renowned photographer whose clients include TV newsreader Trevor McDonald and former Speaker of the House of Commons, Betty Boothroyd.

'Jai Shri Krishna,' Leicester's Gujaratis greet each other, as they go about buying clothes and foodstuff in this perpetual oriental bazaar, stepping into Mirch Masala restaurant for a Jain *bhel* (no onions, garlic or potatoes), buying audiotapes from Jeram Music Centre, drowning sorrows in Club Mumbai Blues and trying out salwar-kameez outfits at the trendy shop, Indi-Kal. Many of these shops are owned and run by Ugandan or Kenyan Indians. Arriving with nothing, they quickly set about trying to rebuild the luxurious lives they had lived in East Africa. 'They never seem to retire,' says Professor Richard Bonney of Leicester University, who has studied the community.

Belgrave Road is the high street of Indian Leicester, and Leicester is the most Indian city in Britain. By 2011, it is believed, the majority of Leicester's population will be of Asian origin, making Leicester the first city of its size in which the white community will be a minority. In a dramatic reversal, Leicester is not alarmed by it; rather, it celebrates it. Last year, the city council apologised for those advertisements it had placed in Ugandan newspapers in 1972. Ross Wilmot, the leader of the council last year, told the BBC: 'It was clearly a mistake. Of course, there are people in our society who still have very strong, negative and racist views. But I know in Leicester the experience of living in a multicultural city has helped educate people to live together in peace and harmony.'

Today, Indians are as important to Leicester as the Jews, fleeing Tsarist pogroms, were to Manchester, or the Huguenots, fleeing French Catholic vengeance, were to London's Spitalfields district. Remarkably, the textile trade played an interesting role. Huguenots in the East End traded in silk; Mancunian Jews focused on waterproof clothing; and Leicester had its hosiery and knitwear trade, a business Indians understood intimately.

Today, Indians account for some 25 per cent of Leicester's population, and 15 of its 56 councillors are Asians. The community's success has not aroused resentment or envy, but there are some rumblings. Internally, community elders complain about rising divorce rates. Over snacks at a restaurant, several of the old men complained of 'our girls' wanting to marry boys they meet in pubs. One man complains that he saw somebody's daughter at a bus stop in broad daylight hugging and kissing 'a foreigner' (which could mean a Muslim, a black or a white youth). While the city council has embraced the Diwali celebrations and pays for *dandiya ras*, a folk dance performed with sticks, the city's non-discriminatory policies mean that Leicester's Hindus cannot prohibit others, particularly Muslims, from participating. 'Then those boys meet our girls, and trouble starts,' one man laments. Another man recounts how he saw an Indian teenager smoking, and asked him not to smoke, but the teenager shot back: 'Mind your own business!' '*Arre*, even Idi Amin was better. He only took away our assets. This country is taking away our children!' he sighs.

One peculiar issue has emerged, galvanising some Indians into action. Some Hindus feel strongly that they should have the right to immerse the ashes of their dead relatives in the river around Leicester, an Avon tributary. Britain allows such immersions in three rivers, and Leicester's Asians would like theirs to be the fourth. Such discussions exasperate Ramnik Kavia, who will take over as Leicester's lord mayor in May, the third Asian to hold that august office in its 300-year history. Kavia says: 'There are alternatives available, such as sending the ashes to India, where a priest will perform the proper ceremony in the holy Ganga. What is the need for insisting upon doing it here?' Pravin Ruparelia of the Hindu Swayamsevak Sangh, a voluntary organisation affiliated to India's right-wing Hindu nationalist Rashtriya Swayamsevak Sangh, unexpectedly agrees. 'Hindus need to emerge from this blind faith over rituals. Is the immersion of ashes really the most important issue affecting Hindus?'

He is right. A more important issue affecting all Asians is the glass ceiling. While many admirers praise Asian entrepreneurs and point out how Indian-owned corner shops, Bangladeshi restaurants and Indian-owned pharmacies have transformed the British retail industry, Shailesh Solanki, executive editor of *Garavi Gujarat*, points out: 'Asians are successful in these businesses not because they have a special aptitude for it, but because they found it difficult to succeed in mainstream companies.'

At a discussion forum organised by the Centre for Social Markets in Leicester, one entrepreneur points out how he was persistently overlooked for promotion by a blue-chip British company, which kept sending him to training courses instead. 'I got fed up improving my qualifications, as though I was perpetually the one requiring training.'

British Asians look at the astonishing success of Indian professionals in the United States, where Indian-Americans run many of America's top corporate icons. Rajat Gupta runs McKinsey & Company; Vinod Khosla co-founded Sun Microsystems; Victor Menezis is one of the most senior executives at Citicorp; Arun Netravali heads Bell Labs; Fareed Zakaria edits *Newsweek* magazine, and Indra Nooyi is president of Pepsi, the highest-ranked Indian woman executive in the US. There aren't any similar Asian corporate achievers in the UK among comparable, iconic British companies.

Result: many Indians have formed their own businesses. And now, some have formed the British Asian Uganda Trust, which raises money for British charities. The trust's logo shows an hourglass in which the Ugandan flag turns into the Union Jack. Madhvani, who chairs the trust, said last year: 'We came here 25 years ago full of anxiety in an unknown land. The British people extended a welcoming hand, enabling us to make this country our home. Very few people tend to say thank you. We intend to be different.'

Ugandan President Yoweri Museveni has also appealed to the Asians to consider investing in Uganda again. 'Amin was wrong; don't punish your home,' he said in an emotional speech at the impressive Swaminarayana Temple in north-west London a few years ago. 'You may not forget what happened, but can you forgive?' Museveni asked plaintively. Some British Asians have made investments in Uganda since that visit.

Last year, riots engulfed Burnley, Oldham and Bradford in the north of England. Disaffected and jobless Asian youths had gone on a rampage targeting white areas of the three cities, and white youth, in turn, tried tormenting Asians. It was a long, hot summer. The right-wing British National Party put up candidates in the troubled cities and won some support, including a handful of seats.

Leicester City Council has commissioned a study to identify the city's strengths, which have prevented such violence in Leicester. Kavia believes Leicester's dynamism will prevent the situation from turning ugly. 'The BNP won't have a leg to stand on if it comes here,' he says. 'They thrive in depressed areas, and Leicester is not depressed.'

There is another element, too, one that may be politically incorrect to cite. Unlike Bradford and Burnley, the majority of Leicester's Asians are not Kashmiris, Bangladeshis or Pakistanis, but Indians. And while there are Muslims among the Indians, many of them are from the Gujarati community of Bohras, who are traders first. Disaggregating the Asian community in this manner may run counter to multicultural clichés about communities, but it helps identify and clarify issues. As Britain becomes a more multi-cultural society, and that multiculturalism spreads beyond London to other parts of the country, clearer understanding of communities is vital. To do that, multiculturalism will have to be divorced from political correctness. It is nobody's case, except paranoid right-wingers who still fear Powellian rivers of blood, that migration is fundamentally bad for Britain. Societies which remain open to migrants – the United States is the foremost example, but others such as Canada, Australia and Singapore too have relatively open borders – are able to maintain a vitality and dynamism that make other societies appear sclerotic. The success of the Ugandan Asians in overcoming the catastrophic consequences of expulsion is the soundest argument against restrictions on immigration. Asians from East Africa proved that, far from being a drain on the resources of host countries, immigrants often become creators of wealth and employment. This is a lesson the US has known for more than two centuries.

Australia-born and bred Patricia Hewitt, a minister in the Blair Cabinet and Member of Parliament for Leicester West, wrote last year: 'We should remember that our diversity brings not only cultural richness, but also economic and competitive advantage. In this global economy, the globe is at home in Britain. The new generation of British Asian, Caribbean and African professionals and entrepreneurs not only grow businesses here, they also create trade and investment links abroad.'

Britain took about 30,000 immigrants from East Africa. Today, in Leicester, which once so opposed the arrival of the Asians, an estimated 30,000 jobs have been created through the rise of Ugandan Asian businesses. The debt, then, has been repaid. ❏

Salil Tripathi *is a writer and freelance journalist*

LEICESTER: CITY OF MIGRATION
JUDITH VIDAL-HALL

MIGRATION HAS TRANSFORMED
LEICESTER FROM A DULL PROVINCIAL
MARKET TOWN INTO THE VIBRANT
CAPITAL OF ASIA IN BRITAIN

My departure early in the 1960s from Leicester, where I was born, more or less coincided with the beginning of a process of transformation that changed the city from a small town in the East Midlands grown complacent on its long prosperity to the vibrant Asian capital of Britain. In the process, it was to be physically brutalised by overzealous developers and, for a time, to suffer the reputation of the most racist city in the UK.

When I returned for an extended stay in the 1980s, the landscape of my memory had been swept away; the house where I grew up was now the city's leading sari emporium. In repeated visits to family and friends over the past decade, I have had to relearn the city, try to fathom the complex economic, social and ethnic geography that has today earned it the title of 'beacon city', a place others look to for lessons in racial harmony and pointers to the achievement of that elusive target 'cultural cohesion', a new take on what we once called 'multiculturalism'.

But all that was a long way in the future in the year of my birth, 1938. Let me remember. In 1801, the population of Leicester was a modest 17,000; by 1901 it had grown to 212,489. They came for jobs from all over the UK and Ireland to work in the thriving hosiery, knitwear and boot and shoe factories, and the engineering works that provided the machines for these industries on which Leicester's wealth was built. They lived in spreading acres of terraced houses thrown up in the latter part of the century to accommodate them.

But, to all intents and purposes, Leicester remained a provincial market town, its medieval street plan and many of its timber-frame houses more or less intact. Despite the Victorian incursion with its factories, villas and teeming streets of workers' housing, it was not a creation of the Industrial Revolution. Nor was it dependent on a single heavy industry and vulnerable to the vagaries of recession.

Leicester railway station: city of change. Courtesy: Leicester Promotions

The population grew only another 60,000 or so in the following century. Most of the new arrivals came in the past 50 years, many of them from Africa. Their arrival in this provincial town brought changes more lasting and profound than anything since the Romans.

The town I walked with my schoolmaster grandfather was the ancient town of the Romans, with medieval streets and buildings dating from the time of the Crusades. We would stroll from the Castle Gardens at the foot of the remains of the castle by the river to the timbered Guildhall, the houses and almshouses built by city merchants, narrow streets with huddled shops smelling of tobacco and liquorice. These led, finally, into the Victorian façades of department stores and gents' outfitters – and, of course, the vast (or so it seemed then) Leicester Co-operative Society store that dominated the high street of the modern town.

Today, most of the old town has gone. The winding streets have been swept away in doubtless necessary slum clearance; much more has been sacrificed to a 1960s orgy of road-building. The Magazine stands marooned between the lanes of an urban freeway, accessible only by underpass; the castle, its gardens and the monuments of my childhood are cut off by swirling motorways and elevated roads. They have become a 'heritage park', no longer a living part of the city, a backwater for tourists and a throughway for students at De Montfort University. The murky waters of the Soar have been cleaned up and offer a riverside walk and, so the brochure tells me, a unique variety of river flora and fauna. Leicester is the UK's first ecological city and is doing its best with what is left, but the destruction of the 1960s razed more than just slums. It is too late now for the once shabby but characterful seventeenth- and eighteenth-century city-centre façades, replaced with bland, anonymous reconstructions in the 1960s and 70s.

In 1936, Leicester, I was told, was the second richest city in the Empire; by 1953, it could still claim the distinction of having the second highest per capita income of any city in Europe. We grew up being told by my banker father we should be proud to live in such a city. But it didn't translate into anything we wanted to do. Joe Orton, a local boy, said it was the most boring city in England and got away as fast as fame would carry him; JB Priestley, on a brief visit, stayed only long enough to remark that there were many worse places in which he'd rather stay. We agreed with them: it was a cultural wilderness, the result, perhaps, of the inward-looking nonconformist temperance spirit that had ruled the city council for decades and lingered still. The city fathers of the 1950s had no more time for culture or entertainment than they were to show for architectural heritage. The last three commercial theatres – the Theatre Royal, the Opera House and finally the Palace of Varieties – closed, depriving us of pantomime, the Royal Ballet and other visiting delights. It was long after my day, in 1973, that the Haymarket Theatre opened and restored Leicester to the theatre circuit. We had music in De Montfort Hall, named for a long-dead earl; swimming in the open-air Lido; expeditions to the countryside, and long months spent vegetating in Lincolnshire with our grandparents. Our school was the best the city had to offer – but it was dull, provincial, and we longed to escape.

Which I did, in 1957, to university. And only then did I find out that Leicester is not what you see; at least not what I had seen. For all its complacency, Leicester had another side, invisible but discovered with shock when I delivered Christmas post in the vacations. The mean streets of working-class housing, by now down at heel and many still without bathrooms or inside lavatories, crowding up with the factories to the iron railings of our own house were familiar enough. But they hid much worse. Slums that could have come out of Dickens.

When I returned, the transformation of these places was even more dramatic than the loss of the city landscape I had once known. What I wandered through seemed nothing less than a small miracle. With the help of local council grants, whole neighbourhoods had been regenerated, houses as well as factories. Grey, depressing streets of mouldering Victorian housing had burst forth in candy colours and were once again thriving local communities – of Asians. Corner shops sold food and spices from India alongside the stock-in-trade of any neighbourhood store; the *Leicester Mercury* rubbed pages with publications in Gujarati and Punjabi; colourful bilingual books and wall posters for children displayed the alphabet and numbers in several languages.

It was the same with the factories and inner-city churches. Mills where the looms had long fallen silent were back in business, with the names of their new Asian owners superimposed on the ghostly letters of former household names; others had been divided into a myriad of small manufacturing units and workshops for Asian enterprise. Churches, nonconformist meeting houses, even in one case an old factory site, had become temples and mosques serving the neighbourhood.

The same was true of other old inner-city housing areas that had escaped demolition in the nick of time and had been rescued by the arrival of Asians from East Africa. The brand new Sikh gurdwara built on the site of Holy Bones, disappeared site of my ancient city, summed things up: not an appropriation, but a restoration of the city to itself. Economically and socially, the migrations of the late 1960s and early 70s – largely of Gujaratis fleeing 'Africanisation' in Kenya, Uganda and most recently Malawi – had, it seemed to me, saved a dying city. Along the Belgrave Road, for instance, the neglected shops of the old city centre were now Leicester's 'Golden Mile', a glittering strip of shops dominated by jewellers and goldsmiths. Asians from all over the UK come here for their wedding finery, I was assured, rather than make the trip to Bombay. Diwali brings huge crowds into the area to celebrate the Hindu festival of light when this part of the city is lit up with a million lights and the explosion of fireworks. The biggest celebration outside India, it brings people into this once enclosed city. Leicester is no longer the self-regarding, inward-looking place it was, but looking out and welcoming a wider world.

Leicester is no stranger to migration. As Cynthia Brown of Leicester University's Living History programme points out, people have been coming here since early in the nineteenth century. Then it was in pursuit of work; latterly, that went hand in hand with flight from war and persecution. Many, like the Poles who had fought in World War II and now found themselves unwelcome back in Communist Poland, settled in Leicester after the war; the late 40s saw the arrival of immigrants from the Caribbean plus the first Asians.

In 1951, the Asian population was just 624. Migration was hastened by the Commonwealth and Immigration Act of 1962: fuelled by people anxious to pre-empt its more restrictive conditions, migration had risen by 1961 to 4,624. They settled in the older inner-city areas, where cheap housing was available in the wake of the departure of English residents offered the chance to escape the decay by moving to council estates around the city. It was this early settlement that acted as the magnet, drawing dramatically increased immigration from Africa. Only a decade later, the arrival of Asians, largely Gujarati from Kenya, had swelled Leicester's Asian population to 20,190. Despite warnings by Leicester City Council printed in Ugandan papers and inflammatory headlines speaking of disaster in the influential *Leicester Mercury*, it was inevitable that a ready-made community of their own kind and Leicester's reputation as a 'friendly' city would draw the majority of Idi Amin's Asian refugees to the city. The appeal of friends, family and their own community, as well as the promise of jobs, increasingly in Gujarati-owned enterprises, were not the only reasons, it seems. 'I travelled all over the UK,' says one African Asian, 'and I made up my mind if I could choose anywhere I could come that I would settle in Leicester . . . I particularly liked Leicester . . . I was attracted to the flatness of the city.'

Of the 30,000 Asians expelled from Uganda in 1972, 6,000 came to the city. By 1981, the New Commonwealth population was 59,709 in a population of something over 250,000. The arrival of the new settlers in the '70s coincided with Leicester's first serious economic downturn. The city's staple manufactures were being replaced by cheaper goods from abroad: factories were in decline and closing; unemployment was rising. Resentment among the white population burst into open racism and discrimination, at the workplace as well as in the streets. Bolstered by Enoch Powell's dire warnings of the dangers of unbridled immigration, the National Front targeted Leicester and inserted itself into local politics. In 1976, it won 18 per cent of the vote in local elections; in 1979, in a climate of racial hostility fostered by the NF, Leicester witnessed one of worst racial confrontations in the country. Shocked and shamed out of complacency, it actively began to work at escaping the opprobrium of being labelled the UK's most racist city.

NIRMALA'S STORY

KEVIN FEGAN

Take an ordinary street, somewhere in the East Midlands. Where I live. One morning,
on my way to work, I decide to knock on every door and greet my neighbours. Not just
'Hello,' but 'Tell me your story, how you arrived here, on this street. I am the son of
a migrant Irish family that moved here for the want of work. What brought you here?
The mines, steelworks, family ties, war, oppression, love? What about your children?
And your children's children?' By the time I reach the end of the street I have met half
the populations of the world – and they're just like me.

The River Ganges is a gift from God:
it winds its way down from the heavens
of the Himalayas to the Bay of Bengal;
if you bathe in the Ganges
it will wash away your sins
so all Hindus aspire to become pilgrims
at least once in their lifetime.
As a family, we would regularly
visit Haridwar, a green and luscious place
on the banks of the sacred River.
I watched my baby brother's head
being shaven and dipped into the water;
I remember a monkey stole my shoes
outside the temple, I didn't know what to do.
Years later, we returned to scatter
my father's ashes on the River.
My name is Nirmala, I was born in Delhi
and we moved to Poona when I was five years old.
My childhood was saturated
in languages, books and religions,
our neighbours were Muslims and Christians,
Buddhists and Sikhs,
Zoroastrians and Jews;
I speak Hindi and Marati,
Gujarati and Urdu,

English and French, I grew up privileged,
reading PG Wodehouse and Agatha Christie.
We lived in what used to be, under the British Raj,
the Poona Hotel. Thanks to the Empire's largesse,
I would sit and look out of the window
at the trees and hills and write poetry.
In the monsoons, the grass would grow
taller than us and we'd pretend it was a wood;
my brothers would play the wolf
and I'd be Little Red Riding Hood.
My parents treated me as an equal
To my brothers, but celebrated
the differences. My mother would exclaim,
'All five fingers on one hand are not the same.'
I played football and took flying lessons,
I learned to ride a motor scooter
in the botanical gardens,
I wore jeans and swore like my male friends
and I studied at university.
Imagine then my culture shock
when, at twenty-one, I married
a traditional Hindu student
from another former British colony,
Malawi in Africa.
I arrived in Blantyre
and was told to wear a saree at all times;
to lower my voice, I was too loud;
to avoid all contact with other men;
I was too proud; to learn to cook
what my husband likes, to sit with the women
in the other room, not to ride my bike
and to learn Malawi language.
I lost all my childhood freedom,
I had to conform; but I loved my husband
and respected his family
so I set aside my degree in English Literature,
my post-grad in journalism
and I learned to cook for him

and serve in the family shop.
I'd never so much as made a cup of tea
in my life, we had servants back home.
After four years in Malawi
we moved to England
in the winter of 1986.
I did not enjoy the snow in a saree
and thought, I must have done something really bad
in a previous life to end up here.
But when our second daughter was born,
we moved to Leicester
where I became a reformed woman.
All of a sudden, everyone seemed to need
the many languages I speak:
at first it was Dixon's electrical store
which was fun, then the libraries, now
the university needs me
and newspapers want my features.
I couldn't be the housewife my husband says
he wants, so we went our separate ways.
I'm a working mum with two beautiful children,
I don't see anything wrong in that;
and this is where I belong, in a tolerant
multicultural society,
much like it was growing up in Poona.
I love Leicester, it feels like home.
As I take a walk along the mile straight
of the River Soar, down by Castle Gardens,
I think, perhaps it's time we consecrated
this stretch of the river, a sort of
mini-Ganges for those of us willing
to trust in fate and believe
that, somehow, we're meant to be here. ❏

From Let your left hand sing, *a dramatic poem written and performed by*
Kevin Fegan, *poet and performer*

Background: Diwali celebrations.
Courtesy: Leicester Promotions

Twenty years on, hard work, dedication and commitment from all the communities have ensured that, unlike Oldham, Burnley, Bradford, Southall, Toxteth, Brixton and other places with high immigrant populations, Leicester has not exploded again. A lot of money has been funnelled to minority community projects. Not always the answer, but as Leicester race relations policy officer Paul Winstone said with a certain realism: 'Leicester City Council poured millions of pounds into ethnic groups. Almost every group could get something like £50,000 (US$75,000) more or less just by asking. It wasn't open bribery, but it most certainly was bribery – and it worked. Why should the leaders riot when they had money and an office?'

In retrospect, Winstone describes the 1970s as the years of conflict, the 80s as the bribery years and the 90s as the decade of consolidation. But there is more to it than that. Asked why Leicester has become something of a model multiracial city, why, given that the minority population is now around 38 per cent and forecast to become the first majority ethnic community in the UK within the present decade, it doesn't explode in racial violence, Asians themselves have another explanation. Above all, they point to the fact that they came not from India or Pakistan but from Africa, where they had occupied a privileged position as professionals, businessmen and entrepreneurs. They explode the myth still current in many places that they came with their pockets stuffed with money, but point out that they knew how to do things, did not rely on the local authority for housing or jobs but bought modest properties and eventually built businesses again from scratch. They were not like the uneducated communities of Bangladeshis or fundamentalist Pakistanis who settled in other places.

Something else too, they say: 'Remember, this was our second migration. In Africa we already knew what it was to be an unloved but tolerated minority. We knew how to keep our heads down, blend in and get on with people. We'd learned all that before we came here.'

Sitting in a local pub, once a down-and-out watering hole but now Asian-owned, bright and cheery, I am struck at the convivial mix of people – Hindus and Muslims, Gujaratis, Sikhs from the Punjab, a few white Englishmen. I am struck by the lack of tension. Are there really no sectarian problems in the city? Jay, a Gujarati from Uganda, explains: 'Most of us African Asians had never seen India. Unlike the people who came from the subcontinent, its politics and its religious hatreds were nothing to do with us, and so we didn't carry all that baggage and perpetuate the old quarrels when we got here. The common experience of coming from Africa keeps us close; that is stronger than any religious divide.' And that, he concludes, is something else that keeps his city, Leicester, from the sectarian extremism that divides other communities.

But this mixture of races and religions is rare. Again, Leicester is not what you see when you meet and talk to the dedicated people who work to bring communities together. The city is as segregated and zoned as it ever was in the days of the old working-class and middle-class divide. That it is largely self-segregated raises the question of how these parallel lives will settle down in the long run when the white English are in a minority, as they already are in most of the city's schools. Maybe it's only the next generation, now in the schools, who can answer the question. As one Asian boy put it to me: 'If there are as many of me as there are of you, we don't have to be afraid of anything, do we?'

Meanwhile, as people in the city admit, there are challenges to be met. Asians will say they are not yet strongly enough represented in the upper echelons of local government and industry, despite the presence of a growing number of local councillors from the minority communities. And the mix of poverty and ethnicity on local sink estates is creating tensions between black and white not evident in the city itself.

But, more than anything else, representatives on both sides of the ethnic divide fear the import of religious and political extremism from outside. The Hindu nationalist fundamentalist BJP government in India keeps close contacts in the city; following the outbreak of sectarian violence in Gujarat last year, they have been keen to put their version of events to the Gujarati community in Leicester. In much the same way, the Muslims of Leiceser are disturbed by the ongoing trial in the city of alleged al-Qaida suspects. They feel a threat from the identification in the media and elsewhere of 'terrorism' and Islam. They have become introspective and assertive at the same time, demonstrating a sense of insecurity in a more aggressive assertion of their religion.

But all of this, I am assured more than once, is manageable as long as the city remains aware of it and is sensitive to its handling. There is optimism and a justifiable pride in Leicester's record. 'There are things to be done, but compared to other places we are doing well. And that's official: it said so in the Cantle report that came out after the riots in Oldham and Burnley in 2001.' ❏

DANCE TO THE MUSIC OF WAR
PAULINE BAX

WAR IS NO RESPECTER OF BORDERS,
ESPECIALLY IN CÔTE D'IVOIRE, WHERE THE
CONFLICT FLINGS TOGETHER REFUGEES,
MERCENARIES, REBELS AND TRANSIENTS
OF ALL KINDS AND NATIONALITIES

If there's one thing that unites the population of war-torn Côte d'Ivoire, it's music. The music the rebels dance to in the besieged town of Bouake is the same music that is blaring from loudspeakers in the government-controlled city of Abidjan. 'Stop the shooting,' the Youssoumba Collective sings. 'We want to have fun.'

It is one hit song among many about the conflict. Most lash out at the rebel movements, others have outright nationalistic overtones, urging 'real Ivorians' to be proud of their Ivorian identity. 'Liberate my country,' another hit song croons. Almost call for peace.

The people of Côte d'Ivoire are tiring of the war that split their country in half and plunged it into economic crisis. It has also traumatised a considerable part of the immigrant community, the largest in all of Africa. Almost one-third of the population was born abroad. Yet, despite an agreement between president Laurent Gbagbo and the three rebel movements, real peace seems a long way off.

Village roadblocks thrown up by so-called committees of self-defence are a nuisance to travellers, but everybody has grown used to them now. The curfew has been pushed back to midnight. Army checkpoints are sometimes the only sign that there is a war going on.

But the conflict has irreparably damaged trust between 'real' Ivorians and not-so-real ones. Real Ivorians have parents born on Ivorian soil. Those considered not-so-real Ivorians are people from the north, whose parents originate from countries like Mali and Burkina Faso. That is where most immigrants come from, too. They are usually, but not always, Muslims. The main rebel movement says its reason for wanting to overthrow the government was that northerners are being treated as second-class citizens.

In the cocoa-producing town of Daloa, the president of the Malian community association was killed last year. Soldiers arrested him soon after the army had retaken the town from rebel forces. Two days later, his body was found. Balla Magassa, the association's new president, says he has never been given an explanation as to his predecessor's death. The Malians in Daloa are worried. They don't feel safe.

'We polled the 25,000 members of our community if they wanted to leave,' Magassa says in his dark, breezy office close to the town's central mosque. 'Around 12,000 people said yes.'

Tension is equally high in the town of Agboville, 80km north of the commercial capital Abidjan. In January, it was the scene of the worst ethnic violence since the beginning of the conflict. At least 14 people died when protests against the peace accord escalated. Several shops and petrol stations were burned.

Supporters of Gbagbo threatened to set fire to the mosque. 'They still say they want to burn this building to the ground,' the watchman says. 'But they don't bother us now. It's just that the gendarmerie has been harassing us since the trouble in January. They come to the northerners' quarter at night and knock on our doors, demanding money.'

In the western border town of Tabou, no foreign community suffers more than the Liberians. Most of them don't even dare to talk to a journalist in public. The problem is that Liberian fighters see the Ivorian crisis as a golden opportunity. The two smaller Ivorian rebel movements, holding chunks of the northwest, were apparently the first to ask for the Liberians' support. Gbagbo's army later responded by hiring Liberian mercenaries.

Liberians are hated with a passion in Tabou. The border is only a couple of kilometres away. Villagers are understandably worried about rebel incursions. At the same time, thousands of Liberians have fled to Côte d'Ivoire because of the civil war in their own country. And now they are trapped. They are refugees, but they have nowhere to go. Was it not for the involvement of the Liberians, according to some people in Tabou, the conflict in Côte d'Ivoire would have been resolved.

'We all pray for peace,' says a Liberian who works as an English teacher. Every now and then, he says, a Liberian disappears overnight. Bodies are sometimes found on the beach, clubbed or beaten to death. Who is responsible? 'Maybe local militia, youth who call themselves Ivorian patriots. We are not sure. These people have all developed such hatred. They will not accept us.' ❏

Pauline Bax *is a journalist currently covering the crisis in West Africa*

A censorship chronicle incorporating information from Agence France-Press (AFP), Alliance of Independent Journalists (AJI), Amnesty International (AI), Article 19 (A19), Association of Independent Electronic Media (ANEM), BBC Monitoring Service Summary of World Broadcasts (SWB), Canadian Journalists for Free Expression (CJFE), Centre for Human Rights and Democratic Studies (CEHURDES), Centre for Journalism in Extreme Situations (CJES), Committee to Protect Journalists (CPJ), Democratic Journalists' League (JuHI), Digital Freedom Network (DFN), Glasnost Defence Foundation (GDF), Human Rights Watch (HRW), Indymedia, Information Centre of Human Rights & Democracy Movements in China (ICHR DMC), Institute for War & Peace Reporting (IWPR), Instituto de Prensa y Sociedad (IPYS), United Nations Integrated Regional Information Network (IRIN), Inter-American Press Association (IAPA), International Federation of Journalists (IFJ/FIP), Media Institute of Southern Africa (MISA), Network for the Defence of Independent Media in Africa (NDIMA), Open Media Research Institute (OMRI), Pacific Islands News Association (PINA), International PEN (PEN), Radio Free Europe/Radio Liberty (RFE/RL), Reporters Sans Frontières (RSF), The Southeast Asian Press Alliance (SEAPA), Statewatch, Transitions Online (TOL), World Association of Community Broadcasters (AMARC), World Association of Newspapers (WAN), World Organisation Against Torture (OMCT), Writers in Prison Committee (WiPC) and other sources including members of the International Freedom of Expression eXchange (IFEX)

AFGHANISTAN

Islamic authorities in Afghanistan banned videos, citing the un-Islamic nature of the Bollywood romances and straight-to-video Hollywood action flicks on show, first in the northern province of Konduz on 19 February and in the western province of Herat on 1 March.

On 21 January, Afghanistan's Supreme Court banned cable television as 'against Islamic laws and values'. The Afghan Minister of Information said he would review the ruling as 'freedom of cable is part of the freedom of our press, and none of the cable operators had broadcast anything objectionable'. (RFE)

The Free Press Defence Foundation group of independent journalists was launched in Kabul on 7 January to defend Afghan press freedoms. It is headed by Abdul Qahar Sarwari. Kabul enjoys relatively free media but there are still restrictions in the major cities of Kandahar, Herat and Mazar-e Sharif. (RFE)

ALGERIA

Cartoonist **Ali Dilem** (*Index* 2/02) was fined 10,000 dinars (US$240) by a court on 31 December for his satirical take on the 1992 murder of President Mohamed Boudiaf. It was the first conviction for 'insult' under a May 2001 change to the criminal code, now nicknamed the 'Dilem Amendment'. (*Algeria Interface*)

ARGENTINA

On 12 February, **Clara Britos**, owner and director of the newspaper *La Tapa*, was accosted by three unknown persons on 12 February who threatened to kill her. She earlier received death threats from a driver of a Ford car who followed her on three separate occasions. (*Periodistas*)

On 5 December, Oberá city mayor Rodolfo Dalmau and his bodyguards attacked *El Territorio* journalist **Pablo García** when he quizzed the mayor about his decision to start a presidential campaign while legal action against him was still pending. (*Periodistas*)

UNC-CALF FM radio journalist **Carlos Marcel** received threatening emails and phone calls following a critical report on Neuquén regional governor Jorge Sobisch. On 6 February, the radio station walls were covered in graffiti abusing the reporter. (PFC)

A federal policeman guarding the house of journalist **Miguel Bonasso** was attacked by two unknown uniformed security police officers on 26 November. The attack is linked to the imminent publication of Bonasso's book about the state's role in the December 2001 'IMF riots' that killed more than 24. (*Periodistas*)

Former police chief Alberto Gómez was jailed for life on 23 December for his part in the January 1997 murder of photojournalist **José Luís Cabezas**. (*Periodistas*)

ARMENIA

A Yerevan court on 16 December sentenced former foreign ministry official, journalist and Turkish affairs expert **Murad Bojolian** to ten years in prison on charges of spying for Turkey. Bojolian has withdrawn a confession saying it was extracted under fear of torture and for the fate of his family. (RFE/RL, CJES)

Armenian Public TV and Radio president **Tigran Naghdalyan** was killed by a single bullet to the head on 28 December. Expected to be a strong backer of incumbent Armenian President Robert Kocharian during his 2003 re-election bid, he was succeeded by another loyalist, presidential aide Aleksan Harutiunian. (CJES, *Noyan Tapan*)

There were widespread reports of attacks on journalists and party officials seeking to expose ballot-box stuffing during the election itself. Incumbent Robert Kocharian won re-election after a 5 March run-off criticised by observers from the OSCE and the Parliamentary Assembly of the Council of Europe. (OSCE)

AUSTRALIA

A 10 December Australian High Court ruling that Australian businessman Joseph Gutnick can sue a US-based website for libel at home rather than the US – where US free-speech rights would undermine his case – triggered a global debate about the legal liabilities of publishing on the web. (*Guardian*)

AZERBAIJAN

On 8 December, the opposition paper *Yeni Musavat* was picketed by members of the Association of Army Reserve Officers, who warned the paper against 'dirtying' the army's reputation. Editor **Rauf Arifoglu** went on hunger strike during part of January to protest against 12 state-sponsored lawsuits against the paper. (RFE/RL)

Azerbaijan Democratic Party (ADP) member **Gurban Mamedov**, co-founder of the party daily *Hurriyet*, was released from jail on 5 February. Mamedov was jailed in 1998 for claiming that national security chief Namig Abbasov had plotted to overthrow President Haidar Aliyev. Mamedov is returning to politics and the media. (RFE/RL)

BANGLADESH

Zaiba Malik and **Bruno Sorrentino**, journalists with Britain's Channel 4 TV, and local freelances **Priscilla Raj** and **Saleem Samad** were arrested on 25 November and accused of spying and sedition. On 12 December, Malik and Sorrentino were deported. Raj was released on bail and Samad conditionally released on 18 January. Both claimed to have been tortured while in custody. (RSF, CPJ)

The day after a 7 December bombing in the northern town of Mymensingh, police arrested 'anti-Bangladesh campaigners' for 'suspicious activities' under the Special Powers Act, among them academic **Muntasir Mamon**, rights activist **Shahriar Kabir** (*Index* 2/02) and 15 opposi-

tion Awami League figures. Kabir and Mamon were released on 7 and 9 January respectively. (RSF, CPJ, *Dawn*, *Daily Star*)

Reuters stringer **Enamul Hoque Chowdhury** was arrested on 13 December after quoting Home Minister Altaf Hossain Chowdury as possibly linking al-Qaida to the Mymensingh bombs. The government denied it and arrested him for 'tarnishing' the country's image. He was allegedly tortured in jail. (CPJ, *Financial Times*)

BELARUS

The Federation of Trade Unions of Belarus (FPB) sacked six more journalists from its own newspaper, *Belaruski Chas*, five months after FPB Chairman Leonid Kozik sacked its editor, **Alyaksandr Starykevich**, asserting that he would not work with a newspaper that did not share his views. (RSF)

Viktar Ivashkevich (*Index* 1/03), editor of the independent paper *Rabochy* and deputy chairman of the Belarusan Popular Front, began two years' hard labour for defaming President Aleksandr Lukashenka in a 2002 article accusing him of corruption. The issue in which it appeared had been seized by police before distribution. (RFE)

Mikola Markevich, editor of the independent weekly *Pagonya*, who was sentenced to 30 months' imprisonment for defaming Lukashenka, has had his sentence cut by 12 months. He can serve out his time in his home town of Hrodna, if he stays inside the city limits, registers with the police and, if working, gives 15 per cent of his salary to the state. (Charter-97)

On 3 February, publisher **Romuald Ulan**'s licence to print the independent weekly *Novaya Gazeta Smorgoni* was rescinded. Reporters Sans Frontières said the court order was 'a death sentence against a paper that has become too much of a nuisance to local authorities on the eve of next month's regional elections'. (RSF)

BOLIVIA

Juan Carlos Marañon, formerly of the Unitel television network in La Paz, and **Andrés Gómez Vela**, former news director of the newspaper *La Prensa*, handed a dossier to Vice-President Carlos Mesa on 6 February alleging that minister Carlos Sánchez Berzaín forced their employers to fire them. The journalists seek a government investigation. (PFC)

BOSNIA-HERZEGOVINA

NATO forces searched the Pale-based Serbian Orthodox Church radio station Radio Sveti Jovan on 2 January. The station is owned by **Sonja Karadzic**, daughter of fugitive former Bosnian Serb leader Radovan Karadzic. NATO said it had been investigating whether the station was being used for illegal covert surveillance. (DPA, RFE)

BOTSWANA

Some 100 students of the University of Botswana attacked reporter **Moreri Moroka** and photographer **Moreri Sejakgomo** of the bi-weekly *Mokgosi* on 5 December as they covered a demonstration at the university. Editor **Pamela Dube** said the attack threatened freedom of information in Botswana. (MISA)

BURKINA FASO

Reporters Sans Frontières accused the government of inefficiently investigating the killing of journalist **Norbert Zongo** in February 1998 (*Index* 2/99) and urged UN Special Rapporteur on Free Expression Ambeyi Ligabo to visit the country and press for concrete action. (RSF)

BURMA

On 12 March 2003, detained journalist **U Win Tin** marked his 73rd birthday in Rangoon general hospital, where he is being treated for a heart condition. Transferred from prison to hospital on 22 November, he was visited on 5 February by an Amnesty International delegation, making its first ever fact-finding mission to Burma. (*Index Online*, RSF)

Censors from Burma's Literary Works Scrutinising Committee warned Burma's private press on 19 February not to publish reports about the public disquiet they (correctly) expected to follow the junta's planned announcement of the closure of selected savings and loan institutions the next day. The targeted S&Ls offered better interest rates than state-owned banks. (RSF)

BURUNDI

Editors of Burundi's private radio stations were summoned by President Pierre Buyoya and ordered to halt coverage of the views of rebel faction leaders **Pierre Nkurunziza** and **Agathon Rwasa**. Buyoya said he wanted the ban strictly observed until all rebel groups had agreed a ceasefire. (IRIN)

Recent Publications: *A Framework for Responsible Aid to Burundi*, International Crisis Group, 21 February 2003.

CAMBODIA

Authorities arrested radio station owner **Mam Sonando** and newspaper editor **In Chan Sivutha** on 30 January on charges of incitement following anti-Thai riots in Phnom Penh. Sivutha's paper published a fake quotation from a TV soap opera actress laying a Thai claim to Cambodia's Angkor Wat temple, and Mam Sonando's station broadcast false claims that mobs had killed Cambodians in Thailand. (CPJ)

CANADA

Françoise Ducros resigned as Prime Minister Jean Chrétien's director of communications after she referred to US President George W Bush as a 'moron' in front of reporters. Chrétien initially refused to accept her resignation but was forced to let her go in the ensuing furore. (*Globe & Mail*)

Canadian Jewish groups have called for senior First Nations chief **David Ahenakew** to be charged with hate crimes and be stripped of his Order of Canada medal after he reportedly claimed Jews 'damn near owned all of Germany' before WWII, as explanation for why Hitler 'fried six million' of them. (*Daily Telegraph*)

Fat Girl, a film banned in 2002 by the Ontario Film Review Board because of a lengthy sex scene between a 15-year-old girl and an adult man, was approved for release on 3 January in a decision that the censors presented as signalling its newly progressive policies. (*Globe & Mail*)

CHAD

Publisher **Nadjikimo Bénoudjita** and deputy editor **Mbainaye Bétoubam** of the weekly *Notre Temps* were jailed for six months on 6 February. The paper had quoted court papers alleging that the president's mother-in-law, Hadjé Billy Douga, ordered the torture of men suspected of stealing her jewellery. Police said one of the suspects had died of 'an incurable disease' while in custody. (RSF)

CHILE

TV commentator **Eduardo Yáñez** (*Index* 2/02, 1/03) was given a two-month suspended jail sentence and fined US$460 for showing 'disrespect' for the Chilean judiciary under Pinochet-era laws. In November 2001, Yáñez called Chilean judges 'immoral, cowardly and corrupt' for not compensating an unjustly jailed woman. (CPJ)

CHINA

Beijing university student **Liu Di**, 22, was reported to have been detained on 7 November after posting an internet article urging readers to ignore the Chinese Communist Party. Police claimed she was a member of 'an illegal organisation'. She was charged with 'endangering state security' on 18 December. (RSF)

China's Information Industry Minister Wu Jichuan warned a Shanghai conference on the internet on 25 November of the 'moral hazards' and 'wonderful opportunities' to be found on the internet in China. (ZDNet)

A Harvard report on web blocking in China published in December found that the top ten sites returned by Google for the terms 'Tibet', 'Taiwan China' and 'equality' were all blocked as were eight out of ten using the terms 'democracy China' and 'dissident China'. The report said that up to 19,000 sites are blocked at any one time, often barring access to just part of the site. (BBC)

The number of web users in China is second only to the US and reached 58 million by the end of 2002, up 28.7 million in the last year alone, said a report released by the China internet Network Information Center on 19 December. Wu Suoning, editor of *People's Posts and Telecommunications* said China's internet users are mainly men, the majority below 35 and unmarried. (www.chinagate.com)

The writer, poet and teacher **Liao Yiwu** was arrested at home on 18 December in Chengdu after signing an online petition calling for a pardon for students convicted after the June 1989 protests. Other signatories include **Ouyang Yi** of the banned China Democracy Party (CDP), **Zhao Changqing**, jailed for three years after the Tiananmen Square protest in 1989, **He Depu** (*Index* 3/02) and **Dai Xuezhong** (*Index* 5/00). It was reported on 6 March that all have since been charged with 'inciting to overthrow state power'. (HRIC)

Commenting on a ban on US-based 'weblog' internet diaries, an official from China's Ministry of Information Industry was quoted on 15 January as saying: 'The Chinese government would never tell Western sites what to post or what not to. They have freedom of expression. So it will just take away access.' (Reuters)

Economist and writer **Tao Haidong** was sentenced to seven years in prison in mid-February in Urumqi, Xinjiang Province, on charges of subversion. Tao had posted articles on the internet predicting economic collapse in China. (HRIC)

Gong Shengliang, the imprisoned founder of the South China Church (*Index* 1/03), was reported on 5 December to have been on hunger strike since 14 November. It is understood he was protesting against prison refusals to allow him to write letters or file an official appeal against his sentence. (*Washington Post*)

It was reported on 7 December that a new system administered by the State Press and Publications Administration will require Chinese journalists to be regularly tested on rules covering publishing and party ideology. Those who fail or who 'violate news discipline' will have their certification withdrawn. (BBC)

A delegation from the Paris-based World Association of Newspapers protested on 13 December to Minister of Propaganda Liu Yunshan about press rights abuses and the detention of 30 writers. Li Changchun, the Chinese politburo's top official for media policy, said on 17 January that journalists should concentrate on 'positive propaganda'. He added: 'Being responsible to the party and being responsible to the people are the same thing.' (CNN, *South China Morning Post*, WAN)

Jae Hyun Seok, a South Korean freelance photographer, was arrested in Yantai, Shandong Province, on 17 January while taking photographs of North Korean refugees attempting to leave China by boat for South Korea and Japan. He has reportedly been accused of involvement in human trafficking, although it is not yet known whether he has been charged. (CPJ, RSF)

Prominent US-based pro-democracy activist **Wang Bingzhang** was sentenced to life imprisonment on 10 February in Guangdong for 'organising and leading a terrorist group' and 'engaging in espionage'. He was reportedly meeting with Chinese labour activists in Vietnam when he and his companions were abducted by Chinese security agents and taken to China. Wang is a founder of

the pro-democracy publication *China Spring* and has previously been deported from China for attempting to organise labour and democracy groups. (www.asiamedia. com, Xinhua)

Tibetans **Lobsang Dhundup** and high Lama **Tenzin Delek Rinpoche** were sentenced to death on 2 December after a closed trial at a court in Sichuan on charges relating to a series of bombings throughout the province. Tenzin Delek Rinpoche's sentence was suspended for two years, which usually means the sentence is commuted to life, dependent upon the prisoner's behaviour. Lobsang Dhundup was executed on 26 January immediately after a second trial, despite official promises to visiting Assistant US Secretary of State Lorne Craner that his case would be 'thoroughly reviewed'. (AFP, RFA)

Recent Publications: *Empirical analysis of internet filtering in China*, Jonathan Zittrain and Benjamin Edelman, Berkman Center for Internet & Society, Harvard Law School, December 2002; *Selection of cases from the criminal law: Banned Protestant Groups*, the Dui Hua Foundation, February 2003; *Mining Tibet: Mineral exploitation in Tibetan areas of the PRC*, Tibet Information Network, 31 December 2002.

COLOMBIA

A number of foreign journalists were detained during January in Colombia. Veteran freelance journalist **Robert Pelton** was abducted with colleagues **Mark Wedeven**

and **Megan Smaker** on 19 January during an attack by rebels of the United Self-Defence Forces of Colombia (AUC) on the village of Paya, just north of the Colombian border. They were freed on 23 January. (CPJ)

Two days earlier, rival rebels from the Revolutionary Armed Forces of Colombia (FARC) and the smaller National Liberation Army (ELN) had detained two *Los Angeles Times* journalists. Photographer **Scott Dalton** from Texas and reporter **Ruth Morris**, a British national, were taken in the lawless Arauca region in eastern Colombia. They were released on 1 February. (CPJ, *Los Angeles Times*)

COSTA RICA

The Inter-American Court of Human Rights is to hear the case of journalist **Mauricio Herrera Ulloa** of the San José daily *La Nación*, convicted of criminal defamation in 1999. A ruling in favour could establish whether criminal defamation is permissible under international law. (CPJ)

CÔTE D'IVOIRE

Reuters journalist **Anne Boher** was arrested by government forces and accused of spying for the Côte d'Ivoire Patriotic Movement rebels. Boher was freed the next day after questioning. Since the attempted coup in September 2002 last year (*Index* 1/03), journalists have been detained for up to six days. (RSF)

CUBA

Cuba's Communist Party declared victory after a turnout of more than 97 per cent voted in the country's one-party general election. More than 8 million Cubans voted in the 21 January polls, electing 609 pro-government candidates who ran unopposed, official newspapers reported. (BBC)

On 11 February, Cuban authorities detained Argentine journalism professor **Fernando Ruiz Parra**, who was researching a book about Cuba's independent journalism movement. After the intervention of the Argentine embassy, Ruiz Parra was deported and his research materials were confiscated. (CPJ)

DOMINICAN REPUBLIC

Environment and Natural Resources Secretary Frank Moya Pons paid for a series of advertisements in rival papers accusing editor **Miguel Franjul** of the daily *Listín Diario* of a 'campaign of lies, defamation and misinformation'. The paper had criticised his department's failure to stop illegal sand extraction. (PFC)

On 5 January, unknown individuals set fire to journalist **Julio Gómez's** car in an attack linked to his reports of alleged corruption at the state-sponsored RENOVE programme, created to support minibus operators in the republic's south-western Pedernales province. (PFC)

EL SALVADOR

CINTEC Environment Inc., the Canadian company that manages greater San Salvador's solid waste, is to sue for criminal defamation against two papers, *El Diario de Hoy* and *La Prensa Gráfica*, whose February reports have linked the firm to organised crime and mismanagement of a US$6 million city fund. (PFC)

ERITREA

On 11 February, the Committee to Protect Journalists launched a campaign to free jailed Eritrean journalist **Fesshaye Yohannes**, editor of the weekly *Setit*, jailed in September 2001 and presently one of 18 journalists jailed in Eritrea incommunicado and without charge. (CPJ)

ETHIOPIA

Police rounded up street newspaper vendors across Addis Ababa in February, arresting some and driving the rest off the streets in a clampdown to eliminate 'illegal roadside vendors and tramps'. It was seen as a direct attack on the independent media, dependent on street sales. (*Addis Tribune*)

The government plans a new media law to create a 'strong, responsible' media by the end of the year. The IFJ, among others, condemns the plan and accuses Ethiopia of staging a 'sham debate' about press reform 'while it plans to stifle the media and to gag independent journalists'. (IRIN, IFJ)

EUROPEAN UNION

On 28 January, members of the Council of Europe signed the Additional Protocol to the November 2002 Cybercrime Convention, calling on states to criminalise the dissemination via the internet of racist and xenophobic propaganda and clearing the way to new attempts at EU-wide censorship of the web. (Council of Europe)

The European Commission announced in February its planned new European Network and Information Security Agency, acting as an 'advisory' coordinator of EU defences against virus and hacker attacks — but with additional and unspecified roles in the 'war on terror' as waged on the internet. (www.itregister.com)

FRANCE

Former US Yahoo! website boss **Timothy Koogle** was cleared by a French court of two charges relating to the sale of Nazi memorabilia on his website on 11 February. An earlier court order had sought to ban French browsers from accessing the site. Yahoo! stopped the sales soon afterwards. (ACLU)

Malian journalists **Youssouf Touré** and **Boubakar Diallo** were arrested on 5 January for filming a fight between Malian deportees and French police on a plane at Paris's Charles de Gaulle airport. The pair were removed from the plane but released later that afternoon. (RSF)

Lyon Mag, a local magazine in south-east France, was fined US$375,000 on 10 January for quoting wine expert **François Mauss** describing Beaujolais wine as 'shitty'. Beaujolais producers sued, not for libel, but under a law rarely used against the media that protects commercial products from being denigrated. (RSF)

A dozen journalists were detained for several hours outside the French Foreign Ministry on 20 February while trying to cover a protest against Zimbabwean President Robert Mugabe's presence at the Franco–African summit. Two more were arrested outside the conference hall the next day. (RSF)

Former Turkish army chief General Hüseyin Kivrikoglu failed in a bid to sue Reporters Sans Frontières' secretary-general Robert Ménard for using his picture without permission in a Paris exhibition of 37 so-called 'predators of press freedom'. Kivrikoglu was ordered to pay €2,000 damages and costs. (RSF)

GAMBIA

Banjul Independent chief editor **Abdoulie Sey** and managing editor **Alhaji Yoro Jallow** (*Index* 4/02) were threatened over the New Year by a telephone caller who warned: 'We know every bit of your movements and we will soon get you. For years you have been courting trouble for yourselves and now you will get it.' (*Banjul Independent*)

GEORGIA

Tbilisi police roughed up reporters from Kavkasia TV and confiscated their camera when they tried to film the detention of a group of Chechen residents on 7 December. The camera was returned damaged and without its film. An investigation has been launched. (CIS, RFE/RL)

GERMANY

Three regional courts upheld a law in January requiring internet service providers to block access to certain web content originating outside Germany. Designed to block neo-Nazi propaganda, the law has been condemned by civil liberties groups as heralding wider censorship on the web. (www.vnunet.org)

On 17 January, the German government outlawed the allegedly violently anti-Semitic student group **Hizb ut-Tahrir** after it established links with neo-Nazis, though officials doubted that their common hatred of Jews and Israel would overcome the xenophobia of the far right. (*Boston Globe*)

The German left-wing daily *Tageszeitung* shut down its online forum in December after failing to find a way to keep the debate open without tolerating abusive, sexist and racist comment. A special 'anger zone' failed to improve the tone, so the publication's own staff pulled the plug. (www.europemedia.com)

Chancellor Gerhard Schröder was powerless to stop the British *Mail on Sunday* newspaper deliberately ignoring a German court order on 19 January forbidding it to repeat claims about his private life. German papers were banned by the order from raising the subject on pain of a €250,000 fine. (*Guardian*)

GREENLAND

The pro-independence **Inuit Brotherhood Party** won 25.8 per cent of the votes in a 4 December general election, expressing public frustration at the failure of Denmark – which retains control of the territory's foreign policy – to reflect local concerns over the US Air Force base at Thule on the island. (*Daily Telegraph*)

GUATEMALA

Former Guatemalan paymaster-general Marco Tulio Abadío, who had been sharply criticised by the daily *El Periódico*, began his new job as director of the country's tax administration department (SAT) by calling down a full tax audit on the paper and issuing several subpoenas to the paper's staff. The tax authorities' campaign was condemned as harassment by the Inter American Press Association on 15 January when the SAT followed up by demanding documents from files of the *Diarios Modernos* publishing company. A judge later rejected the tax authorities' claim as unconstitutional. (IAPA, CPJ)

On 23 February, reporter **Elizabel Enríquez** of the Cerigua news agency was attacked by unidentified individuals as she was about to enter the agency's office. Cerigua staff have been the target of a number of attacks, assaults and threats. (APG)

GUINEA

Yacine Diallo, founder of the bi-monthly magazine *L'Enquêteur*, was arrested on 19 December after the journalist reported that Colonel Mamadou Balde, the country's inspector-general of the army, had resigned. Diallo was accused of allying with plotters wanting to bring Balde down. (RSF)

GUINEA BISSAU

On 13 February, private radio station **Bombolom FM** was shut down on orders of officials who accused the station of 'threatening state security'. Police officers came into the studios and forced it off air. Station managers say the raid might have been linked to criticism of the president made on air by an opposition politician. (RSF)

On 8 March, **Ensa Seidi**, editor-in-chief of the state-run National Radio, was assaulted and expelled from his offices by order of the country's information minister. He had been targeted for producing a report about opposition leader and former prime minister **Francisco Fadul**'s return to the country ahead of this year's presidential and legislative elections. (RSF)

HAITI

On 28 November, unidentified attackers opened fire outside a Gonaïves hotel where the Association of Haitian Journalists (AJH) was discussing the safety of the media with a group of threatened radio correspondents and police officials. There were reported injuries, but no deaths. (RSF)

On 25 December, **Michèle Montas**, news director of Port-au-Prince-based Radio Haiti Inter and widow of journalist **Jean Dominique**, murdered in April 2000, was attacked by two gunmen at her home in Pétionville. Bodyguard **Maxime Séïde** was killed in the assassination attempt. (*Miami Herald*)

On 15 February, unidentified attackers tried to burn down the house of Radio Métropole political affairs journalist **Jean-Numa Goudou** by setting fire to a car in his garage. He had gone into hiding the day before after receiving threats. Neighbours managed to put the fire out. (RSF)

After the mother of Radio Métropole journalist **Nancy Roc** was shot at on 16 February, the station called a 24-hour strike on 18 February to protest againt the violence. Up to that point the station had not publicised the attacks on its staff, but were alarmed by the increasing violence. (RSF)

On 21 February, Radio Haiti Inter decided that it had to cease broadcasting because of the increasing number of threats to its journalists and technical staff. News director Michèle Montas announced on air: 'Three of our people have already been killed and we don't want to lose anyone else.' (RSF)

HONDURAS

Germán Antonio Rivas, managing director of Corporación Maya Visión and Channel 7 TV, escaped an assassination attempt at his home in Santa Rosa near the Guatemalan border on 24 February. Rivas said the attack was linked to his work, but would not single out a specific suspect. (PFC)

Recent Publications: *Honduras – Zero Tolerance for Impunity: Extrajudicial Executions of Children and Youths Since 1998*, Amnesty International, 25 February 2003.

HONG KONG

Concerns continue to run high in Hong Kong over drafts of the 'anti-subversion' Article 23 of the territory's constitution (*Index* 1/03). US and British statements in November 2002 calling for fuller public participation were rejected by a Chinese foreign ministry official in Hong Kong as 'meddling'. (AFP)

Hong Kong's Arts Development Council told Hong Kong security chief Regina Ip on 22 November that artists' work might be construed as 'incitement' under the proposed bill. A poll conducted by the Professional Teachers' Union published on 23 November showed almost 75 per cent of 442 teachers opposed the proposals; 53.8 per cent believed they would 'dare not' criticise Beijing or the Hong Kong government in lessons, fearing prosecution for 'thought and word' crimes. (*South China Morning Post*)

Hong Kong Chief Executive Tung Chee-hwa announced on 28 January that the draft anti-subversion law would be scaled back and would no longer outlaw possession of seditious material and would address journalists' fears that they could be charged for using information from state sources that had not been officially released. But on 21 February the Committee to Protect Journalists said the government had disregarded the public consultation process and that 'in its current form, this bill poses a grave threat to freedom of expression'. (AP, CPJ)

INDIA

Syed Iftikar Geelani (*Index* 4/02), *Kashmir Times* journalist and son-in-law of nationalist leader **Syed Ali Shah Geelani**, was freed on 13 January after seven months in detention despite the government's rejection of an intelligence report that denied that he had illegally taken papers of 'security value'. (*Frontline*)

The Hindu reported on 13 January that **Vaiko**, leader of the MDMK party in Tamil Nadu, had filed a petition on the constitutional validity of India's Prevention of Terrorism Act. Vaiko was arrested in July last year (*Index* 4/02, 1/03) for voicing support for the Liberation Tigers of Tamil Eelam in Sri Lanka. (*The Hindu*)

Kumar Badal, of the much-harassed www.tehelka.com news website (*Index* 3/01, 2/02, 4/02, 1/03), was granted bail by the Supreme Court on 13 January. He had been arrested in July 2002 in Uttar Pradesh under the Wildlife Protection and Arms Act while investigating the illegal sale of fur pelts. (*The Hindu*)

In January, Information Minister Sushma Swaraj ordered the National Aids Control Organisation (NACC) to drop advertisements for condoms from state-run Doordarshan TV. Swaraj claimed the ads encouraged sex rather than discouraged the spread of Aids in India, which has the world's second highest number of HIV-positive people. (*South China Morning Post*)

In January, US missionary **Joseph Cooper** and his family were injured by Hindu nationalist thugs outside a Protestant convention organised by the Friends Bible Church of Puliyam. Cooper was later deported for attending the conference in alleged breach of his visa conditions. (*The Hindu*, BBC)

Parvaz Mohammed Sultan, editor of the News and Feature Alliance wire service and contributor to the Urdu-language newspaper *Chattan*, was shot dead in his office on 31 January by two men. No one has claimed responsibility for the murder but the service was often pressed to carry statements by militant groups. (CPJ)

In February, the state of Rajasthan announced a ban on the carrying of the trident as a traditional Hindu icon to protect Muslims and other religious minorities from the threat of hardline Hindu nationalist organisations such as the Vishwa Hindu Parishad and the Bajrang Dal. (BBC)

Almost a year after over 50 Hindu pilgrims were killed in an attack on a train in Ghodra, Gujarat (*Index* 2/02, 3/02, 4/02), the state charged Muslim cleric **Maulana Hussain Umarji** on 19 February under the Prevention of Terrorism Act for allegedly masterminding the incident. His supporters say Umarji was forced to make a confession in custody. (BBC)

Kui tribal poet **Dasuram Mallik**, alias 'Jacob', from Gajapati in Orissa, was arrested on 21 February for allegedly inciting the tribal people of the region through his revolutionary songs and stories. Police said he was a sympathiser of the Kui Labanga Sangha group, linked to the outlawed People's War Group. (IANS)

A film based on interviews with survivors of the Gujarat religious riots was refused a certificate allowing its showing in India or abroad on 13 March. The film board believes the 22-minute documentary *Aakrosh* (*Outburst*) could incite religious tensions in the country. (BBC)

Government censors cut nine times more footage from Indian films than it did from foreign ones last year, Broadcasting Minister Ravi Shankar Prasad told parliament on 10 March. His censors cut 12,121 metres of film from 943 Indian movies, and just 1,367 metres from 290 foreign films. Prasad said censors' guidelines are to be updated after 12 years but did not give details. (IANS)

Recent Publications: *India: Break the Cycle of Impunity and Torture in Punjab*, Amnesty International, January 2003.

INDONESIA

Academic and writer **Lesley McCulloch** (*Index* 1/03) was released from jail in Indonesia on 9 February. She and health worker **Joy Lee Sadler** were jailed on 30 December 2002 for breaking the terms of their tourist visas by meeting with Aceh separatist rebels. Sadler was released in mid-January. (*Guardian*)

German freelance TV journalist **Seyam Reda** was sentenced to ten months in jail on 18 January for breaking his visa conditions by filming, it was alleged, ethnic rebels undergoing military training in the eastern Poso (Central Sulawesi) and Ambon (Maluku) regions. (*Jakarta Post*)

IRAN

Journalist **Ali-Reza Jabari** was arrested on 28 December after he was quoted in an interview he gave to the paper *Charvand*, claiming that Iranian spiritual leader Ayatollah Ali Khameni wanted the current crisis in Iran to worsen for his own political advantage. (RSF)

On 12 January, journalist **Alireza Eshraghi** of *Hayat-e-No* was arrested for republishing a cartoon – first printed in the US in 1937 and depicting a US Supreme Court judge under the thumb of then president Franklin Delano Roosevelt – that the courts regarded as having too great a resemblance to the late Ayatollah Ruhollah Khomeini. (RSF)

Three papers were suspended in the early months of 2003: *Hayat-e-No, Bahar* and *Nowrooz*. *Hayat-e-No* was allowed to reopen, but limit its reporting to economic matters. *Nowrooz* was due to reopen on 25 January under a different title, *Ruz-i-No*, but was banned indefinitely before it could start publishing. (RFE)

On 6 February, journalist **Emadoldin Baghi** was released after two years in prison. He had previously written for the banned newspapers *Neshat* and *Fath*. He had been arrested and imprisoned for alleged subversion. (RSF)

The death sentence handed down to Iranian academic Professor **Hashem Aghajari** (*Index* 1/03) for apostasy and questioning clerical rule in November 2002 was quashed on 14 February after mass student protests. He must be retried by the same court that ordered his execution and may yet face flogging and years in jail. (WiPC)

Tehran's Peykan football club let women journalists and female relatives of players attend a first-division league match on 8 January, in the latest relaxation of the rule that has generally barred women from soccer matches since the 1979 Islamic revolution. (Reuters)

Film magazine journalists **Kambiz Kaheh, Said Mostaghasi** of *Haftenameh* magazine, **Mohammad Abdi**, editor-in-chief of the monthly *Honar Haftom*, **Amir Ezati** of *Mahnameh Film* and film music critic **Yasamin Soufi** were arrested in raids between 26 February and 1 March, Soufi by the Adareh Amaken 'morality police'. (RSF)

IRAQ

An Iraqi web enthusiast known as '**Salam Pax**' has had his 'weblog' diary, 'Where_is_Raed?', blocked in Iraq, thanks to the authorities' use of a web filtering program made by US firm 8e6 Technologies. The pages had become a widely regarded alternative perspective on the imminent war in Iraq. (www.itregister.com)

Washington officials ordered out Iraqi News Agency UN correspondent **Mohamed**

Hassan Alaoui on 14 February, accusing him of activities 'considered prejudicial to national security'. The Iraqi authorities retaliated by expelling US Fox TV correspondent **Greg Palkot**. (RSF)

Soon after the fighting got under way in Iraq, the media suffered its first casualties: veteran British ITN correspondent **Terry Lloyd**, 51, cameraman **Fred Nerac** and local producer **Hussein Othman**, apparently victims of 'friendly fire' at Iman Anas. Belgian freelance **Daniel Demoustier** was wounded in the same attack. Australian cameraman **Paul Moran**, 39, was killed on 22 March by a booby-trapped car explosion in Iraqi Kurdistan, at a checkpoint near the Iranian border. (Reuters)

IRELAND

Details of Irish citizens' phone calls, faxes, email and internet usage could be retained for up to four years under a draft law published in November. Presently, data may be retained only by Irish telecom and by web firms for billing purposes for up to six months; it must then be destroyed. (*Irish Times*)

ISRAEL

Israeli Arab film director **Mohammed Bakri** thanked Israel's Film Ratings Board for indirectly promoting his documentary about the occupied Palestinian town of Jenin by banning it. The board said it was a 'one-sided propaganda film'. It was shown on 18 November in Palestinian-controlled Ramallah and to a selected audience of Tel Aviv

OUT OF THE BLUE: ISRAEL

State of Israel, Newspaper and Media Censorship, Office of the Chief Censor,
PO Box 7003, Tel Aviv 61070

To: Scoops Forum and Fresh News Site (www.fresh.co.il)
Subject: Censorship instructions – American Attack on Iraq

Given the current security situation, you are reminded that it is required to submit
(for the Censor's review) all materials that could pose a threat to the security of the
State of Israel and its residents, in accordance with the list of topics that is in your
possession. In particular, it is prohibited to publish the following details without prior
permission of the Censor:

- Precise locations of missile impacts. In live broadcasts, it is permitted to identify
  impact locations as the Tel Aviv region, the Haifa region, or the Jerusalem region
  exclusively. Anything more than that requires the permission of the Censor, or
  publication of an authorised announcement from the Homefront Command. In
  any event, it is forbidden to publicise the fall of a missile into the sea or in locations
  designated as strategic.
- It is prohibited to publish the type of missile until publication of an authorised
  announcement from the IDF Spokesman, and it is prohibited to publish
  correspondents' reports on the subject, given the danger to human life from
  an unauthorised report.
- IDF operations in any sector, operational plans, mobilisation of reserves.
- Collaboration with foreign parties.
- Cabinet discussions.

In these times, your extra sensitivity to fulfilment of the Censor's instructions is
requested. Given the circumstances, I know I can count on your full cooperation,
as required.

Censorship facilities: Tel Aviv Censorship Base; Jerusalem Censorship Base
In addition, censors will be working 24 hours a day in the two media centres – in the
Foreign Ministry in Jerusalem, and in the David Intercontinental in Tel Aviv – and you
may also turn to them.

I request that you direct reporters in general, and field correspondents who broadcast
live as well as relevant internet sites in particular, to follow these instructions.

Sincerely
Brigadier General Rachel Dolev, Chief Censor ❏

*Translated from the Hebrew by the Federation of American Scientists (www.fas.org). A copy of
the original faxed message can be viewed at http://www.4law.co.il/L532.html*

university students on a law and politics course led by former education minister Shulamit Aloni. University officials barred other students from attending the showing. (*Ha'aretz*, Reuters)

Israeli prime minister **Ariel Sharon**'s attempt to refute opposition charges of party corruption on TV backfired when election officials shut down the live broadcast on 9 January. Israeli law bars party broadcasts a month before elections, which were scheduled 19 days later. (*Guardian*)

Likud party members on Israel's election commission attempted to ban Arab Knesset members **Ahmed Tibi** and **Azmi Bishara** from standing in the 28 January poll, claiming that the two supported military action against Israel in the occupied territories. Israel's Supreme Court later overturned the ban. (*Daily Telegraph*)

An exhibition by Tel Aviv architects **Rafi Segal** and **Eyal Weizman** that placed the design of illegal Jewish settlements in a political context, blocked by Israeli architectural grandees from an allotted space at a Berlin congress in 2002, was recreated and opened for seven weeks in New York on 12 February. (*Index Online*)

Rabbi Menashe Miller told a rabbinical court in Haifa in January that he would divorce his wife if she voted Labor. 'I fought for this country and I will not accept my wife voting against my will,' said the Likud-voting rabbi. The court, called to arbitrate, said the wife would have to surrender her vote. (*Ma'ariv*)

Israeli officials issued a two-year ban on the Islamic weekly *Sawt al-Haq wa al-Hurriya* newspaper on 22 December after Israeli security services claimed the paper was a mouthpiece for Hamas. The paper is published by the Islamic Movement, a political party with two seats in the Israeli knesset. (RSF)

Two Palestinian Associated Press photographers were attacked in Nablus on 21 January after they tried to photograph Israeli soldiers driving a jeep with two Palestinians forcibly seated on its bonnet. The AP men were beaten and told: 'If we see a picture of us published anywhere, we're going to kill you.' (*B'Tselem*)

Censor-in-chief Rachel Dolev ordered websites with a taste for 'scoop' news, including www.rotter.net and www.fresh.co.il, not to publish sensitive information on missile attacks on Israel or its covert cooperation with other states during the Iraq conflict. Some site editors warned that they would find ways round the censor if the rules were unfairly applied. (ZDNet)

ITALY

Intellectuals including **Enzo Biagi** and **Umberto Eco** (*Index* 4/02) petitioned parliament to protest against its 10 December plan to control the selection of school history books. Right-wingers say it will balance the Communist Party's historical influence over history teaching; left-wing parties denounce it as censorship. (*La Repubblica*)

State TV RAI decided not to broadcast live coverage of anti-war protests in February which may have drawn up to 3 million people in Rome alone. Prime Minister Silvio Berlusconi's private TV stations did cover the protests but this did not silence allegations of politically influenced censorship. (*Guardian*)

Senator **Franco Bassanini** warned that many television journalists avoided being seen to criticise the prime minister for fear of losing their jobs. 'They have no alternative,' he said. 'If they are excluded from RAI, they cannot go to the other major stations, because they are owned by Mr Berlusconi.' (*Guardian*)

JAPAN

Japanese publisher *Yamakawa Shuppan* won government permission on 16 February to edit a new schoolbook's references (*Index* 3/01) to the 1937 Nanjing Massacre in China. Text that put the number of people killed by the invading Japanese 'in a range between tens of thousands and 400,000' was altered to read, 'many Chinese people'. An official said the revision 'was due to concerns that the original explanation may obstruct students' proper understanding'. (AFP)

A redrafted privacy protection bill tabled in February extended protection from prosecution to professional writers and freelance journalists holding private papers obtained for a story, although Japanese free-speech campaigners still believe officials could apply sanctions arbitrarily. (*Japan Times*)

JORDAN

The weekly newspaper *al-Hilal* was closed and journalists **Nasser Qamash**, **Roman Haddad** and **Muhammad Mbideen** were arrested under the controversial security law 150, which allows the criminal prosecution of journalists, for an article on 'the mythology of sex in Islam'. On 17 February, Mbideen was jailed for six months and Haddad and Qamash were fined. (Index Online, *Jordan Times*)

KAZAKHSTAN

On 7 December, 1,000 copies of the paper *Assandi-Times* intended for local opposition activists were seized at Pavlodar airport in north-east Kazahkstan on the orders of local National Security Committee officers. Two days later the city's daily, *Vesti Pavlodara*, had its website blocked after publishing critical reports about local governor Daniyal Akhmetov. (CIS, CJES)

On 19 December, President Nursultan Nazarbaev founded a Public Media Council to report to him on the formulation of state information policy. It will allegedly advise him on improvements to media legislation and the protection of the interests and rights of the media sector and its workers. (CIS, CJES)

Free-speech groups voiced support for human rights activist **Sergei Duvanov**, jailed for three and a half years for 'rape of a minor' on 28 January. The groups cite several inconsistencies in prosecution evidence and

contest the procedural handling of the case. Duvanov says he was framed. (OSCE, RSF, CJES)

Canadian coroners who travelled to Kazakhstan to investigate the 2002 death of **Leila Bayseitova**, daughter of journalist **Lira Bayseitova** (*Index* 4/02), concluded that she died from injuries consistent with hanging while in police custody. Her death had been linked to Lira's reports on secret Swiss bank accounts held by top Kazakh officials. But the Canadian Journalists for Free Expression group noted that the coroners' report did not address the possibility that 'someone other than Leila was involved in the act – or that she was forced into it'. (CJFE)

KENYA

A bid to seize the assets of *The People* newspaper was halted by a High Court order on 5 March. The Nairobi paper had been fined 23 million shillings (US$300,000) for libelling a former minister in 1999 articles about the controversial Trukwell Gorge hydroelectric dam. (*The People*)

KUWAIT

Information Minister Sheikh Ahmed al-Fahd al-Sabah told foreign journalists based in Kuwait to cover the war in Iraq that they would be prosecuted if they were caught stringing for Israeli media as well as their own. Over 1,000 foreign journalists were accredited in Kuwait ahead of 20 March, but none is Israeli. (RSF)

KYRGYZSTAN

RSF reported on 24 January that journalist **Aleksandra Chernykh** of the daily *Moya Stolitsa* suffered head injuries in an attack by two men as she took her 11-year-old daughter home. A series of court orders and asset seizures against her paper have been condemned as 'judicial persecution' by media rights groups. (RSF, CJES)

Voters approved a new constitution by a three-quarters majority in a 2 February referendum. Opposition leaders say the political changes to reinforce regional decision-making will also reinforce a north–south divide and give President Askar Akayev more political leverage over their activities. (www.eurasianet.org)

LEBANON

International broadcasts by **New Television** were blocked in January on order of Prime Minister Rafik al-Hariri. The station had planned a report assessing the negative impact on Saudi Arabia of a US-led war on Iraq and the equally negative consequences on the Lebanese economy. (ABC)

LESOTHO

Candy Ratabana Ramainoane, editor of the weekly *MoAfrica*, won the right to retain a 16-word note on his front page that links Prime Minister PB Mossili to the murder of Deputy Prime Minister **Selometsi Baholo**. A November ruling had ordered its removal while the murder case was in progress. (MISA)

LIBERIA

Throble Suah, a reporter with the independent *Inquirer* newspaper, was reportedly flogged by five uniformed security personnel on 14 November. At one point, he said, the troops put a gun to his head and told him they would kill him. Suah was later found by fellow journalists who took him to hospital. (*Inquirer*)

MALAWI

Radio journalist **Maganizo Mazeze** was arrested on 19 January and charged with 'broadcasting false information likely to cause public alarm' after interviewing a man who said he had been attacked by a vampire. A persistent village rumour claims that the state has hired vampires to collect blood to sell to foreign aid agencies. A judge later dismissed the charges. (*Guardian*)

Penelope Paliani-Kamanga, deputy chief reporter for the *Daily Times*, was hit in the knee by a rubber bullet by Blantyre anti-riot police on 27 January, as they dispersed demonstrators against the tabling of a parliament bill aimed at allowing President Bakili Muluzi to serve a third term in office. (MISA)

MALAYSIA

Police seized all 19 computers from the *Malaysiakini* news website office on 20 January, after it posted an anonymous letter criticising the ruling party. The state-run company that owns the office tried to evict them and editor **Steven Gan** has been charged with sedition and incitement to racial hatred. (*Malaysiakini*)

Footage of women kissing each other in the Oscar-winning movie *The Hours* has been banned by film censors from being shown in Malaysia. The head of the country's Film Censorship Board said it was protecting 'the interests of the country and people from bad influences and negative elements shown in films'. (BBC)

MALDIVES

On 14 February, Reporters Sans Frontières called again for the release of email newsletter journalists **Mohamed Zaki**, **Ibrahim Luthfee** and **Ahmed Didi** (*Index* 2/02, 4/02), jailed for life, and editorial assistant **Fathima Nisreen**, jailed for ten years, for 'committing acts hostile to the government' in July 2002. (RSF)

MEXICO

Seven Mexican journalists received court orders attempting to force them to reveal their sources in November and December. **Daniel Moreno**, news director at the daily *El Universal*, refused in court to reveal his sources for an article on corruption at the state-owned oil giant Pemex. (RSF)

On 31 January, Governor Antonio Echevarría Dominguez of the north-western state of Nayarit ordered independent **Radio Korita** off air just as the station's controversial *Consensos* programme, known for its criticism of the governor's administration, was due to start. (RSF)

MIDDLE EAST

Former Jordanian information minister Saleh Qalab, director of Arab satellite TV news channel al-Arabiya TV, launched in March, says it will be less provocative than its rival, al-Jazeera. Arab information ministers, many of whom are critical of al-Jazeera's independent style, met in Cairo in June 2002 to discuss a US$20 million campaign to counter Israeli and US media influences. (IHT)

Recent Publications: *National Security vs. Openness: An Overview and Status Report on the Johannesburg Principles*, by Toby Mendel, Article 19, January 2003.

MOROCCO

A war of words between Morocco's media took a violent turn on 26 January when **Rachid Mahamid** of the satirical weekly *Douman* was assaulted by journalists from the daily *al-Ahdate al-Maghribia*, as he tried to photograph a brawl at a meeting called to show solidarity with Iraq. Journalists from *al-Ahdate al-Maghribia* are in dispute with *Douman*'s French edition, which has mocked their paper as 'pornography'.

MOZAMBIQUE

On 31 January, five men accused of killing journalist **Carlos Cardoso** (*Index*, 1/03, 4/01, 3/01, 2/01) were convicted and jailed for 23 years each. A sixth man, hit-squad leader Anibal dos Santos Jr, escaped pre-trial detention in 2002 but was recaptured in South Africa on 30 January. He was sentenced to 28 years' imprisonment. (MISA)

DON'T BE SHY. SAY HOW YOU FEEL

Yahya Abu Zakaria

I am completely convinced that the Arab ruler, in his cruelty, repression and oppression of the peoples, bears most, if not all, the responsibility for the collapse of the Arab [world], politically, economically and culturally. The Arab ruler has not managed to come up with a political plan to advance the country and the people.

This Arab ruler made the country his, and his alone; he turned it into a commercial company and appointed his sons and relatives to be supervisors. In addition, the Arab ruler treats the Arab people with disdain. We have rulers in the Arab region who came to power on a tank. Some came out of a British tent, and some out of an American tent, and they have ruled us for decades.

If they had even a grain of shame, they would withdraw from the political arena and leave it to the young political leaders . . . But the Arab ruler has turned into a slaughterer and a thief, and he gambles with the livelihood of the peoples. He has become a thief who steals the people's bread.

The Arab ruler who goes to sleep with his slave girls, and whose prisons are full of prisoners, is a contemptible ruler. The Arab ruler who sleeps with his masseuses while the people lie on the open ground and sleep in the streets is a thieving ruler. The Arab ruler who murders his opponents in the streets, confiscates minds and pushes the people into exile is a ruler of dubious origin. The Arab ruler who opens his borders, on land, sea and air, to the Americans is a bastard ruler.

The Arab ruler confiscated all our powers and laid us low. This Arab ruler must now withdraw. They ruled us for 30–40 years, and nothing has changed. The debt increased, the prisons filled up, the number of universities shrank, the number of those exiled reached the maximum, the number of those living in grave[yards] increased, the Arab citizen began to look for bread and cannot find it.

O Arab ruler, before the Americans enter your palace to search it, let the Arab street enter this palace to trim your moustache. Get out, because you are the reason for our cultural, social and political catastrophes, and all our catastrophes, the last of which was that the American master is coming to gnaw away at the region directly, after some of its rulers were CIA officials . . .

Ahmad Othman

I disagree with this completely. The problem is not the rulers . . . If we replace the rulers and bring new ones tomorrow, they would do the same thing, because the people itself and the Arab nation are in a state of cultural and moral collapse.

If we look at the beginning of the last century, we will see that a revolution has taken place. Then there was cultural activity, there were moral values, there were political values, there were [political] parties and organisations in the [Arab] nation. There was British and French occupation. But the Arab nation struggled to build itself. There was a flowering of ideas . . . We expected to attain independence after World War II . . . but what happened? Today we are in complete collapse in the sphere of ideas. How can you say that the Arab ruler is responsible? Who enabled this ruler to sit on his throne? We did. Who knelt before this ruler and made him a demigod? Who turned the man who is an officer, the man who is a prince, or the man who is a sheikh, into an emperor and leader? We have done all this.

The Arab has no honour, no thought, no culture. We have turned these images into regimes, and were we to replace them, others just like them would come in their stead. We must, first of all, change ourselves. We must establish cultural values . . .

Why do we want to defend Saddam Hussein? Why do all the Arab regimes use the Arab people as a human shield for the greatest dictator of them all? If you object to dictatorships – who in the [Arab] regimes is a greater dictator than Saddam Hussein? How can the Arab people, who are persecuted by their regimes, be asked to defend the murderer who killed hundreds of thousands of the Iraqi people . . . ? How can we defend Saddam Hussein and remain a free people ourselves? [A people] that defends a dictator is not a free people . . .' ❏

*Excerpts from a discussion on the Qatari-based TV station al-Jazeera titled: 'Why the Arabs Have Become the Joke of the World'. **Yahya Abu Zakaria** was identified as an Algerian journalist, an 'Islamist' and resident of Sweden. Egyptian historian **Ahmad Othman** was identified as a 'liberal'*

Translated by the Middle East Media Research Institute (www.memri.org) and used with permission

NEPAL

Gobinda Acharya, editor of *Janadesh*, and **Chandra Shre-stra**, editor of *Janadisha*, were released from two different prisons in the Kathmandu Valley on 16 December. Both men had been detained because of their alleged sympathies with Maoist rebels. (*Nepal News*)

On 17 January, **Dipendra Rokaya** (*Index* 1/03) of the weekly *Janadesh* reported that the paper's equipment had been stolen after he and his colleagues were detained in 2002 (*Index* 1/03). **Rewati Sapkota** of the daily *Rajdhani* said he was tortured during his one-month detention last year for alleged Maoist sympathies. (*Kathmandu Post*)

Journalists **Om Sharma** and **Krishna Prasad Khana**, both affiliated with Kath-mandu-based pro-Maoist newspapers, were freed on 7 February. Sharma, a Federation of Nepalese Journalists council member, spent nearly 15 months in prison. Of nearly 150 journalists detained during a nine-month state of emergency in 2002, a dozen journalists remain behind bars. (CEHURDES)

Recent Publications: *Situation of Basic Human Rights – A Baseline Survey Report Among Selected Communities of Nepal*, Informal Sector Service Centre, Kathmandu, January 2003.

NEW ZEALAND

So-called 'Pakeha' (non-Maori) journalists were barred from the commemoration of the signing of the 1840 Treaty of Waitangi on 6 Feb-ruary. Senior members of the Ngapuhi tribe, traditional custodians of the event site, have complained about 'adverse reporting' by journalists of European descent in the past. (NZPA)

In March, a parliamentary select committee recommended a broadening of the censor's powers to ban or restrict films and videos. It wants censorship laws to cover the way films, videos and publications deal with mental illness, suicide, sexual orientation and HIV. (NZPA)

NIGER

Journalist **Ibrahim Manzo** and marketing director **Cisse Omar Amadou** of *Le Canard Déchaîné* were released without charge on 27 November after four days in detention. The paper had linked the army's chief of staff with the arrest of a key opposition figure. (RSF)

NIGERIA

Former minister Haji Wada Nas advised the Nigerian media to focus on issues rather than religious or ethnic identities when covering Nigeria's presidential election. He said the failure of President Olusegun Obasanjo 'was not because he is a Yoruba and Christian but rather because he was Obasanjo'. (*This Day*)

PAKISTAN

In January, the government announced plans to allow the licensing of private radio and TV stations for the first time. The stations will be limited to music and entertainment pro-grammes at first, but media experts think that it is simply a matter of time before independent news channels will also be permitted. (BBC)

Fazal Wahab, author and outspoken critic of radical Islam, was shot dead by four armed men in the hill town of Mingora, in Northwest Frontier Province, on 21 January. His murder followed efforts by the Islamist government in the province to curtail free expression. (BBC, Amnesty International)

Demands for the shutting-down of cable TV, video and music shops allegedly spreading 'obscenity and vulgarity' have intensified in conservative Northwest Frontier Province. In February, police in Peshawar detained two dozen video shop owners as part of a campaign against pornographic movies. (PTI)

On 10 February, the Supreme Court overturned military leader Pervez Musharraf's order barring candidates defeated in last October's elections (*Index* 1/03) from standing in upcoming Senate polls. The court said candidates should have been told before the vote what the consequences of defeat would be. (BBC)

The News reported on 23 February that the Pakistan Telecommunications Company Limited had banned 103 pornographic websites. The move came a month after the minister for information technology and telecommunications ordered the blocking of websites showing 'vulgar and indecent' material. (*The News*)

Asadullah, a photographer for the daily *Express*, was beaten by police in Jhang Bazaar on 24 February while trying to cover a story about a youth being tortured. The police were not involved in the torture, but a senior officer reportedly beat Asadullah when he refused to hand over his camera. (*Dawn*)

PALESTINE

On 6 February, Palestinian Authority secret police arrested al-Jazeera Gaza correspondent **Seif al-Din Shahin** after a live broadcast by the station included a phone-in caller's comment that the Fatah Movement's denial of responsibility for two recent suicide bombings was 'defeatist'. (PCHR)

PARAGUAY

On 17 December, Channel 9 TV news director **Benjamín Fernández Bogado** was found guilty of defamation in connection with broadcast comments that linked lawyer Adalberto Fox with organised crime in December 1996. Bogado was fined US$1,200 and ordered to pay compensation of approximately US$1,400 to Fox. (PFC)

PERU

Journalist **Javier Tuanama Valera** was released from prison on 16 November. He was sentenced to ten years in jail in 1994 on charges that he was a member of the Tupac Amaru Revolutionary Movement. (WiPC)

On 17 December, former politician **Miguel Ciccia Vásquez**, apparently upset by being filmed at President Alejandro Toledo Manrique's daughter's 15th birthday party, attacked *Ojo* reporter **Domenique Favre** and Canal N journalists **Marco Sifuentes** and **Paola Ugaz Vásquez**. (IPYS)

On 20 January, Peruvian National Police Captain Arturo Parra Tella threatened Radio Anaconda journalist **Henry Pinedo Rojas** after Rojas criticised the police for alleged lack of concern in the handling of the case of five high school students who committed suicide. (IPYS)

On leaving Radio Studio 99 on 6 February, journalist **Juan Espinoza Linares** was attacked and left seriously injured. The attacker and motives are unknown. (IPYS)

PHILIPPINES

On 7 February, the government and the US ambassador reached an agreement to allow American teachers to teach English in the Autonomous Region of Muslim Mindanao. Five hundred Muslim teachers who met the government last year welcomed the proposal. (*Philippine Star*)

Eraño Manalo, executive minister of the controversial Iglesia ni Cristo sect, went to court on 27 February to challenge a lawyers' group petition to ban religious leaders from endorsing political candidates. The lawyers say it would break the separation of church and state. (*Philippine Star*)

Police officer Guillermo Wapille, the alleged killer of Pagadian City journalist **Edgar Damalerio**, was reported to have escaped from custody shortly after a local judge hearing his case ordered his arrest on 30 January. Wapille was supposed to be detained within the camp precincts. Damalerio's widow Gemma has sued the commander for dereliction of duty. (CMFR)

POLAND

In January, *Gazeta Wyborcza* published partial transcripts of a 2002 meeting between editor **Adam Michnik** and an alleged cabinet intermediary who demanded US$17.5 million to amend media laws so that the newspaper's parent company could buy a private Polish TV station. A state inquiry has been launched. (*Gazeta Wyborcza*)

British media lawyer **Geoffrey Robinson** and Dutch law professor **Egbert Dommering** are to monitor legal proceedings against Presspublica, the publisher of Polish independent daily *Rzeczpospolita* (*Index* 1/03), which currently faces a dozen state-sponsored law suits allegedly aimed at reining in its coverage. (WAN)

QATAR

On 24 February, Jordanian journalist **Firas Majali** had his death sentence confirmed by the Qatari appeals court. Majali was originally arrested in February 2002 in Doha for 'spying' for his country. He was sentenced by the Supreme Court of Doha to the death penalty on 22 October 2002. (RSF)

ROMANIA

Romanian free-expression advocates met Justice Minister Mihaela Rodica Stanoiu on 21 January and urged the removal of 'insult' laws and penal code clauses that could make people who handle non-secret state documents liable to treason charges. They said a de facto ban on the public criticism of government officials should be lifted along with a privacy law that has seriously limited the ability of journalists to investigate and expose wrongdoing. (CfIJ)

RUSSIA

Russian senators threw out a bill to establish Russian as the 'state language' and bar obscene words from public speeches – a habit among populist politicians, including premier Vladimir Putin. It would also have barred the use of foreign words where Russian equivalents exist. The upper house of the Russian parliament said the bill as passed by the lower Duma was an anachronism. (*Moscow Times*)

Journalist **Grigorii Pasko** (*Index* 4/02, 2/02), jailed for revealing how the Russian military fleet dumped nuclear pollution in the Sea of Japan, was named winner of the Reporters Sans Frontières–Fondation de France annual prize on 10 December. The prize was accepted by his wife Galina in Paris. (RSF)

On 13 January, a Russian court upheld a US$10,000 fine imposed on an advertising agency for provoking street violence by showing a clip from the US movie *The Big Lebowski* in which a man

smashed up a car with a baseball bat. It was shown on a giant screen moments after the broadcast of Russia's defeat by Japan in the 2002 World Cup. One man died and scores were injured in the riots that followed. (Reuters)

Two police officers were arrested for the assassination of military affairs journalist **Vladimir Sukhomlin**, beaten to death with baseball bats on 4 January. They reportedly confessed that they had received US$1,150 for the murder and named the man who paid, the director of a St Petersburg company. (*Moscow Times*)

Anna Politkovskaia (*Index* 2/02), the independent Russian journalist fêted for her reports from Chechnya, was announced as the winner of the 2003 Prize for Journalism and Democracy in Copenhagen. The prize, awarded annually by the parliamentary assembly of OSCE, includes a US$20,000 award. (Yahoo! News)

RWANDA

On 16 January, the International Criminal Tribunal restarted the trial of Radio-TV Libre des Mille Collines founders **Ferdinand Nahimana**, **Jean-Bosco Barayagwiza** and **Hassan Ngeze**. All plead not guilty to charges of genocide, conspiracy to commit genocide and crimes against humanity. (*Hirondelle*)

Ismael Mbonigaba, editor of *Umuseso,* was detained on 22 January and charged with incitement to discrimination after the paper reported that former prime minister Faustin

Twagiramungu would challenge President Paul Kagame at the next elections. Mbonigaba was released on licence on 28 February. (www.allafrica.com)

SAUDI ARABIA

A draft proposal in which the Crown Prince proposed wide-ranging political reforms, including enhanced popular participation in politics, was officially 'leaked' to the Saudi press in January. Human Rights Watch was allowed to conduct a groundbreaking visit to Saudi Arabia in February, plans for a Saudi Journalists' Association to support media rights were approved in March, and Arab media report plans for economic, educational and women's rights reforms to be announced, along with cabinet changes, in early June. The effect on the plans of war in Iraq is not known. (*Beirut Daily Star, Straits Times*)

Saudi officials denied visas to staff from Qatar-based al-Jazeera satellite TV, preventing it from covering the annual Hajj in the city of Mecca. No reason was given, but the Saudis have long criticised al-Jazeera's frank coverage of the Saudi royal family (*Index* 4/02) and its foreign policy. (*Washington Post*)

SENEGAL

African Television News cameraman **Libasse Nuraye** was attacked and injured by police on 18 December in Dakar as they forcibly broke up a demonstration by relatives of victims of a September 2002 ferry disaster that claimed more than 1,000 lives. (WAJA)

SERBIA

Following the assassination of Serbian Prime Minister **Zoran Djindjic** on 12 March, the state banned all information about the killing not approved by officials. By 18 March, two daily newspapers, *Nacional* and *Dan*, the weekly magazine *Identidet* and TV Radio Mars were all deemed to have broken the rules — TV Radio Mars for playing music during Djindjic's funeral — and were closed down and fined. (RSF)

Vukasin Obradovic, owner and editor-in-chief of the Vranje-based weekly *Novine Vranjske,* and his reporter, **Goran Antic**, reported that they had received death threats on 4 March for reporting allegations of sexual abuse made against Serbian Orthodox Bishop Pahomije. (CPJ)

SOMALIA

It was reported on 17 January that Somali **Radio TV HornAfrik** was taken over by armed militiamen and taken off air. The men were acting on the orders of a businessman who was offended by a news report about a book mentioning connections between Somali businessmen and terrorism. No staff were hurt and the station was returned to the air after a few hours. (IFJ)

SOUTH AFRICA

On 23 January, SABC TV journalists **Lexi Herholdt** and **Nthabiseng Makhongoana** were attacked by the staff of a school near Loanyaneng in North-West Province as they interviewed students angered by the principal's decision to withhold students' report cards on non-payment of fees. (MISA)

The International Press Institute has condemned the government's decision to close the media's offices in parliament, a facility open to the South African press for 100 years. The Institute claims that closure will obstruct the electorate's and the media's rights to access parliamentary proceedings. (IPI)

On 19 March, South African parliamentarians discussed banning TV from showing MPs sleeping or yawning in session. Parliament's camera crews are suspected of singling out certain parties. No decision was made and the planned ban was sent back to a committee. MP **Pandeli Nefolovhodwe** argued that telling MPs to wake up would be better than TV censorship. (SABC)

Recent Publications: *Truth & Justice: Unfinished Business in South Africa*, Amnesty International & Human Rights Watch, February 2003.

SPAIN

Police closed down *Egunkaria*, Spain's last remaining Basque-language daily, in a dawn raid on 20 February, arresting ten employees including the paper's editor, **Marcelo Otamendi**. The Spanish authorities accuse the paper of links with ETA, the Basque terrorist organisation, which *Egunkaria* denies. (IFJ)

An 'anti-capitalist group' calling itself The Five Cs was blamed for an attempted parcel bomb attack on the *El País* newspaper office in Barcelona. The bomb was defused by police. The Five Cs are accused of several bomb attacks including an attack on the Italian TV network RT4 in July 2001. (RSF)

SRI LANKA

Sripathi Sooriyaratchchi, publisher of the opposition paper *Lakmina,* was quizzed in December over allegations that a top member of the opposition People's Alliance (PA) had been encouraged by the ruling United National Party to assassinate PA leader and President Chandrika Kumaratunga. (*Lanka Academic*)

The home of **Senathirajah Jeyanandamoorthy**, Batticaloa correspondent for www.tamilnet.com and the daily *Virakesari*, was attacked with grenades on 7 January. He has had death threats from Islamic extremists and angered Sinhalese nationalists with his photographs of a law court run by local Tamil Tiger (LTTE) forces. (www.tamilnet.org)

Thinakural photojournalist **S Sivabalan** and *Eelanadu* reporter **S Manoharan** were assaulted by Sri Lankan soldiers and their equipment destroyed as they covered clashes between troops and unarmed female LTTE cadres at a checkpoint in the Jaffna Peninsula on 12 February. (www.tamilnet.org, AP, Xinhua)

On 13 February, all 23 members of Jaffna town council resigned in protest in the face of LTTE threats over the reopening of Jaffna's Public Library. LTTE want the library closed until an annexe documenting the destruction of its Tamil-language books by Sinhalese mobs in 1981 is built and the Tamil books replaced. (AP)

In late February, the Supreme Court was criticised for sentencing human rights activist **Michael Anthony Fernando** to a year in jail for contempt of court for disputing the right of Chief Justice Sarath N Silva to preside over a procedural hearing in which he had been named as a respondent. Fernando was reportedly tortured in custody and was later hospitalised with serious spinal injuries. (Asian Human Rights Commission, *Colombo Sunday Times*, *Ravaya*)

On 25 February, police forwarded five pistols and ammunition recovered from the offices of the Eelam People's Democratic Party to government analysts who will match them against spent shells found in October 2000 by the body of murdered journalist **Mylvaganam Nimalarajan** (*Index* 1/01, 3/01, 1/02, 4/02). (www.tamilnet.org)

Recent Publications: *The Cost of 'Peace' and the Dividends of Terror: Sri Lanka's Nordic Winter?* – *Information Bulletin No 30*, University Teachers for Human Rights (Jaffna), 3 December 2002; *The Gathering Storm in the East* – *Information Bulletin No 31*, University Teachers for Human Rights (Jaffna), 13 January 2003.

SUDAN

On 28 December, security police closed down the newspaper *al-Watan* and its parent publishing company, accusing the paper of printing 'scores of articles . . . aiming to defame and tarnish the reputation of the government institutions and individuals'. (RSF)

SWITZERLAND

The town of Meilen near Zurich attempted to introduce apartheid-style rules in December to bar asylum seekers from parts of the town, including the main square and municipal swimming pool. A map to indicate the prohibited areas was marked by a symbol of four black men with a line through them. The rules were dropped after protesters raised doubts about their constitutionality, but it was thought they would still be applied covertly. (*Guardian*, *Wochenzeitung*)

SYRIA

On 23 December, London-based journalist **Ibrahim Hamidi** was charged with 'publishing false information' in Syria and faces up to three years in prison and a US$7,000 fine. Hamidi was working on reports that Syria was preparing for the arrival of a million Iraqi refugees during a US-led attack on Iraq. (AP)

On 15 January, a military court charged Syrian-Kurdish poet and journalist **Marwan Osman** and fellow Kurdish Yekiti Party member **Hassan Saleh** with membership of unauthorised organisations, after their arrest in connection with a Kurdish protest in front of the Syrian parliament on 10 December. (www.kurdishmedia.com)

TAJIKISTAN

Rakhim Qalandrov was sentenced to death on 26 January for his part in the May 2000 murder of **Saifullo Rakhminov**, chairman of the Tajik State Committee for TV and Radio. Qalandrov pleaded not guilty and said his confession had been forcibly extracted by police. He is appealing to the Supreme Court. (RFE)

THAILAND

Journalist **Surapong Ritthi**, a correspondent for Thailand's biggest daily, *Thai Rath*, was murdered on 11 February in the southern resort island of Phuket, shot twice in the head at close range by a gunman in the early hours of the morning. Governor Pongpayom Vasphuti said Surapong's reports had uncovered many 'dark corners' in Phuket's business community. (WAN, DPA, Index Online)

TOGO

Sylvestre Dhjjahlin Nicoue, publication director of the weekly *Courrier du Citoyen*, was charged on 26 December for inciting citizens 'to take up arms' against the state with an article that argued that without palpable progress towards change 'the people would rebel in 2003'. (RSF)

TUNISIA

On 30 January, jailed web journalist **Zouhair Yahyaoui** ended a two-week hunger strike in protest at prison conditions. Founder of the website TUNeZINE, he joined fellow prisoner, journalist **Hamadi Jebali**, publisher of the weekly *al-Fajr*, organ of the An Nahda Islamic movement. On 12 February, Jebali, who has spent 12 years in prison and suffers from heart problems, was moved from Nador Prison to Habib Bougafta Hospital for treatment. (RSF)

TURKEY

On 20 December, US author **Margaret Kahn**'s book *Children of the Jinn: In Search of the Kurds & Their Country*, published in America in 1979 and by **Avesta** in Turkey, was banned. Texts in the introduction and preface to the first edition of the book were cited as the reason. (www. kurdishmedia.com)

Ankara University Associate Professor **Necip Hablemitoglu** was shot and killed on 20 December while returning from work. Turkish news outlets highlighted the scholar's publications concerning Islamist groups, but police had no official word on any motive for the killing. (www.kurdishmedia.com)

On 30 November, the 15-year-old State of Emergency was lifted in the last two Kurdish provinces of **Diyarbekir** and **Sirnak**. Under emergency rule, Turkish security forces were granted wide powers to detain without charge and limit press freedom and civil liberties. (*Cildekt*)

On 5 December, the European Court of Human Rights found Turkey guilty of breaching the rights to freedom of expression of **Yalçan Küçük**, author of a book of interviews with Abdullah Ocalan. Küçük had been jailed for a year and fined for 'separatist propaganda' for the book, *In the Kurdish Garden*. (*Cildekt*)

On 24 December, Istanbul's state security court fined **Abdullah Keskin** (*Index* 4/02, 3/02), owner of the **Avesta** publishing house, 3.9 billion lire (US$22,750) and found author **Songül Keskin** not guilty of separatist propaganda over the publication of the books *Kurdish Uprisings* and *History of Kurdistan*. (*Özgur Gündem*)

On 24 December, journalist **Mehmet Sevket Eygi** was sentenced to 20 months in jail and **Selami Çaliskan**, chief editor of the daily newspaper *Milli Gazete,* was fined for publishing an article entitled 'Enemies of the Head Scarf', adjudged to have violated the Turkish Penal Code. (*Özgür Gündem*)

Former head of Turkey's Human Rights Organisation (IHD) **Kiraz Bicici** was reported jailed on 15 January for three years and nine months for making public comments on the pro-Kurdish Medya-TV network. She had been interviewed about the December 2000 police assault to break the Bayrampasa jail protest. (*Radikal*)

The trial of **Sanar Yurdatapan** (*Index*, 3/02, 1/02, 4/01, 2/99, 5/98, 3/97, 1/03) and **Yilmaz Çamlibel** for publishing the book *Freedom of Thought 2001* continued on 22 January. They are the only two among 11 high-profile figures, including US political critic Noam Chomsky, to be charged so far. (TIHV)

On 1 February, chief editor **Seyfullah Karakurt** of radio Voice of Anatolia was reportedly jailed for 32 years and newsreader **Selda Demirsis** imprisoned for breaking a state media ban on coverage of the 2001 F-Type protest hunger strikes by jailed leftists. (FAZ)

In February, lawyers for jailed Kurdish parliamentarian **Leyla Zana** (*Index* 4/02, 1/01, 6/99 5/99, 4/99, 5/98, 1/97) applied for her release from a 15-year sentence, citing a new law that provides for retrials of cases subject to judgements by the European Court of Human Rights. (IMK, DPA)

Tayyip Erdogan, leader of Turkey's ruling Justice and Development Party, was cleared by a constitutional amendment in February to stand as a candidate in a by-election in March. Erdogan was refused permission to stand for election in November because he had a criminal conviction for inciting religious hatred. (FR)

Recent Publications: *Turkey: End Sexual Violence Against Women in Custody!*, Amnesty International, February 2003; website: Kurdish Women Research Resources, http:// fcis.oise.utoronto.ca/~mojab web, 13 January 2003.

TURKMENISTAN

Turkoman state TV's November coverage of hearings called to investigate an attempt to assassinate President Saparmurad Niazov was criticised by the OSCE, which drew parallels with the show trials of the Stalin era. It added that the state continues to 'humiliate and terrorise' its critics. (RFE, CJES)

Environmental activist **Farid Tukhbatullin** was jailed for five years on 4 March for illegally crossing a border – officials 'forgot' to stamp his passport – and concealing a serious crime: attendance at a conference on human rights that President Saparmurad Niazov's secret police claimed was a cover for terrorist plotting. The day before, Niazov had personally told an OSCE delegation that Tukhbatullin 'will be released soon'. (RFE, CJES)

UGANDA

Vincent Matovu, managing editor of the weekly *Mazima a Luganda,* pleaded not guilty to two counts of sedition on 6 January over articles on Joseph Kony and the Ugandan LRA rebels in November and October 2002, including reports on the defeat of Uganda government forces by the rebels. (www.allAfrica.com)

In January, Uganda's new Media Council announced plans to visit media organisations to vet the qualifications of journalists, and order the dismissal of those they deem under-qualified. The state wants staff without formal journalism qualifications barred from working in media houses. (*The Monitor*)

Information Minister Basoga Nsadhu clamped down on radio stations that run outside broadcasts from the hugely popular 'Question Time' style debates called 'ebimeeza'. Those that continue will be closed under 1996 broadcast laws, but Nsadhu says he

would use sedition and anti-terror laws if all else fails. (*The Monitor*)

UKRAINE

Parliament press freedom committee head Mykola Tomenko says a new bill tabled in January would protect journalists from dubious lawsuits, impose penalties on officials who deny journalists access to information, and redefine censorship. The bill is, he said, based closely on Council of Europe recommendations. (AP)

Kyiv newspaper *Hrani Plus* has published a letter from a group of policemen accusing former interior minister Yurii Kravchenko and his subordinates of organising the killing of journalist **Georgii Gongadze** (*Index* 2/01, *passim*) two years ago, allegedly on the orders of Ukrainian President Leonid Kuchma. (*Interfax-Ukraine*)

UNITED KINGDOM

Leading academics called on MPs to block changes to a new communications bill that could allow Rupert Murdoch's News Corp to take control of the country's Channel 5 TV. Critics of the bill to liberalise media ownership and set up a new regulatory body also say the bill may stifle musical diversity. (*Guardian*)

A boycott by top British children's writers, including **Gillian Cross** and Carnegie Medal winners **Melvin Burgess** and **Tim Bowler**, forced Nestlé to scrap a teenage book award. The boycotters claimed that the Swiss multinational was

breaching codes on the marketing of powdered baby milk in the developing world. (*Independent*)

The BBC unwittingly allowed contributors to a BBC online message board to break an injunction barring the publication of the name of a football player allegedly linked to a sex scandal. The name was removed by the BBC but not before the player threatened legal action. (*Guardian*)

BBC Radio barred pacifist British folk group **Seize the Day** from its annual world music awards in February claiming that it used peace websites and email lists to campaign for votes and would use its acceptance speech to promote anti-war messages. The band denied the claim; the BBC denied censorship. (*Guardian*)

The BBC banned senior news staff from attending an anti-war march in London on 15 February. BBC director-general Greg Dyke reminded staff they should remember their duty to be 'independent, impartial and honest' ahead of the country's expected war with Iraq. (*Guardian*)

A government report released in December said big business was using libel laws to shut down websites set up by disgruntled customers or protest groups. The law puts internet service providers under pressure to remove sites as soon as they are told the material on them might be defamatory, regardless of whether the information is in the public interest, or true. (*Independent*)

A computer program set up to filter incoming emails for porn links and bad language blocked more than 900 emails to British MPs in its first week of operation, including one containing the text of a new sexual offences bill and a Liberal Democrat consultation paper on censorship. (BBC)

Former UN Bosnia commander General **Sir Michael Rose** warned against too much 'kiss-kiss' between the media and the military ahead of the war in Iraq. 'NATO had far too easy a ride during Kosovo and I expect the press to be far more rigorous in covering what they see in the future,' he said. (*Guardian*)

The Independent Television Commission conceded in November that it had over-zealously applied its rule barring the portrayal of living people in advertisements without their permission when it banned adverts for a satirical cartoon series that portrayed US president George W Bush as stupid. (*Guardian*)

UNITED NATIONS

UN officials used a blue sheet and flags to cover a tapestry of Picasso's epic anti-war painting *Guernica* on 5 February before US Secretary of State Colin Powell arrived to make the US case for war on Iraq. Officials said the cover was put up to provide background for TV crews in the corridor. (Reuters)

State delegations at a Geneva conference to prepare for the December 2003 UN World Summit on the Information Society (WSIS) excluded 390 civil society groups from sessions to discuss a draft declaration and action plan — an act that the International Federation of Journalists said 'stifled voices of dissent'. (IFJ)

At the Asian regional preparatory session for the WSIS conference there was a last-minute change to its final declaration, withdrawing a pledge to support the development of non-commercial open-source software at the behest of the US, acting in turn for its giant computer corporations. (*Info World*)

UNITED STATES

The FBI has asked schools and universities across the US to provide personal information about all non-American students and teachers as part of its anti-terrorist investigations, provoking protests from institutions and from two Democratic senators. (*Washington Post*)

On 15 November, the Supreme Court upheld a 1998 law extending copyright to between 70 and 95 years, overruling claims that it would violate First Amendment rights and 'inhibit the progress of science', cheering entertainment industry giants fearful of loss of income due to product 'piracy'. (*Financial Times*)

A 21 January ruling by a Federal judge obliges internet service providers to disclose the identities of alleged music pirates, raising concerns about internet privacy. (*Financial Times*)

Washington Post reporter **Jonathan Randal** won an important legal battle in December when his refusal to testify in The Hague against former Yugoslav prime minister Radoslav Brdjanin was accepted by an appeals court on the grounds that testifying would endanger war correspondents. (*Financial Times*)

The University of Oregon's student radio station was urged to drop a syndicated chat show on 12 December on 'hate speech' because the show's producers could not be asked to moderate the tirades without their First Amendment rights being compromised. (AP)

Stephen Downs, 61, was charged with trespass in a shopping mall in Albany, New York, after he refused to take off a T-shirt reading 'Peace on Earth' and 'Give Peace a Chance'. When police told Downs and his son **Roger** to remove their shirts or leave the mall, he refused and was arrested. (AP)

On 20 February, Tampa university professor **Sami al-Arian** was indicted on charges of financing Islamic terrorism, following months of dispute since he was suspended after appearing on a TV talk show shortly after the 11 September attacks. Evidence against al-Arian, who strenuously denies the charge, is based on years of covert taps on his telephones, and is released for the use of the prosecution under the USA Patriot Act of 2001. Al-Arian's case is expected to rest on whether government agents violated his Fourth Amendment constitutional rights through 'unreasonable search and seizure'. (*Knight-Ridder*)

New York State's school English exams were found to have altered a passage from Franz Kafka and sanitised another by Aldous Huxley, cutting lines on 'unpunctual Orientals'. State officials had previously promised to stop the excision of potentially offensive references from texts used to test students. (Newsday)

In sharp contrast to a November court ruling in Australia theoretically allowing internet libel cases to be heard anywhere in the world, a US court of appeal found on 19 November that two Connecticut papers could not be sued for libel in the state of Virginia simply because the stories could be read on the web there.

The Supreme Court rejected an appeal by Mattel Inc. that the Danish pop band **Aqua**'s 1997 hit 'Barbie Girl' infringed the dollmaker's trademark. The court upheld an earlier ruling that the song, featuring a doll-like voice calling herself a 'blonde bimbo', was parody and therefore covered by the First Amendment. (AP)

A new US State Department list of countries that deny religious freedom omitted three conspicuous violators – Saudi Arabia, Turkmenistan and Uzbekistan. The trio are all allies of the US in wars against Iraq and Afghanistan. The list, dated 5 March, named Burma, China, Iran, Iraq, North Korea and Sudan. (HRW)

Recent Publications: *United States: Beyond the Law, an Update to Amnesty International's Memorandum to the US Government on the Rights of Detainees Held in Guantanamo Bay and Other Locations*. Amnesty International, December 2002.

URUGUAY

Radio journalist **Oscar Ubiría** of CW 158 San Salvador Radio was given a suspended sentence of seven months in prison for criminal libel after criticising the management of charity funds raised during a fashion show in the eastern city of Dolores in the eastern department of Soriano. (IAPA)

UZBEKISTAN

After posting a 13 January article by analyst **Usman Khanazarov** criticising President Islam Karimov's rise to power and linking him to Afghan warlord Abdul Rashid Dostum and various Uzbek 'clans' engaged in drug trafficking, the website **www.centrasia.ru** was reported blocked in Uzbekistan. It remained accessible from abroad. (RFE/RL)

Ergash Babajanov, a journalist and member of the Birlik pro-democracy movement, was arrested on 17 February on charges stemming from his published articles. He was released but charges have not been dropped. (RSF)

On 18 February, a Tashkent court sentenced journalist **Gairat Mekhliboyev** to seven years in jail for membership of the banned Islamist party Hizb ut-Tahir, possessing illegal writing materials and using his journalistic activities to promote religion and public discussion. (RFE, RSF, CJES)

VENEZUELA

President Hugo Chávez told five private TV stations in February that their output would be monitored for statements deemed to 'incite rebellion and disrespect of institutions and its authorities'. Any offenders would be fined, suspended or closed down. (CPJ)

VIETNAM

Nguyen Khac Toan was jailed for 12 years on 20 December, the longest sentence yet handed down for internet activities. He was charged with spying after emailing Vietnamese human rights groups based abroad. The trial, held in secret, lasted less than one day and Toan was not allowed private access to his lawyer. (RSF)

ZAMBIA

Editor **Arthur Simuchoba**, entertainment editor **Calvin Kaleyi** and chief reporter **Chali Nondo** of *The Monitor* were arrested on 21 January and quizzed about an article of 18 October linking the president's brother, Harry Mwanawasa, to a corruption case. Reporter **Douglas Hampande** was interviewed on 22 December but business editor **Mervin Syafunko** went into hiding after he was summoned. (MISA)

After an intervention by the Afronet human rights group executive director **Ngande Mwanajiti**, *Monitor* reporter **Chali Nondo** was released on 10 Febuary without charge after being detained, said police, on suspicion of 'publishing false news with intent to cause fear and alarm to the public'. (MISA)

DIPLOMATIC LICENCE
CRAIG MURRAY

Uzbekistan is not a functioning democracy, nor does it appear to be moving in the direction of democracy. The major political parties are banned; parliament is not subject to democratic election, and checks and balances on the authority of the executive are lacking.

There is worse: we believe there to be between 7,000 and 10,000 people in detention whom we would consider as political and/or religious prisoners. In many cases they have been falsely convicted of crimes with which there appears to be no credible evidence they had any connection.

Uzbekistan's strategic situation has put it in the forefront of countries struggling to deal with problems such as terrorism and narcotics trafficking. But let us make this point: no government has the right to use the war against terrorism as an excuse for the persecution of those with a deep personal commitment to the Islamic religion, and who pursue their views by peaceful means. It is not only Muslims who suffer; the British Embassy yesterday observed the trial of a Jehovah's Witness, being prosecuted for pursuing his beliefs. It should not be a crime to practise your religion, or to tell others about it.

And a number of those imprisoned are ethnic Russian human rights defenders, colleagues of some of my audience. I am very conscious that I stand here in a very privileged position, in the literal sense. You on the other hand daily risk persecution to stand up for the rights of your fellow citizens. You have my deepest respect and one day your countrymen will be in a position to show you their gratitude.

Uzbekistan is to be congratulated on a good record of ratifying key UN Conventions on human rights; unfortunately, there appears to be a gap between obligation and practice.

World attention has recently been focused on the prevalence of torture in Uzbek prisons. The terrible case of Muzafar Avazov, apparently tortured to death by boiling water, has evoked great international concern. But all of us know that this is not an isolated incident.

Brutality is inherent in a system where convictions habitually rely on signed confessions rather than on forensic or material evidence. In the Uzbek criminal justice system the conviction rate is almost 100 per cent.

It is difficult not to conclude that once accused by the Prokurator there is no effective possibility of fair trial in the sense we understand it.

Another chilling reminder of the former Soviet Union is the use of commitment to lunatic asylums to stifle dissidents. We are still seeing examples of this in 2002.

Nor does the situation appear to be getting any better. There is little sign of genuine positive change in human rights. And that is what we want to see: genuine change. By that I mean change which actually increases the liberty of Uzbek citizens in their daily lives.

Uzbekistan's international obligations require genuine respect for human rights. For example, officially censorship has recently been abolished. But you would not tell this by watching, listening to or reading the media which is patently under strict control and contains no significant volume of critical comment or analysis of central government policy.

Let us try a small experiment. I hope you will agree this short speech has not been uninteresting. I am making copies available to the media in English, Uzbek and Russian. I trust that the proceedings of this event will be fully and fairly reported.

What then are the components of the real change we wish to see? They are not difficult but they require political will. I believe that people are born with an instinct for liberty and that freedom and democracy come naturally to people everywhere, once they are given the chance. Giving people freedom does not mean that anarchy and instability will follow. Indeed, it is repression which, by allowing no outlet for pressures in society, risks causing resentment, alienation and social tension. ❏

Craig Murray is British Ambassador to Uzbekistan

Excerpt from a speech given by Ambassador Murray on 17 October 2002 to an audience of Uzbek officials, diplomats and human rights activists. 'The shock value of these statements,' said one observer, 'cannot be overstated.'

Index on Censorship *has joined other free-expression groups in urging the European Bank for Reconstruction and Development, which holds its annual meeting in Uzbekistan in May 2003, to press for change and ensure the meeting is not seen as an endorsement of the country's record.*

On 24 February, Reuters correspondent **Shapi Shacinda**, Zambia Independent Media Association chairman **Dickson Jere**, the BBC's **Penny Dale**, **Amos Malupenga** of the *Lusaka Post* and **Wendy Mpolokoso** of Radio Phoenix were barred from the trial of former president Frederick Chiluba for the alleged theft of 190 billion kwacha (US$38 million) of public funds. (MISA)

On 24 February, Information and Broadcasting Services Deputy Minister Webster Chipilli accused the Catholic Church-owned Kitwe radio station Icengelo of acting as a mouthpiece for opposition Patriotic Front leader **Michael Sata** and threatened to withdraw its licence. (MISA)

ZIMBABWE

Award-winning Zimbabwean journalist **Geoffrey Nyarota**, former editor of the independent *Daily News*, was awarded a Nieman Fellowship for journalism at Harvard University in February. During his time as editor he was known as a fearless critic of President Robert Mugabe's Zanu-PF government. (www.allafrica.com)

Zimbabwe Union of Journalists senior member **Kelvin Jakachira** told a 24 November conference that the country's government was sowing the seeds of genocide via the national broadcaster by filling the minds of the nation with anti-white, anti-opposition propaganda. (*Zimbabwe Standard*)

Two sets of charges of publishing false information against *Zimbabwe Standard* editor **Bornwell Chakaodza**, reporter **Farai Mutsaka** and entertainment editor **Fungayi Kayuchi** were dropped on 4 December. The cases, outstanding since May 2002, involved reports on state purchase of anti-riot gear from Israel and a story about police freeing arrested prostitutes in exchange for sex. (MISA)

On 3 January, **Norma Edwards**, editor of the Masvingo-based weekly *The Mirror,* was arrested and charged with contravening section 80 of the country's repressive AIPPA act, following an article of 19 December 2002 concerning the arrest of National Constitutional Assembly activists. Four were detained in prison for two days and had their houses searched under the accusation that they were responsible for 'civic disobedience'. In her article Edwards had described the activists' arrest and ill-treatment by the police. (MISA)

Daily News reporter **Fanuel Jongwe** and Lutheran World Federation officials **Kathleen Kastilahn** of the US, **Gustav Rolf** of Finland, **Pauline Mumia** of Kenya and **Falk Orth** and **Ute Heers** of Germany were arrested on 24 January in Zvishavane and charged with practising journalism without a licence. They had been visiting Lutheran-sponsored famine relief and Aids projects. The charges were dropped for lack of evidence on 29 January but the five foreigners were all deported. (MISA)

Minister of Information and Publicity Jonathan Moyo claimed that Zimbabwe's section 20, the constitutional right to freedom of expression, covered individuals not organisations. Moyo claimed that consequently newspapers such as the opposition *Daily News* could not claim a right to free expression. (MISA)

Journalist **Simon Briggs** of the London *Daily Telegraph* was denied entry to Zimbabwe on 19 February. Despite official accreditation, immigration officers at Harare International Airport ordered him to return to Johannesburg. (MISA)

On 26 February, *Daily News* journalists were barred from covering parliament from the press gallery. The government claims that the paper has not registered with the state, and therefore its staff cannot be accredited as journalists. The paper has said that the state has blocked its registration. (MISA)

Compiled by: James Badcock (North Africa); Ben Carrdus (East Asia); Gulliver Cragg (Western Europe, North America); Hanna Gezelius (Britain and Ireland); Monica Gonzalez Correa (Central Asia and Caucasus); Frances Harvey (South America); Andrew Kendle (India and subcontinent); Najlae Naaoumi (Russia, Poland, Ukraine and Baltic States); Gill Newsham (Turkey and Kurdish areas); Ben Owen (South East Asia and Australasia); Shifa Rahman (East Africa); Jason Pollard (Gulf States and Middle East); Yugo Stoyanov (Eastern Europe); Alsi Yalçin (Western Africa); Mike Yeoman (Central America and Caribbean)
Edited by Rohan Jayasekera and co-ordinated by Natasha Schmidt

MEDIA & MIGRANTS

MIGRANTS EXPECT MORE FROM THEIR MEDIA THAN JUST NEWS FROM HOME; THEY NEED NEWS RELEVANT TO THEIR NEW LIVES ABROAD

London 1997, 'in their own words': migrants' media. Credit: Alex Majoli / Magnum Photos

EXCLUSION ZONE
PIERRE VERMEREN

EVERY YEAR, ENTICED BY THE FANTASY EUROPE
BEAMED INTO THE MAGHREB VIA SATELLITE,
MORE THAN 100,000 ILLEGAL MIGRANTS RISK
DEATH TO REACH THEIR DREAM CONTINENT

Departure and migration dominate the lyrics of *'Ya rayah wein musafir?'*
('Traveller, where did you go?'), a 1990s hit in Morocco, Algeria and
Tunisia. A song of exile, it reflects people's widespread longing to leave
home for Europe or Canada. The launch of the European Union's
Schengen zone in 1990 drastically reduced the number of available visas and
left young North Africans feeling trapped. Hence the rise in illegal immigration, mainly from Morocco to Spain via the Strait of Gibraltar.

Such crossings, in small 40hp–60hp fishing boats known as *pateras*, are
high-risk. Increased surveillance means that smugglers have to be daring: the
perilous crossing, 12km at its shortest, sometimes turns into a trip of several
hundred kilometres. Distances expand even further when the destination is
the Canary Islands, the Spanish territories off the coast of Morocco. In April
last year, the bodies of seven Moroccans were recovered after a boat
capsized near Agadir on Morocco's south-western coast.

Spanish and Moroccan police often pull migrants' bodies from the sea:
some are thrown overboard when smugglers are frightened by patrol boats;
others drown when *pateras* capsize. In 2000, 72 bodies were retrieved on the
Spanish side of the strait, while survivors reported 271 other deaths. The
Moroccan press covers the tragedies off the coast: one disaster on 26 September 1998 claimed the lives of 38 people.

According to AFVIC (Associations of friends and families of victims of
clandestine immigration), 3,286 bodies were recovered on both sides of the
strait between 1997 and 2001. If that represents one of every three who
died, the number of migrants who died in the strait is closer to 10,000.

The situation is tense in the Spanish *presidios* (military enclaves) of Ceuta
and Melilla on Morocco's northern coast. With their thriving smuggling
trade, these are accessible to residents of northern Morocco on presentation
of an identity card. Ceuta, where 25,000 smuggling trips take place every
day, has sought to protect itself by building a fence around its perimeter, an

electrified iron curtain. The *presidios* face intense migratory pressures, particularly from children, thousands of whom are turned back every year. Mariano Rajoy, the Spanish interior minister, says: 'The Moroccan authorities show no concern for the wellbeing of their minors.'

Moroccan authorities say the migrants come from all over Africa, as well as the Middle East and Asia; the Spanish police claim 80 per cent of them are Moroccan. Pan-African migrants are an everyday sight in Morocco, especially in Tangiers and Rabat, despite the harsh living conditions. Arriving from Algeria by way of the Sahara, they are transported by smugglers to the coastal cities of Tétouan or Nador where they are given shelter before setting off in the *pateras*. Sometimes they are turned back at the Algerian border without legal process, and entire groups are sometimes denied entry, a violation of international law. Some 10,000 'residents' were recently released from a camp on the Algerian border while several thousand would-be migrants are being detained in Ceuta and Melilla.

Prospective Moroccan emigrants have many options. For children from upper-class homes, enrolling in foreign private schools is the safest way to qualify for unrestricted travel. For other schoolchildren the situation is trickier. Last year, 14,000 *baccalauréat* holders – almost one in four – applied at the French embassy in Rabat to study in France; Spain and Canada are also popular places to study. Graduates are frequently in demand: last year, foreign firms recruited every computer science graduate from Morocco's prestigious Mohammedia engineering school. Over the past few years well-established young professionals, including doctors and engineers, have sold up and left the country, mainly for Canada and France.

For the average Moroccan the situation is more complex and costly. One strategy involves obtaining a Schengen visa and overstaying its expiry date. Members of Moroccan sports teams competing abroad often vanish. Last winter a French rugby federation found to its dismay that it had granted several dozen visas to a bogus Moroccan team. But obtaining documents is not easy: according to AFVIC, false papers cost US$4,600–US$5,600.

Some young Moroccan women relocate to the Persian Gulf to work as prostitutes. Connecting flights can be used to disembark in Europe: some migrants book flights to Australia or China and then stop over in Paris or Rome, where hired accomplices sneak them out of the airport. Although this may cost as much as US$6,500, it is the safest option. Land routes are also used: every year 100,000 lorries cross from Morocco to Spain via the Strait of Gibraltar and every week in Rabat's industrial district young people with meagre provisions try to board lorries carrying textiles to Europe. For US$4,600, passage can be arranged in collusion with bus drivers. Crossing via Tunis and the Strait of Sicily costs US$2,800; passage via Turkey and Greece is also possible.

Then there are the individual solutions: these include marriage, family reunions, employment sponsorship in Italy and travel by private car.

But it is the *pateras* that transport most of the illegals. They come primarily from economically disadvantaged rural areas: from Oujda (in the Rif mountains) to Nador; from Beni Mellal-Casablanca and Marrakesh-Casablanca and more. According to survivors, people from these regions have often never seen the sea and have no idea of the risks they face.

Well-organised local operatives recruit potential migrants in remote regions and transport them to the coast in lorries; other intermediaries provide shelter until the seas are calm. The boat operators – often go-betweens who do not own the vessels – receive US$185–US$280 per passenger. After paying US$930–US$1,200 to the mafias that organise the crossings, the *harragas* ('those who burn their past') are brought to the boats at night. Trafficking in human beings earns these mafias annual revenues of up to US$100 million, less than the fortunes earned from smuggling cannabis.

Lodgings for new arrivals are provided either near Tarifa at the southern tip of Spain or in the Canary Islands. The traffickers operate as part of a highly structured international ring: by some accounts, the human smuggling is overseen by expatriate Moroccans with Spanish assistance, but the scale of the trade means individuals on both sides of the strait must be involved.

Last year, 44,841 illegals in Spain were deported or sent back to their countries of origin – Moroccans, Colombians and Ecuadorians topped the list. 22,984 people without documents, of whom 21,706 were Moroccans, were detained; 12,976 foreigners, primarily Moroccans, were deported following legal proceedings. So far this year 6,579 have been deported. This is a result of the new Spanish immigration law that came into effect on 23 December 1999. Traditionally a country of emigrants, Spain received very few immigrants in the 1980s; last year, however, it officially welcomed 1,243,919 foreigners, 46 per cent from non-EU countries.

Immigration has become a pivotal issue in Spain: the current impasse in Moroccan–Spanish relations (Morocco recalled its ambassador last October) is about illegal immigration and cannabis smuggling.

Tarifa, Spain, 2000: stopped in their tracks, waiting for the police van.
Credit: Michel Lozano

According to the Council of Europe, illegal immigrants in Spain filed 246,000 applications to legalise their status between 3 March and 31 July 2000. Although 90 per cent of the applications filed in Ceuta and Melilla are rejected (the average Spanish rejection rate is 50 per cent), Moroccans remain Spain's largest minority group, though the Spanish government gives priority to migrants from Latin America and Poland who work as agricultural labourers in Andalusia in southern Spain.

Yet north–south differences in growth, wealth and demographics are so great that migratory pressures never diminish. Wealthy regions such as Spain's Costa del Sol contrast with the despair of Morocco's Rif Mountains; the Kettama area has been abandoned and is now exclusively devoted to cannabis growing.

In 2000, riots broke out in El Ejido, a small Andalusian town where manhunts were organised targeting 'Moors'. After watching the resulting violence on television and listening to interviews with agricultural workers, many Moroccans realised for the first time that their fellow citizens were working overseas. After that, the queues at the Spanish consulate in Rabat were longer than ever.

The EU provides Spain with financial assistance to deal with migrants and to guard the borders of the Schengen zone: Spain gets US$280 for every Moroccan illegal sent back home. Protesting about this and deploring the lack of European assistance, Morocco maintains it has cooperated and shown goodwill.

After three years of drought (1998–2001), times are hard in Morocco. Almost 20 per cent of the population lives below the threshold of absolute poverty (less than US$1 a day). Spanish statistics show that 70 per cent of those caught while taking the illegal route are unemployed; a few professionals who have exhausted the legal channels, including lawyers and doctors, also attempt to cross the strait.

One survivor of the crossing told the Moroccan weekly *Demain* magazine: 'The straits are the last chance. They're the final frontier between hell and a supposedly better world. Those who attempt the crossing know what to expect. It's a game of life and death.' One of AFVIC's interviewees said: 'I've tried the *pateras* three times. Once we were arrested, twice we capsized. Six people died but I'd try it again. If I die I'll be an economic martyr. Everything I do is for my family.' Given such desperation, illegal immigration acts as a safety valve. Going into exile is one way of giving up the fight at home. It also frees up jobs – official unemployment figures fell last year – and increases the hopes of those who stay behind.

But it also reflects the failure of the nation-building projects that the countries of the Maghreb began after independence. This crisis is more moral than political. Relatively speaking, the people of the Maghreb were economically self-sufficient until the 1980s. The countryside had little if any contact with the outside world and state-run radio and television encouraged a form of patriotism unrelated to European consumer-based models. With the exception of emigrants and social elites, foreign travel was uncommon and contacts with foreigners deliberately limited. After attempting to open Morocco to tourism in the 1970s, King Hassan II limited the number of tourists to 1 million Europeans annually.

The sudden popularity of television satellite dishes in the late 1980s changed people's image of the outside world. Tunisians now learn Italian thanks to RAI, the Italian radio and television network; Algerians keep abreast of current events in France; and Moroccans are gradually envisaging new horizons. The West, as fabricated on TV, is a highly visible phenomenon. In the late 1990s, European satellite channels flooded the region with non-stop programmes for Arabic-speaking viewers.

Moroccan TV sometimes features profiles of successful Mahgrebi emigrants such as Jamel Debbouz, the Netherlands-based entrepreneur, the singer Nadia Fares and sportsmen such as Zinedine Zidane. Many emigrants revisit Morocco each year (1.5 million last summer). They arrive in gleaming cars bearing consumer goods, feeding the myth of Europe as an El Dorado whose doors must be prised open.

The Maghreb is the Mexico of the EU. Last year, Mexico had 100 million residents at home and 35 million in the US (including ten million illegals with a further 1 million arriving every year). Today, the Maghreb has a population of 70 million, with an estimated 10–15 million living in Europe. Morocco has 30 million inhabitants and 5–7 million people abroad; a further 100,000–200,000 leave every year. This flow shows no sign of slowing down and will continue unless the traffic is fought.

Khalil Jemmah of AFVIC warns: 'The fight against illegal immigration should not be waged at the borders but in the communities and the minds of immigrants. It must come from north–south cooperation and balanced dialogue. It should not be based on unilateral policies dictated by the north. There should be immigration policies, not immigration police. The south should not be reduced to begging.' ❏

Pierre Vermeren is a journalist and the author of École, élite et pouvoir. Maroc–Tunisie, XXᵉ siècle *(Editions Alizés, Rabat, 2002) and* Le Maroc en transition *(La Découverte, Paris, 2002)*

Translated by Luke Sandford and reproduced courtesy Le Monde diplomatique

SEEN FROM CASABLANCA

Big Brother (*Loft Story* in its French incarnation) has arrived on Morocco's television scene. Pirate decoder cards for the French satellite services TPS and Canalsat sell for less than €5 (US$5) on the alternative Derb Ghallef market in Casablanca, so it's easy to follow the fortunes of the housemates (or 'lofters', as they are known). The poverty of Morocco's two national channels, 2M and TVM, does not entirely explain the hold these representatives of the French way of life have over the imaginations of local society. For the 70 per cent of young Moroccans who want to abandon their country for greener pastures abroad, *Big Brother* provides an unparalleled window on to those El Dorados 'with no poverty and no unemployment' that Morocco's disinherited youth dream of.

The presence of housemates of North African origin among France's 'lofters' has encouraged Moroccans to identify with them. However, their early expulsion from the house helped to reinforce the image of French hostility to foreigners and French Arabs. When one housemate, Kenza, had a little love affair with a fellow contestant, the 'shamelessness' of her behaviour shocked Moroccan viewers. But Kenza was, none the less, forgiven: the guy was from the Maghreb, after all. As always, women are condemned, while men are encouraged in the expression of their virility – a reflection of taboos back home and a denial of the westernisation of these young people.

And there are the usual rants about the low intellectual level of the 'representatives of the community', which ignore the fact that it's just about on a par with that of the other contestants of more 'solid French stock'. The theory of a French media conspiracy against Arabs is gaining ground again, combined with the contempt of Morocco's French-speaking elite for the immigrants: 'those bums who can't control their kids and tarnish the image of Moroccans in France'.

Ultimately, people are pretty happy to see them leave the Loft, 'expelled' by the *vox populi* of that France that so clearly expressed its anxiety about its North African community at the last election. Moroccan audiences identify with these Maghrebis who are 'just like us', only to reject them. And among the intelligentsia who 'follow the Loft' it is de rigueur to be a connoisseur, speculator and analyst of this phenomenon.

Moroccans are natural voyeurs, the perfect audience for reality shows. This goes hand in hand with a boundless appetite for gossip, the social currency of a bored society devoid of any political debate and without real passion for a cause around which they can mobilise, other than the lure of extremism or the Palestinian question. Moroccans are not easily moved to take their own fate in hand.

Loft Story fills the gap in a society suffering from its own indolence and fatalism. The mediocrity of the programmes on offer on national television and the practically non-existent cultural programming push Moroccans headlong into a televisual landscape that is not their own.

Other contestants in the Loft are judged less severely, more thoughtfully, than their compatriots who are circus animals observed by Moroccans with a mixture of contempt and restrained affection. They find them so different and yet so similar. At the end of the day, *Loft Story* does have the merit of bringing people together. Vanity, foul play, love, sorrow and anger are the same for everyone – at least in *Loft Story*'s version of France, soft, sanitised and rich; and in Casablanca. ❑

Younes Alami
Translated by GC

A 'lofter' poses outside the Loft Story studios.
Credit: AFP

'THEY WERE ALL ASYLUM SEEKERS'
DAVID MILLER

REFUGEES FROM IRAQI TYRANNY ARE
AMONG THE VICTIMS OF A PROPAGANDA
CAMPAIGN TO JUSTIFY A WAR ON IRAQ

In the spring of 2003, three separate currents of ideology came to flow into a single ideological pool. The issue of asylum seekers and immigration came to share space with the 'war on terror'. A government propaganda campaign aimed at turning public opinion behind a war in Iraq tried to link Baghdad to al-Qaida and 'Islamist terror' and failed. Instead, it increased hostility towards asylum seekers.

A wave of arrests under Britain's new Terrorism Act has swept up a number of Arabs. In one raid in Manchester a policeman was stabbed to death. Announcing the suspects' arrest on 18 January the *Daily Mail* was able to reveal triumphantly that 'they were all asylum seekers'. Only in the context of a campaign against asylum seekers and refugees could this be thought significant. If 'terrorists' used tourist visas to enter Britain, could we expect headlines like 'they were all tourists'?

Press reports on a series of anti-terrorist raids in the past six months have consistently linked asylum seekers to al-Qaida or Iraq. While the first arrests on 9 November were reported with little fanfare, within two days Tony Blair was warning of a 'real' threat to London from a terror attack. Then on 17 November the *Sunday Times*, working from a briefing given by Britain's MI5 security service, linked the arrested men to a suspected plot to drop a gas bomb on the city's underground railway.

'Fleet Street scrambled to follow up the sensational tale,' wrote *Observer* columnist Nick Cohen later. His own paper 'said the men had been charged with plotting to "release cyanide on the London Underground", as did pretty much everyone else. Broadcasters repeated the story.' The *Sunday Times* reiterated its origin from 'reputable security sources'.

Reputable maybe, but how accurate? In the end the Algerians were only charged with having false passports. No evidence whatsoever of gas bombs was produced. When an equally unproven scare story popped up on 3 December, this time warning of a possible attack with a smallpox germ weapon, former *Times* editor Simon Jenkins complained. 'I was outraged by the smallpox scare story. It was a clear repeat of the previous weekend's lobby story of "gas horror on London Tube", itself an echo of the Home Office "dirty bomb" story two weeks earlier,' he wrote. 'Terror stories are always the easiest for government to sell.'

Faisal Bodi drew parallels with Northern Ireland in the *Guardian*: 'For all the hysterical headlines warning of a bin Laden in our back yard, the reality is a picture of political repression of Muslims that is starting to resemble the experience of Northern Ireland's Catholics throughout the Troubles.' As in Ireland the arrests are high-profile and the outcomes usually much less dramatic. Also like Ireland the media coverage ensures the possibility that a fair trial will be prejudiced, leading most probably to unsafe convictions.

By May 2002, official figures showed 144 arrests under the Terrorism Act 2000, leading to 46 people being charged with offences. Writing on 21 January, Bodi noted this figure had since risen to nearer 200, adding that 'the fact still remains that there has yet to be a single conviction'.

In a deportation case last year against nine men detained without trial for over seven months, the defence asked *Observer* home affairs editor Martin Bright to analyse the prosecution evidence linking the defendants to terrorism. He found that 'by far the largest proportion' of evidence was simply a collection of cuttings from newspaper articles drawn from 'Whitehall sources'. Information from intelligence briefings becomes common currency and repeated by journalists starved of any real information, Bright wrote. In this case it had simply been re-presented to the court in 'almost absurdly circular' fashion. 'Whenever the readers see the words "Whitehall sources",' he noted, 'they should have no illusions about where the information comes from.'

It would be wrong to see this as a wide-ranging conspiracy in which the government, the police and a secret state are all engaged. In a later comment he added: 'I believe that the police and intelligence services are genuinely concerned and that the threats are largely real (in their minds at least they really believe an attack is imminent and inevitable) . . . But I do not know for sure and I don't believe the police have any understanding of Islamist politics and so what they perceive as a threat may be nothing of the sort.'

Even Tony Blair can't be sure. As he put it in an interview with BBC TV's *Newsnight* programme on 6 February: 'I mean this is what our intelligence services are telling us and it's difficult because, you know, either they're simply making the whole thing up or this is what they are telling me.'

It doesn't seem likely that they are making the whole thing up, but the past record of the intelligence and defence establishment encourages scepticism. The day after Blair's *Newsnight* interview Downing Street had to confess that parts of a government dossier on Iraq, supposed to be based on intelligence sources, was in fact plagiarised from a PhD student thesis and compiled by Downing Street officials. Supposedly damning reports on Iraq have been successively dismissed as either based on old academic research or selectively recycled reports by human rights groups blown up out of all proportion by Downing Street and British Foreign Office spin doctors. Even MI6 was driven at one point to repudiate publicly government suggestions that al-Qaida was working with Iraq.

The difficulty lay in Tony Blair's public position and private intent. He set out his objective in a key address to the House of Commons Liaison Committee: 'I think it is important that we do everything we can to try to show people the link between the issue of weapons of mass destruction and these international terrorist groups, mainly linked to al-Qaida.' Moments later he spelled out the reality: 'I know of nothing linking Iraq to the 11 September attack and I know of nothing either that directly links al-Qaida and Iraq to recent events in the UK.'

Downing Street persisted with the spin campaign, attempting to keep Blair's public pronouncements on the right side of truth while feeding the media with more dramatic fare off the record. It signally failed to convince the majority, as evidenced by the largest ever protest demonstrations in recent British history on 15 February.

All that was left was a possibly unintended but wholly predictable ratcheting up of hostility towards refugees and asylum seekers. The safety and wellbeing of refugees, many from Iraq, have been sacrificed in the name of a failed effort to scare the public into endorsing a war against tyranny in Iraq. As Simon Jenkins put it: 'I resent the government trying to terrify me, week after week, trying to dominate the news agenda . . . Scaremongering is not a spin-doctoring pastime; it plays on the basest human instincts of group paranoia, xenophobia and ghoulish panic.' ❏

David Miller is a member of the Stirling Media Research Institute

Martin Bright's deposition to the court ⇨ http://www.observer.co.uk/
libertywatch/story/0,1373,758265,00.html
David Leigh, 'Britain's security services and journalists: the secret story'
⇨ http://www.bjr.org.uk/data/2000/no2_leigh.htm

JUST A QUESTION OF MONEY?

MOUSSA AWUONDA

WHILE SWEDEN CHAMPIONS THE ROLE OF
COMMUNITY MEDIA 'OUT THERE' IN THE
DEVELOPING WORLD, IT SHOWS LITTLE
INTEREST CLOSER TO HOME. A NEW REPORT
URGES THE GOVERNMENT TO PAY MORE
ATTENTION TO ITS MINORITY PRESS

Believing in the crucial role of the media in furthering integration in her new homeland, Turkish journalist Dilek Yaras started *Prizma*, a magazine intended to end the isolation of the Turkish community in Sweden. 'Mentally and physically, they are scattered, separated from each other and from their new environment in Sweden. With *Prizma* we may stop this trend,' she said at the launch four years ago.

In many ways, Yaras has seen her dream come true. *Prizma*'s mix of stories affecting the Turkish minority – jobs, schools, food, sexuality and politics – has proved popular and, with the growth in Islamophobia after 9/11 and the impending invasion of Iraq, Yaras, who is not attached to any particular religion, senses an even greater need for outlets for Muslim opinion on controversial matters of general interest. 'As usual, Swedish mainstream media doesn't offer opportunities for broad and diverse opinions,' she notes, citing readers' responses in *Prizma*. With a loyal and growing readership of 10,000, the obvious next step for Yaras is to expand her print run to reach more of the 70,000 Turkish-speaking community and turn the magazine into a viable commercial operation.

A fellow Turkish journalist agrees. Tandogan Uysal, correspondent for *Hurriyet*, Turkey's leading daily, says: 'It's self-evident: Turks need publications like *Prizma* that can improve their access to all kinds of information. The Turkish community can do with more publications. Several generations have grown up since the community first came here in large numbers as guest workers in the 1960s. There's a need for writers who can tackle issues seriously and offer in-depth analysis.'

In the sense that it empowers the voices of marginalised and excluded social groups, Yaras's type of journalism is not very different from that of the grassroots community media now mushrooming across Africa, Asia and Latin America. In many cases, these are funded by Western aid agencies and governments to help consolidate the processes of multiparty democracy. Swedish support for media projects abroad over the past ten years has blossomed, reaching around Sek500 million (US$59.5 million). SIDA (Swedish International Development Agency), a government aid department, allocated Sek35 million last year alone to a range of media operations, mainly in Africa and Asia. A further Sek4 million was devoted to supporting the cash-strapped independent media in Russia and Ukraine.

Charles Nyambuga, a lecturer at Maseno University in Kenya, considers the empowering role of the community media one of the defining characteristics of post-Cold War global media development. 'Advocacy journalism,' he says, 'is the in thing with Western donors. Funding for community media, especially for operations that raise awareness of those who lack a voice in the mainstream, of gender equality and the eradication of poverty, has become the most popular concept.'

Were *Prizma* located in Turkey, a country often at loggerheads with the West over lack of press freedom and the persecution of journalists, it might well have found itself lavishly supplied with cash.

On the contrary, for Yaras and many of her colleagues advocating the rights of ethnic minority communities in Sweden, the going is tough; apart from small grants under the 'cultural' rubric, institutional and professional support is almost zero. Yet Sweden is also distinguished for its generous subsidies to its domestic press – Sek510 million last year, of which the country's second largest daily, the conservative *Svenska Dagbladet*, bagged Sek65 million. Yaras comments: 'I know about those fat subsidies and I also know Swedish organisations such as the Swedish Union of Journalists are helping journalists in Turkey. I fail to understand why the same principles don't apply to us.'

Sounding bitter during an interview in the sitting room of her council flat that also serves as an office, Yaras paints a pessimistic picture. She has learned to juggle multiple responsibilities in order to get *Prizma* out – reporter, editor, advertising rep and subscription clerk in one – but doubts if she can continue like this. 'The politicians are aware of the role of the migrant press in influencing public opinion,' she says, fingering an issue of the magazine that features coverage of September's general election on its cover. 'The political parties publicise their manifestos to get the minority

Success story: the work of fashion designer Senem Yazan gets a cover feature.
Courtesy: Prizma magazine

votes. But after the elections the leaders don't show any further interest.'

Those sentiments echo the views of publishers of 120 publications in 37 languages working with shoestring budgets and permanently under threat of liquidation. *Sesame*, a weekly magazine popular with newly arrived migrants who can manage its simple Swedish, folded last year. At the same time, state-run Swedish Television announced plans to phase out *Mosaic*, a programme built around cultural diversity.

Until the 1980s, the 'minorities debate' in Sweden was largely about refugees and tended to centre on exclusion in jobs, housing and schools, discrimination and racism. Compared with neighbours such as Finland, Sweden's liberal policy rated rather well. But with the collapse of the Berlin Wall, the internet revolution and globalisation, the spotlight has shifted to the intellectual and cultural exclusion of minorities from the mainstream media and other power centres such as universities and government. The concept of 'migrant ghettos' assumed a new dimension in the shape of the growing 'information divide' separating native Swedes and minorities. Sweden has one of the highest per capita newspaper readerships globally. Yet readership among minorities has plummeted. Thanks to unemployment, many households have no telephones let alone an internet connection.

For reasons such as these, debate on Sweden's multicultural policies has focused on the negative stereotype of minorities portrayed by Sweden's mainstream media and on their absence from any positive context. It is this imbalance that the minority media aims to redress. 'Sweden is a segregated society and the Swedish media reinforce this segregation,' wrote Swedish media scholar Ylva Brune in the hard-hitting anthology *Black Magic in the White Media*, published as part of the EU Campaign Against Racism some five years ago.

Partly in response to the heated public debate at that time, the minister of culture, Marita Ulvskog, commissioned the Swedish Press Subsidies Council to study the conditions of the ethnic media. It published its findings last September under the title *Minority Media*. This provides the first in-depth survey of the full range of radio, TV, print and webcasts employed by Sweden's minorities – from the Sami, Sweden's indigenous people, to more recent newcomers such as Somalis and Bosnians. It also looks at the experience and practice of the UK media – the BBC and newspapers such as *The Times*, *Observer* and *Guardian* as well as Britain's most successful black weekly *The Voice* – as a possible model for Sweden.

Among its conclusions, the report stresses the importance of putting migration within its historical context; the various roles the ethnic media play in building multicultural society; and the need to provide professional and financial training for migrant journalists that will contribute to making their media viable in the long term – in other words, an integral part of the Swedish media scene.

By highlighting the fact that Sweden itself was once a country of emigration – almost one-fifth of its 8.9 million population left for the United States in years gone by – the report underlines an aspect of Sweden's official policy that is unlike that of other European countries, especially Britain and France which were once colonial powers: it encourages a positive view of migration as a natural, universal and human process that has, overall, been beneficial. Given a social climate hardened by economic reforms since Sweden joined the EU, the official status of *Minority Media* goes a long way to boosting the confidence of minority communities that have often been told by racists to pack up and return home.

However, five months after its launch, the Swedish government has shown no intention of acting on its findings. The most that can be said is that it has set the ball rolling. This, at least, is the view of Joe Frans, a member of the ruling Social Democratic Party elected to parliament last September. A former TV journalist with roots in Ghana, Frans says he is prepared to take up the matter of press subsidies with Ulvskog. 'It's simple: Swedish Press Subsidies are there to support diversity in the media and freedom of speech. This country is proud of this tradition and small communities with only a few thousand people have been able to start and run their community press. It is the same with political parties. If dailies like *Svenska Dagbladet* get help annually from the Swedish taxpayers, the small players should not be denied this same public service. It's a matter of justice.'

Frans could provide the leadership and direction the minority media badly need. Despite their heroic initiatives, ethnic minority groups have often been criticised for their infighting and lack of unity when it comes to standing up for their rights. It's not so long since women and the working class in Sweden were as marginalised as today's migrants. It took committed leadership and public mobilisation to win equality – and one important element in their ultimate success was the foundation of their own newspapers to counter the dominance of the privileged classes. ❏

Moussa Awuonda is a Kenyan journalist based in Stockholm

MULTICULTURAL MOSAIC

SIDHARTH BHATIA

CANADA, ARCHETYPAL LAND OF
IMMIGRANTS, WELCOMES SKILLED
FOREIGNERS AND ENSHRINES THEIR
RIGHTS IN ITS CONSTITUTION. WHAT
POSSIBLE PROBLEMS CAN THERE BE
FOR THE NEWCOMER?

Every newcomer to Canada – and there are roughly 250,000 people who make Canada their home every year – learns a few things quickly. The first, and probably the most brutal, truth that hits the recently arrived immigrant is that his academic qualifications and skills, which entitled him to that coveted residence permit in the first place, provide no guarantee that he will get a job, any job, not necessarily what he is qualified for.

Thus stories about former physicians driving taxis or qualified account-ants cleaning toilets are not mere urban legends but probably true. The cold gust of reality hits like the famed Canadian winter and the first few months after arrival can be full of humiliation, doubt and regret about leaving a more settled life back home for one full of uncertainty.

Soon after, the new immigrant finds out that modern Canada is mostly a land of immigrants. Everyone is an immigrant or a child of previous immi-grants: from the governor general to the chief executive of a corporation to the janitor, all came from somewhere else, either recently or a few genera-tions ago. Why, that person across the table rejecting you for that job too is a child of immigrants, though that is no comfort to the new immigrant. But it gives hope that sticking around and working hard can lead to success, especially for the next generation. And since most people move to Canada to provide their children with a better life, the vast majority of immigrants stay on and persevere.

To those who do, Canada provides an easy life. Health care is free, state education is of a high standard and the country boasts superb infrastructure. Not for nothing has Canada been consistently voted among the best coun-tries in the world for quality of life; not for nothing does it attract immi-grants from all over the world. Canada is a magnet for immigrants wanting to start a better life. Nearly 3 million people made Canada their home in the last decade and the latest census revealed that 18 per cent of Canadians were born outside the country. Visible minorities make up 13.4 per cent of the Canadian population, but in the bigger cities such as Toronto and Vancouver almost every second person is non-white, most of them from China and India, both rapidly becoming the largest ethnic minorities in the two cities, where in some suburbs whites are definitely the visible minority.

To beckon skilled foreigners and keep them in the country, Canada also offers multiculturalism, a word that new immigrants learn to recognise quickly, even if it was not a concept particularly well known in their homelands. Multiculturalism, Canadian style, is not merely a populist slogan, but was enshrined in the constitution in 1971 under Pierre Trudeau. A new immigrant is encouraged to become a Canadian, but equally afforded the opportunity to maintain each and every aspect of his native culture, which the state fosters through word, deed and cash subsidies.

Every Canadian is a mosaic tile who adds to the big picture but maintains a unique identity and any discrimination on the basis of being 'different' – in terms of race, ethnicity, gender or sexual preference – is illegal. The state promotes the idea of diversity and has set quotas for inclusion of 'visible minorities' in the workplace. Canada, it is proclaimed, is a patchwork quilt as opposed to a melting pot and, to its credit, the country has succeeded at promoting the diversity idea as the underpinning of its nationhood far better than other countries which have large multi-ethnic immigrant populations. The bigger cities are a colourful blend of all racial types and overt racism is rare, even if visible minorities often complain that it exists institutionally, behind the ultra-polite façade. The Toronto police, for example, has been under severe attack for racial profiling, especially of black youth. But the notion of the Canadian identity – even if hyphenated – has taken root among immigrants, who find the country's benign nationalism appealing.

Yet immigration as an issue does not get the visible attention in the public space that, say, Canada's ties with the US or even health care gets. Not even the right-wing opposition parties see fit to touch the subject. It is not as if immigration is a hot potato, or that no one wants to be seen as anti-minority for fear of appearing politically incorrect. It is just that the country as a whole appears to have accepted the need for immigration, to keep the population young, to attract much needed skilled labour and of course to keep the economy going. Each family is supposed to bring in at least

Can$12,000 and, obviously, all of them buy television sets, cars and even houses. The real-estate boom in Toronto, Vancouver and other cities is almost totally predicated on the continued influx of newcomers.

Attacking immigration, or indeed raising questions about the changing face of Canada, will not pay any political dividends and though there would be some resentment among sections of Canadian society, especially in the non-urban areas, it is not a political issue. Ruling politicians use every platform to sing the praises of more, not less, immigration and some ultra-liberal papers call for the country to open its doors even wider, to let in more and let them in quicker, because it can take up to four years in certain countries before an applicant can hope to get his case cleared. The hows and whats of the issue are open to debate; the why is rarely asked.

So, come on, all those who want to make a new life, Canada welcomes you. But then comes the awkward question: what to do with them once they get here? The entry requirements are high and only the most qualified and skilled get in – the list of needed professionals ranges from medicine to accountancy to bricklaying – but integrating them economically into society is quite another matter. Many find their qualifications are simply not recognised by local professional associations, which function as guilds of yore. Under-employment is rampant; doctors become physiotherapists, chartered accountants find jobs as bank tellers and many just fall through the cracks. Studies have found high levels of depression among immigrants, who can neither go back to where they came from nor get a job that matches their qualifications.

It becomes difficult, if not impossible, for the first-generation migrant to join the 'mainstream' in any significant way. Institutionally, the country remains a sea of white, with a few brown, yellow and black specks here and there, mainly thanks to the government's efforts to promote diversity. But jobs go to those who were born here or at least studied here; newcomers have to queue up and will perhaps see only the next generation make it anywhere in the mainstream.

Critics have complained that multiculturalism is the system's way of ghettoising people, especially from non-white communities, celebrating 'saris and samosas' but ensuring that visible minorities stay away from the mainstream. Income levels among immigrants, especially of colour, remain at lower levels than those of Canadians, and some communities that have not had easy access to English (or French) find it difficult to break into the job market.

Perhaps for them multiculturalism comes in handy, offering the space where they can feel comfortable among fellow Chinese, Somalis, Serbians, Sri Lankans or Sikhs. New communities are also forged, though these are not always organic or realistic. Thus South Asian includes everyone from Sri Lanka, Pakistan, India and Bangladesh, even though there is barely any kinship among them, while the 'Muslim community', an amalgamation much in the news after 11 September, could consist of Shia Iranians, Sunni Pakistanis, French-speaking Algerians and even Malays, none of whom would otherwise have anything in common with each other.

This is the view of mainstream Canada – seemingly discrete groups that have a common identity based on religion, race, ethnicity, language or even country of origin. Their separateness is celebrated and sometimes they may even wield some political influence, but they show up little on the mainstream radar.

At the ground level, all these groups maintain their own exclusive universe, reflected in their media. There are literally hundreds of publications, small, big and medium, in a variety of languages, offering a familiar pastiche of stories about the local community, stories about 'back home' and, inevitably, news and advice about immigration. They help create windows through which the immigrant can access some part of his new home: health services, mortgages, even employment, while trying hard to maintain some level of cultural roots. They peddle nostalgia and compensate for the sense of loss they must feel. They usher the immigrant slowly into the Canadian way. The bigger television channels give a point of view that is often bewilderingly North American – multicultural channels try to fill the gap.

Media for the migrants is not as powerful and all-pervasive as the mainstream, but provides the hinterland that the immigrant so sorely misses. Most immigrants realise this quickly enough – they may have come to Canada but, often, Canada has not yet come to them. ❏

Sidharth Bhatia *is an Indian journalist and writer living in Canada. He is an associate press fellow of Wolfson College, Cambridge, UK*

MAKING CONNECTIONS
DONALD R SHANOR

IT'S THE US MAINSTREAM, MORE THAN
THE MIGRANTS THEMSELVES, WHO
NEED WHAT THEIR BURGEONING
MEDIA HAS TO TELL

Franz Schurmann, professor emeritus at the University of California at
Berkeley where he taught history and sociology, likes to take visitors to San
Francisco's Chinatown to an intersection that once marked the shoreline of
Oakland Bay. Above are the nineteenth-century buildings of the old
Chinese immigrant associations, and below, on landfill, are the office towers
of the financial district. The Chinese kept their links to their homeland
across the Pacific from the time they arrived in the United States, Schurmann says, and this bridge over the ocean still connects China to their
communities in this country: 'They may go back to their homelands rarely
or not at all, or they may be dotcom entrepreneurs who commute weekly,
but they still have the bridge as part of their consciousness.'

Schurmann and Sandy Close are using these bridges in a project called
New California Media (NCM), a news service aimed at bringing the news
and insights of the ethnic media in the Bay Area and beyond to a general
audience that doesn't speak Chinese or the dozens of other languages that
Schurmann and Close pick up and translate on the service. They're tapping
into more than 350 newspapers, internet sites and broadcast stations, ranging
from Iran Today to India West and including five Chinese dailies and a 24-
hour Chinese television station. 'They tell the daily stories of people in their
communities in California as well as in the countries they come from,'
Close says. 'The ethnic media really are producing something the mainstream media can't duplicate, and that is this incredible new virtual geography, the neighbourhood and homeland all in one.'

Close, a veteran editor and activist, saw the importance of the changes in
California's ethnic composition long before the 2000 census showed that
the state had become the second in the nation in which minorities consti-
tute the majority (after Hawaii, which has never had an Anglo majority).
Latinos led the increase, making up 33 per cent of California's population in
2000, compared with 25 per cent in 1990 – three-quarters of the 4.1 million

people California gained. Asians added about 1 million in the decade between the two censuses, giving them an 11–12 per cent share of the population instead of 9 per cent.

NCM covers these changes and their ramifications in stories sold to newspapers and available on the internet (www.ncmonline.com) and public radio and television programmes. It connects ethnic papers and broadcasters to the mainstream media as well as to one another. There is polite disagreement at NCM over which connection is more important. Some editors argue that the project's main role should be to bring its diverse range of minority viewpoints to the majority who seldom get to hear them, including the readers of the *San Francisco Chronicle* and other newspapers.

NCM's television, a weekly half-hour, covers the spectrum of the ethnic media, from Asian-American film to the Kashmir dispute and Muslim women's voices. Mexico is a common topic because of the border and the immigrant flow that has helped make Latinos the largest minority in the US. NCM-TV's Emil Guillermo anchored a programme about the 2000 Mexican elections that showed how Mexican issues are intertwined for all Californians, whatever their ethnic background. 'Immigration, the economy, jobs – how the candidates tackle these issues is a concern for the new California,' he said. José Luís Sierra of Los Angeles's *La Opinion* said on the programme that in Mexico 'there's real change now – some sense of democracy, something they haven't had for decades'.

Many other NCM viewpoints come from Asia, from the Japanese, Indian and Pakistani press. Chinese media are the most prominent, especially *Sing Tao Daily*, a newspaper based in Hong Kong with editorial operations in six US cities, which has a reputation for independence that balances its more opinionated pro-Taiwan and pro-Beijing rivals in the US.

For more than four decades, *Sing Tao* has reported on one of the world's most important stories – and for its readers, *the* most important – mainland China, in a way that its editor, Wellington Cheng, describes as neutral. *Sing Tao* shows its independence in every issue: critical of US treatment of scientist Wen Ho Lee, but also of Chinese government violations of human rights since the Tiananmen massacre.

Cheng says the English newspapers in the Bay Area seldom pick up anything from his columns, local or international, but on an important story, *Chronicle* reporters sometimes interview *Sing Tao* editors. The latter agree Americans are under-informed about China, but have no quick solutions: an English-language page attracted few non-Chinese readers.

Los Angeles: news for everyone.
Credit: © Ferdinando Scianna / Magnum Photos

About half the content of *Sing Tao* – printed in bright colours in its text, photographs, headlines and ads – is about China and the rest of Asia. The other half is US news, with sports and a vibrant business section competing with a big news slot for national, foreign, local and regional issues of interest to Chinese. And not only Chinese. With the advent of NCM, the work of *Sing Tao*'s Larry Li and other reporters in the US and Asia has been getting picked up and translated into English in press round-ups or used in analysis pieces.

KTSF-TV first attracted San Franciscans' attention when Chinese troops massacred demonstrators in Tiananmen Square in 1989. It broadcast half-hour special reports in Cantonese and Mandarin, the two most widely spoken Chinese languages, some of which were picked up by the English media. The station had gone on the air a few months earlier with the US's first live Chinese television news, *Chinese News at Nine*.

Since then KTSF-TV has grown into a 24-hour station that reaches the entire Bay Area, where 1.6 million Asian-Americans live, with news in Vietnamese, Japanese and 11 other languages as well as Chinese. NCM's website provides links to Anglophone audiences.

NCM's most prominent showcase is in a section every Sunday, appropriately named 'Bay Area Bridges', in the *San Francisco Chronicle*. The stories in 'Bridges' are a mixture of local and foreign news – a Vietnamese-American soldier of fortune imprisoned in Thailand, job offers in Shanghai for Americans laid off in Silicon Valley, and emergency water supplies left in the desert to save the lives of Mexican immigrants crossing borders.

NCM has been providing this kind of news since 1996 on its website and broadcast programmes, translating the best of what Close calls the explosion of ethnic media that serve California's new majority. NCM does more than translate. Schurmann reads Chinese, Farsi and Arabic among many other languages, and uses these skills to keep English-only readers up on trends and news in the Middle East, China and the rest of Asia. Unlike the European immigrants on the East Coast and in the Midwest, Schurmann observed, San Francisco's Chinese and many other ethnic groups, distinguished by their skin colour or features, 'never melted into the general US population, are never going to and are going to maintain, as logically and easily as they have always done, a dual cultural identity'.

Close says she wants to promote more contact between ethnic communities. 'We're trying to encourage Indian papers to print news about China and vice versa,' she said. 'It's already happening in areas such as sports and big elections.' Editors are careful to screen out advocates who write for political parties or interest groups, although NCM does encourage open debates, such as those it sponsored between Indian and Pakistani journalists on nuclear weapons.

NCM proved its worth in the aftermath of the World Trade Centre and Pentagon attacks, presenting a broad spectrum of the foreign media's reaction to the disasters and the hate crimes against foreigners and US citizens of foreign background that followed them. They provided a more nuanced view of the attacks and their consequences than did most of the mainstream US media. 'Japanese-Americans, who were forced out of their homes on the West Coast after the bombing of Pearl Harbor and incarcerated in concentration camps, are likely to relate to the fear and anxiety burdening those of Arab, Muslim, Sikh and South Asian descent,' *Nichi Bei*, the Japanese-language newspaper, wrote.

Iran Today urged intelligence operations against the terrorists rather than massive military attacks that would alienate the Muslim world. The AllAfrica website criticised US arrogance and bullying. The leftist *Confidencial* of Nicaragua warned against all extremist forms of religion, whether Islamic or US fundamentalist. The Chinese-language *World Journal*, which supports Taiwan, took the unusual step of criticising the Bush administration's policy as designed 'to dominate Asia, contain China and on the Middle East to ask no questions'. Both the London-based Arabic newspaper *Al-Sharq al Ausat* and *Sing Tao*, in translations by Schurmann carried on NCM's site, criticised the tightening of US detention laws designed to fight terrorism. *Sing Tao* reported fears in the Chinese community about the new anti-terrorism law. 'For some,' Schurmann wrote, 'the bill conjures up historical discrimination measures such as the Chinese exclusion act that banned immigration of Chinese labourers and banned citizenship' until it was revoked in 1943.

New California Media is an idea that is bound to spread to the rest of the US, impelled by the same forces that caused it to take hold in California: the changing composition of the US population. As minorities grow in number and influence, the majority will need more information, more insights, more understanding about them. It's fortunate that the minorities are producing their own talent – media entrepreneurs, editors, producers and reporters – to do this informing and explaining, and that majority journalists are making use of the news they provide to reach a broader public. After NCM, New New York Media may be next, with New Texas, New Illinois and New Florida not far behind. ❏

Donald Shanor *is Cabot professor emeritus at the Graduate School of Journalism of Columbia University and teaches an online writing course at the University of Phoenix. A former* Chicago Daily News *and UPI foreign correspondent, he is the author of* News from Abroad, *a study of US foreign coverage (Columbia University Press, forthcoming August 2003)*

CULTURE

Illustration from Vladimir Sorokin's Trick Lard.
Credit: Genia Chef

VLADIMIR SOROKIN'S 'TRICK LARD'

Vladimir Sorokin's *Trick Lard* (*Goluboe salo*, also variously translated as *Blue Bacon Fat, Blue Lard, Gay Lard*) was published by ad marginem in 1999. Shortly afterwards, the text was scanned and put on the internet by a third party. Sorokin and ad marginem took Andrei Chernov to court for providing a link to the unauthorised website, and duly lost, since they were unable to show that Chernov had either made a copy (by downloading the novel to a computer hard disk or server) or had 'published' the novel (merely by providing a link) or distributed it (since there was no evidence of pirated printing).

The novel's second court appearance relates to a campaign by the youth grouping Idushchie vmeste, variously translated as Walking Together or, more mischievously, the Fellow Travellers or Solidarity (*Index* 2/2002). In July 2002 this group, an apparently Kremlin-orchestrated Putin fan club, mounted a demonstration near the Bolshoi Theatre in Moscow at which, rather than burn the offending book, they tore a number of copies to pieces and threw them into a mock toilet bowl. Excerpts from the novel were shown to children and elderly ladies before the book was taken to the offices of the Moscow prosecutor where criminal charges were brought against Sorokin, who could face up to two years in jail for disseminating pornography. (Sorokin and ad marginem have in their turn counter-sued Walking Together for US$150,000 for unauthorised copying of excerpts from the book.)

Vladimir Sorokin has been raising eyebrows for many years now with writings that Vsevolod Ivanov once described as Russian literature singing in the toilet, and which Sergei Biriukov has more recently characterised as rectal socialist realism. The Booker Prize judges at one time dismissed his style as a dead end, and some critics have seen his relentless scatology as at best immoderate and at worst commercially motivated. Some of Russia's most prominent writers are lavish in their praise, however, and see him as outstandingly talented.

There is no doubt that Sorokin is a consummate parodist who boldly goes where none have ventured before. He forthrightly denies being a pornographer, however: 'There's a big difference between pornographers and writers. The pornographer aims to help the reader achieve an erection, but the writer's task is to provide the reader with aesthetic pleasure.' The controversy over his novel has uncomfortable reverberations for the intelligentsia in Russia, where many works now generally regarded as major literary achievements of the twentieth century were reviled or banned in their time. Prosecutor-General Vladimir Ustinov commented: 'Regardless of whether pornographic elements are to be found in Sorokin's novels, to me it is clear there is a problem. It is time to screen out second-rate "art".' He had not read the novel 'and I must admit I don't plan to. What I've heard about it doesn't make me want to pick it up.' Conspiracy theorists detect unseen forces of the Putin era directing the denunciations of Vasilii Iakimenko, organiser of the League of Itinerant Youth, much as Vladimir Semichastnyi of the Young Communist League was part of a wider campaign by conservative forces to swing the barometer from thaw towards freeze under Khrushchev.

Sergei Biriukov writes that real literature is always left-wing, obliged in the name of originality to oppose any form of stable conservatism. The avant-gardists of the post-revolutionary period, he notes, found themselves caught on the hop when the ultra-left revolutionary government became conservative and right-wing. He disputes that Sorokin belongs to the 'true' avant-garde, but the comedy being played out around *Trick Lard*, in which the political forces deal in stereotype and spin while the writer and his publisher deal in the ineffable (and spin), is a true dialogue of the deaf.

What is *Trick Lard* about? Sorokin will say no more than that it is about the death of Russian literature. He refused to give evidence to the police, he told reporters, 'because I consider this matter absurd, vicious and humiliating to me as a writer and humiliating to Russian literature as a whole'. A novel cannot be paraphrased. Those who want to know what it is about should read it. Critic Viktor Sonkin, writing in *Russkii zhurnal*, sketches out a helpful map, however, to guide a reading. Russian literature is dead, but clones of the great writers – Tolstoy, Dostoevsky, Chekhov, Pasternak, Akhmatova, Mandelshtam, Platonov, Nabokov – are still writing and producing a by-product of trick lard which is not subject to the normal laws of physics. The novel includes examples of the pastiche which these clones produce, and one writer may have more than one clone, each with his or her variations of style. The cast of characters includes Stalin, Khrushchev, Hitler, Eva Braun, Leni Riefenstahl, Beria, Yevtushenko, Akhmadulin, Rozhdestvenskii, Brodskii *et al.* They are not, however, what they seem. The 'Count Nikita Khrushchev' who, in the scene which has been at the centre of the *skandal*, has sex with Stalin, is a figure with long grey hair, and the interaction of the two personalities is clearly not historically based. Are we really to suspend disbelief sufficiently to imagine Hitler having sex with Stalin's daughter? The vagaries of the trick lard are central to the plot.

Sonkin sees a major achievement in the novel's language. Sorokin, like Anthony Burgess in *A Clockwork Orange*, has wittily invented a vocabulary of the distant future, this time drawing on Chinese.

Sales of the novel have increased dramatically. A spokesman for Moscow's Dom knigi bookshop noted that they were now selling more than 120 copies a day 'while before we were lucky to sell 16', demonstrating that in today's Russia, too, there is no such thing as bad publicity. ❏

TRICK LARD

VLADIMIR SOROKIN

Khrushchev slowly undressed Stalin who was lying on an enormous disassembled bed. The Count's bedroom was brightly lit – three candelabra illumined walls covered in lilac chiffon and three large portraits in carved gilded frames. The middle one, from the brush of Picasso, depicted in greys, pinks and pale blues Lenin's comrade-in-arms, Larissa Reisner, sitting in a gold bathtub filled with milk; symmetrically to either side hung Stalin and Lenin, painted by Isaak Brodskii in the classical style in darker blues, reds and browns. From the radio came a muffled broadcast of Ambroise Thomas's opera *Mignon*. Birch logs crackled in the fireplace.

'The aroma of your eau de cologne . . . ' Stalin said, stroking Khrushchev's smooth cheekbone, 'I haven't yet tired of being driven wild by it.'

'I am glad, my little boy, that I still have something to amaze you with.' Khrushchev finished unbuttoning Stalin's shirt, parted the delicate silk with his powerful, hairy hands, and pressed his lips to the Leader's hairless chest.

'What I feel for you, mon ami, is like nothing else.' Stalin closed his eyes. 'It is . . . like fear.'

Illustration from Vladimir Sorokin's Trick Lard.
Credit: Genia Chef

'I understand, my little boy,' Krushchev whispered into Stalin's small nipple and carefully took it in his large, sensual lips.

Stalin moaned.

Khrushchev carefully unbuttoned his trousers, slipped down the see-through black underpants, freeing the Leader's tense, swarthy penis. Spitting on his fingers, the Count began delicately worrying Stalin's nipple with them while moving his lips down over the Leader's body to the tumescent penis.

'Oh . . . how often I think about you,' Stalin murmured. 'How much space you have occupied in my limitless life.'

'Masculinum . . .' The Count's lips touched the maroon glans. Stalin cried out and clutched Khrushchev's head. The Count's lips, at first delicately but then ever more lustfully, began toying with the Leader's knob.

'Spiral, spiral . . .' Stalin moaned, pressing his fingers into the Count's long silvery hair.

Khrushchev's strong tongue began spiralling over Stalin's glans.

'You know . . . my sweet . . . no . . . sacre . . . I . . . but no . . . The tip! The tip! The tip!' Stalin thrashed about on the down-filled pillows.

The Count's tongue carefully touched the tip of the Leader's penis and began parting the urethra.

'But . . . no . . . I mustn't! Don't let me!' Stalin rolled his eyes.

Khrushchev gave the Leader's tightening balls a hard squeeze.

'It mustn't flow . . . Oooh . . . Tell me not to! Tell me like you used to! Only do it gently! Do it gently!'

'Give me your rosebud, sweet boy,' Khrushchev ordered gently, holding Stalin firmly by the balls. Whimpering, Stalin turned over on to his stomach.

'Your little boy is frightened . . . kiss my back.'

'My little boy's back shall be kissed . . .' Khrushchev slipped the shirt from Stalin's shoulders and began to cover them with slow kisses. Stalin moaned into the pillow.

Khrushchev gave him a big wet kiss between the shoulder blades, moved his lips to his ear, and whispered:

'What is my little boy frightened of?'

'A big fat worm,' Stalin whimpered.

'And where does the big fat worm live?'

'In mister's pants.'

'What does the worm want?'

'To rush inside.'

'Inside where?'

'Inside my little bottom.'

Khrushchev unbuttoned his trousers and pulled out the long uneven penis with its lumpy glans, on whose gleaming skin there was tattooed a pentacle.

The Count spat in his hand, lubricated Stalin's anus with the spit and, mounting him from behind, began with gentle prodding to insert his penis in the Leader.

'Mister, you're . . . No . . . Be gentle! Be gentle!' Stalin whimpered.

'My sweet little tin soldier . . .' Khrushchev whispered in his ear.

'Why . . . suffering . . . Oooh . . . why do we need . . .' Stalin bit his lip.

'In order to forget . . . in order to forget everything, my little boy . . .' The Count's penis had fully penetrated Stalin. Cupping the Leader's balls in his left hand, the Count took the penis in his right hand and began unhurriedly to masturbate him.

'You . . . it's . . . you . . .' Stalin groaned. 'What is mister doing to his little boy?'

'Mister is fucking his little boy in the ass,' Khrushchev whispered hotly.

'What? What? What?'

'It's so sweet . . .'

'Did mister tell me to? Did mister tell me to . . . strictly . . . ?'

'Mister strictly told you to.'

'Mister told me to?' Stalin whimpered.

'Mister told you to. Mister strictly told you to . . .'

'And will mister tell me again?'

'Mister will . . . hundreds of millions of times mister will tell his little boy what to do . . .'

'What? What? What?'

'He will tell you to . . . but not yet . . .'

'What? What? What?'

'Gradually . . . gradually . . . gradually . . .'

'But . . . but . . . little boy already . . . little boy already . . .'

'What, little boy?'

'Little boy is ready . . . he is . . . he is . . .'

'Only when I tell you . . . Only when I tell you . . .'

'Little boy is . . . little boy is . . . bring it here! Bring it here, you wrecking saboteur!'

Hugging Stalin from behind, Khrushchev toppled sideways with him to the edge of the bed.

'Adzhuba!' the Count shouted in a breaking voice. Adzhuba appeared, bearing a golden chalice encrusted with six large sapphires. Kneeling down by the bed, he positioned the chalice beneath Stalin's purple penis.

'Little boy, come now!' Khrushchev roared. They came together with cries and moaning. Adzhuba caught the thick gobbets of Stalin's sperm in the chalice.

'I didn't miss! I didn't miss!' Stalin cried in a high voice.

'No! No! No!' the Count roared, his whole body shuddering as he rammed his penis into Stalin's quivering buttocks.

When the agony of orgasm had receded, the lovers lay motionless in a semi-daze.

Adzhuba continued to hold the chalice in place, observing attentively as Stalin's wilting penis yielded its last turbid drops.

'Eternal recurrence . . . symbiosis . . .' Stalin murmured and laughed.

'I love you,' Khrushchev gasped wearily into the pomaded hair of the Leader.

Stalin took his hand, raised it to his lips and kissed it. Khrushchev began carefully to extract his penis from the Leader's anus.

'Stay, I beg you,' Stalin kissed the bony fingers with their overly convex nails. 'Your sperm is hot. Like lava. To feel it inside me is unbelievably delightful . . .'

Khrushchev stayed stock still.

Adzhuba caught the last, most viscous drop with the rim of the chalice, placed it on the bedside table, which was cluttered with books, and departed.

'Do you read a lot?' Stalin's gaze fell on the books.

'What else is there for a recluse to do?'

'I have forgotten what books are.'

'That is forgivable for a Leader.'

'Are there interesting writers around?'

'Yes, but no interesting books.'

'What do you mean?'

'Well . . . something is happening to Russian literature, but I don't for the moment understand what.'

'Is it decaying? I expect so.'

'Well, yes, we are all decaying. As soon as a person stops growing he begins to decay.'

'Books are not people.'

'Are you saying that books do not decay?'

'You are a sophist, Joseph!' Khrushchev laughed, and his shrivelled penis popped out of Stalin's anus.

'What is this? *One Day in the Life of Ivan Denisóvich?*' Stalin read the title of a manuscript lying on the floor beside the bed.

'Denísovich,' Khrushchev corrected him, flopping over on to his back. 'It's a novella by some weirdo. He brought me it. He came on foot all the way to Arkhangelskoe from the Crimean Forced Love camps.'

'From the Lovelag?'

'Yes. Said he had worn out four pairs of boots on the way. I had doubts about him immediately.'

'Was he doing time there?' Stalin took a bunch of grapes from a golden bowl, pulled one off and placed it in Khrushchev's lips.

'Yes, about seven years as I recall. After that he was in exile, in Koktebel. Well, and then he wrote this novella. About life in the Lovelag.'

'I heard everyone's falling over themselves to write about that now. Hot topic. Is it any good?'

'Weird. The writing seems vivid and authentic, but . . . there's something unconvincing about it from the outset.'

'Tell me.' Stalin devoured a grape.

'Well, what is there to tell?' Khrushchev yawned. 'Ivan Leopoldovich Denisovich, a dyed-in-the-wool kike from Odessa, gets sentenced by OSO to ten years in the Lovelag for third-degree sexual perversion. He worked as an accompanist at the Odessa Philharmonic. Lured schoolgirls from the senior classes to his home and got them drunk on liqueur and sedatives. When they fell asleep he fucked their every orifice, stuffed their vagina with his own shit and sewed it up with a golden thread. Then he would kit them out in a wedding dress, take them to Luna Park, and sit with them on a hobby horse, riding round and round until they woke up. What really turned him on was the expression on the schoolgirl's face just as she woke up. Well, so the novella describes one day of his life in the camp. How he screwed and how he got screwed.'

'So what's unconvincing about it, mon cher?' Stalin set to feeding Khrushchev.

'In the first place, in a hundred pages there's not a single Italian word. There's nothing at all in French. English phrases here and there, but only very occasionally. Are the prisoners all supposed to speak Russian? What sort of arrogant nonsense is that?'

'That is weird,' Stalin said, looking into his face.

'In the second place, he's describing some kind of innocent childish relations there. No kidney fucking, no shit stabbing, no subcutaneous fucking. And where is the classical fucking an old man through his catheter that you get in every camp?'

'Even my Vesta knows about that.'

'In the third place, there's the food. This Denisovich splutters that Hungarian-style chicken and asparagus soup, which they are fed practically every day, makes him feel sick. Their brigade leader (they have forced beadwork and lace-making in the camp) suffers from indigestion and gives up his helping of "rancid, over-cooked truffles burned to eyeball-sized bile" to another prisoner who "sets joyfully about it". They are said to get only Crimean wine, no chance of French. And the cocaine in the coke café is cut with sugar.'

'Well, that takes the biscuit! They get first-rate Colombian cocaine in the Lovelag, quality-controlled by the MGB. All the barmen in the coke café are state security officers who would never dream of cutting the ice . . .'

'In short, there's something not right about those camps. And I took an instant dislike to the man himself. He's shifty. Russian writers shouldn't be shifty. Rude, brazen, obnoxious – no problem. But not shifty. My boilerman Varlam has spent half his life in the Crimean Lovelag. He's a real character. He has a split penis for nostril fucking. His hands are bent to fit round a human head. He has screwed tens of thousands of people's nostrils. I gave him it to read. He told me straight up: "That's not like any camp I was ever in." And then, in the fourth place . . .'

'In the fourth place, I love you.' Stalin kissed his chewing lips.

Khrushchev responded with a long kiss. Then he stood up briskly, took the chalice and downed it in a single draught.

'Mon cher ami, I've just got something to show you,' Stalin said, glancing at his small suitcase beside the bedroom door. 'Something very important. Something you and I have been waiting for for sixteen years.'

Khrushchev froze into immobility with the chalice in his hand before slowly turning to Stalin.

. . .

Khrushchev opened the little suitcase and looked at the trick lard.

'Why didn't you mention this all evening?'

'All night, more like!' Stalin grinned, coming up behind and putting his arms round him. 'If I had shown you it straight away you wouldn't have wanted me any more. You'd have wanted the trick lard.'

Khrushchev covered his face with his hands, uncovered it and covered it again.

'At moments like this I understand that our world is a dream.'

'I understand that every minute, and have since my earliest childhood.' Stalin kissed his hump, moved away and began lighting up a cigar. He had on Khrushchev's black Chinese dressing gown.

Khrushchev sat down, naked, on the edge of the bed, locked his fingers and looked at them in concern.

'We have wasted time. You should have come to me straight away.'

'With a block of ice? And let Beria work everything out?'

'I am quite sure he knows anyway.'

'Mon cher, there's no need to flatter Beria. He is no clairvoyant. I acted everything out as if following a script.'

'We have wasted time, though! . . . verflucht noch mal!' Khrushchev slapped his muscular knees, jumped up and began pacing around the bedroom. His long hands dug into his hairy hips, and his hump jutted up menacingly from his twisted back.

'Du calme, mon ami,' Stalin exhaled his smoke into the open suitcase. 'Time is on our side.'

'They won't allow us to leave! They'll hunt us like the bears in Arkhangelskoe . . . Beria has already sniffed arses with Zhukov. They've got the entire Soviet army, plus Lubianka! That petit con Zhukov, that regimental whore! And to think I saved that insect in 1937 from Ezhov. They will go to any lengths, how can you not see?!'

'Do, I beg you, take yourself in hand.' Stalin admired the cigar smoke which, billowing in the suitcase, had turned sky-blue.

'Why didn't you think of anything? Why didn't you contact me from the theatre?! We should have arrested them all in the theatre, all of them,

in one go! My Ninjas and Circassians would have had it sorted in three
minutes!'

'There was no need for that.'

'Right now, while you are here, they have the entire army! Do you not
understand?! The entire army, all of Russia, the whole MGB is in the hands
of Beria and Zhukov!'

'While we have the whole universe in our hands.' Stalin turned to him.
'The whole universe will fit into this small suitcase.'

'You won't get a chance to use it!'

'Calm yourself. They knew nothing and they still don't. I am fully
aware of what I am saying.'

'Schweine . . . verdammte . . . Schweine!!!' Khrushchev yelled.

Stalin went over and hugged him:

'Mon ami, I implore you. All will be well.'

'I don't believe it . . . I can't believe that insect Beria . . .'

'All will be well.' Stalin looked into the Count's now bloodshot eyes.
'It is Stalin telling you this. Do you trust Stalin?'

Khrushchev responded with a grumpy and less than trusting look.

'Do you trust Stalin?' the Leader asked again.

'Of course I do,' Khrushchev murmured reluctantly, averting his eyes.
Stalin took him by his pointed chin and turned his face to himself.

'Do you trust me?'

Khrushchev looked long into the steady eyes the colour of strong
Indian tea, melted, took Stalin's hand and kissed it.

'I trust you, Joseph.'

'Bon. Then get ready.'

Stalin crossed to the telephone and lifted the receiver.

'The Kremlin. Stalin's apartment.'

Sisul answered the phone.

'Hello?'

'Sisul, where is the family?'

'Hello, boss. The children all at school. Nadezhda sleeping at home.'

'Send for the children immediately.'

'I do it, boss.'

'Wake Nadezhda. Tell her "Drum".'

'What you mean drum, boss? What drum?'

'Just "Drum". She knows which one. And make sure they are all ready
by twelve.'

'I do it, boss.'

Stalin hung up, went over to where his clothes were lying on the bed, threw off the dressing gown and began quickly to get dressed.

'What an exquisite colour . . .' Khrushchev leaned over the suitcase. 'It's the colour of the fourth principle of thermodynamics . . .'

'You are no romantic. It's the colour of the Other.'

'For me the the Other is the New.'

'New is new. And Other, mon cher, is other.' Stalin finished buttoning his shirt, sat down and began pulling on his long black-and-red stockings.

'Sixteen years . . .' Khrushchev went over to where the fire had gone out and hugged himself in an attempt to keep warm.

'Has that parcel gone?'

'Yes. Time post. Probably the slowest. And the most expensive.'

'Do you remember us reading their leather book?'

'At yours? In the bathhouse? In the bathroom?'

'You suggested reading with a torch under a blanket. You were a grand conspirator!'

'That was when I strangled the guard.'

'Who came in at the wrong moment?' Stalin stood up, pulling on his tight trousers.

'I remember his young Adam's apple as if it were yesterday.' Khrushchev ran a hand wearily over his face. 'Do you know . . . to tell the truth . . . I never believed any of this was real. I thought it was all an enormous sham, a trap. But I couldn't see the logic of it. And who was it for? I couldn't see that either. The Germans? The Americans? The Japanese?'

'Well, I believed it all from the very beginning. Just as soon as I saw that horned boy.' Stalin put on his waistcoat, went over to a dressing table with an oval mirror, took his necklace with the emerald and began putting it round his neck.

'Let me, my angel . . .' Khrushchev went over, fastened the necklace and carefully arranged it round his shirt collar.

The faces of the two friends reflected in the emerald's forty-two facets.

'Tu ne peux pas t'imaginer combien tu m'es cher, mon ami,' Stalin said, gazing into the mirror.

'Un ermite comme moi aime entendre de telles choses,' Khrushchev slowly kissed the silky white shoulder of the Leader. ❏

Translated and introduced by Arch Tait

DIASPORA CHIC

DIRAN ADEBAYO

I have in front of me an invitation to speak at a forthcoming
Windsor conference whose theme is 'The Imaginary Homeland: Has
Commonwealth Literature Had its Day?' My session is entitled 'Britain
as the last colony of the British Empire'. Various notables of the 'post-
colonial'/Commonwealth diaspora literary scene – Abdulrazak Gurnah,
Aamer Hussein, Ben Okri – are due to attend, as well as older gods such
as Wilson Harris and Peter Porter. I know that, amid the academics and
writers and what have you, my early 30s self will probably be the youngest
one there, and this will contribute to a certain sense of distance, a lack of
full commonality that I tend to feel at gigs like these. But I expect I'll go.
Among other reasons, I'd be foolish not to. This is the market, you see,
but increasingly I'm not sure that it's me.

The 'post-colonial' school has been the main lens through which non-
white writers of any international antecedents have been discussed these
past 20 years. As someone whose parents emigrated from Nigeria, who
grew up with Heinemann's African Writers Series as well as British classics
on the family shelves, I readily accepted induction into the diaspora circle
when my first novel was published. Like most other writers, I wanted
critical and commercial comforts, and I was certainly mindful of how the
post-colonial school was big in the academy. Given the unlikelihood of
serious novelists making big commercial breakthroughs, especially ones
with 'strange' names – I'm always mindful of GK Chesterton's *mot* that the
British public will never greatly buy a book by an author whose name they
can't pronounce – it's as well to keep the academy onside. You have half an
eye on a tenured academic post, like Gurnah's at the University of Kent or,
better still, like Caryl Phillips, overlooking New York's Hudson River. Just
the kind of thing a writer might want in his mid years, when the demands
of a family, say, have sapped his novelistic energies.

But, of course, I am as much a Briton as a diasporan. I came into the
writing game partly to record this British/black British world around me,
only to see quickly that such an obvious ambition did not sit easily with
the dominant diaspora chic.

I should have known. Looking for literary 'role models' as an apprentice
writer, what was most striking about various eminent diasporans – your

Okris, your Caryl Phillips – was that, despite living in Britain, hardly any of them engaged on the page with the British, black British world around them. Of course, any writer can only answer to their own concerns, nevertheless it strikes me, now as much as then, that to be hailed as an important non-white writer, one's work has to fall into what you might call a 'once removed' category: either removed in place – set your work in places that are exotic to the key Western market, with exotic mythologies or world views operating (Okri, Arundhati Roy) – or in time. If I had a dollar for every book that has replayed the slavery experience to general acclaim (Tony Morrison's *Beloved*, Phillips's *Cambridge*, Fred D'Aguiar's *Feeding the Ghosts*, etc etc), I'd be a rich man.

No doubt this tendency has much to do with the long tradition of well-known writing in these areas, a tradition that most diaspora critics would have grown up in and gained their professorships on. They tend to champion those who easily lend themselves to the kind of discourse that is their own bread and butter. One should never underestimate the influence that art patrons have on the type of art that is produced. A friend of mine, a UK Chinese artist, found that, among all the different applications she used to send in to the Arts Council for funding for diverse video projects, the only ones to meet with success were the ones whose themes were riffs on Chinese restaurants and 'Takeaway' culture. So now 'Takeaway' stuff is all she does.

The tendency is also enhanced by people's – the readers', the diaspora mafia's – general reluctance to deal with any sensitive matter that is right in front of them. And race – encounters between whites and non-whites – is sensitive. It's far easier for a reader to feel pity for a slave than to be moved by the story of a twenty-first-century young black British male when it's these same males she fears when she walks out on to the street.

Hanif Kureishi was different. Seeing his film *My Beautiful Laundrette* was one of the great moments of my apprentice years. Here, at last, was a diasoporan, an Anglo-Pakistani, who was setting his stuff in modern Britain, in all its multi-coloured, edgy splendour. Now, Kureishi is more about sex; then, he was more about race – although as I then saw, to my disappointment, in his debut novel *The Buddha of Suburbia*, about a certain type of racial encounter that I was less interested in chronicling. In that novel, his two main characters, the Asian father and son, spend most of their time in white circles – the dad is a guru-figure to white suburbanites while the son, when he's not listening to David Bowie, expends his

Great moments: My Beautiful Laundrette *showed modern Britain in a new light.*
Courtesy: Channel 4 Films

energies trying to make it as an actor in the liberal circles of the Royal
Court Theatre. The book, like *Laundrette*, was a hit and it occurred to me
that to have a black-British hit you had to provide white lines of entry into
the work. The runaway success of Zadie Smith's *White Teeth* and the Asian
comedy series *Goodness Gracious Me* is, of course, further evidence of that.
Being a progressive and rather contrary-minded, in my second novel I set
about writing a book set in Britain that had no white points of entry, partly
because it reflects a truth – lots of black people here, like the characters in
my novel, see few if any whites in their everyday lives – and partly because
the reception of such a book would tell me whether or not black people
had arrived as full members of the human club. White contemporary tales,
of course, with no black points of entry are frequently seen as being
'universal' or of wide social significance.

My Once Upon a Time deployed the noir private-eye tradition to tell a
state-of-the-nation, London story. The novel had strong Yoruba religious
flavours to it too, the Yoruba religion being the one that, quiet as it's kept,
in its modern guises of *voodoo*, *santeria* and *candomble* informs black lives in
the diaspora as much as any other carry-over from the old country. It was
an old world/new world tale and one I was exceptionally proud of, not
least because I'd put down every part of me.

The novel was well received where it was reviewed. Unfortunately, the
only newspapers that didn't review it on publication were the ones my
potential readers tend to read – the liberal left ones; the ones, interestingly,
where diaspora chic is strongest. I suspect that my novel, to mix some
metaphors, dropped into the cracks between various stools. The rather
sniffy diaspora-critical gatekeepers out there would not have seen enough
orthodox diaspora stuff in a novel that had slang and shootings in London
clubs, while its literateness and my own education would have precluded a
certain 'all hail the primitive/black guy straight off the streets' approach –
that other long-standing exotica tradition. And as for Yoruba mythology –
well, few would take voodoo's ancestor seriously. There is nothing like the
respect for African culture, African religions, that there is for their Asian
counterparts: the diaspora is not a level playing field. And so a certain type
of black work is still released into what feels like a critical vacuum.

I suspect too, from various times I've crossed paths with the diaspora
mafia, that they have a certain unease when faced with the new, emerging
black-British school, as if they know that their old certainties may no
longer apply in the new, upcoming world. And they're right to feel so, for

one of the most striking things about my generation of black Britons is how little solidarity it feels with newer British-based diasporans, such as the North Africans, such as the Sudanese or Somalians who came here in the 1990s, or the Eastern European asylum seekers. Eritrean cabbies have told me of brutal robberies where their black-British fares turned assailant and screamed at them, 'You fucking refugee!' while burglaries are routinely blamed on the new Kosovars in the neighbourhood. Complaints about the refugees taking the council houses and slowing down their kids' progress at school or their treatment in a doctor's surgery have become a regular refrain. Diaspora chic may be big in the academy but not on the streets. Perhaps a sense of Commonwealth, post-colonial solidarity was prevalent in the 1960s and 70s, but certainly not now, in this increasingly British black Britain. The only black diaspora that most of my peers feel part of is their own native country and, always, America – the place where black people are glamorous and millionaires.

So new diasporas are emerging, old ones with their old assumptions fading, friends and enemies all less obvious than before. Professional diasporadom will no doubt adapt to survive but it will have to do some serious reorienting, and rid itself of certain inequities, if it is to keep any deserved place at literature's High Table. ❑

Diran Adebayo's *novels* Some Kind of Black *and* My Once Upon a Time *are published by Abacus*

A SMALL WAR YOU MAY HAVE MISSED
FRANCES PLATT

December 2002

I'm typing this sitting up in bed, it's a chilly Kathmandu morning, there's no heating in the house. I've been living here for the past ten days, after a sudden removal from Dhulikhel, a town 30km to the east, because of the deteriorating security situation. I had a small flat on the roof of an apartment building directly opposite the town's recreation ground, a green space the size of a football field above a grassy embankment. About a year ago, it was taken over by the army as a temporary camp. At first, just a couple of sandbagged shelters appeared, then trenches were dug, trees lopped, the fountains were fenced off and youngsters were no longer allowed to do their morning martial arts practice up there.

When I returned from the UK last summer, the changes were startling: guns were trained on our house because it blocked the view to the jungle beyond; the bunkers had grown in size and number; and, as the weeks of autumn passed, I watched further changes like the rise of mercury in a thermometer, registering the growing fear that there would soon be a big Maoist attack. When my landlord reported strangers in town – code for insurgents – we'd lock the gate to the street early. There's been a dusk-to-dawn curfew for nearly a year almost everywhere outside the Kathmandu valley, and it's strictly enforced. My friends who work in the local hospital have confirmed rumours that innocent people have been shot and wounded or killed by security forces. Any social life in the evening entails an overnight stay.

Rereading reports that were written nearly three years ago, when I first came to work in Nepal, has brought me up short: I'd forgotten how much my personal freedom has been eroded with the growth of the Maoist insurgency. Where once I walked alone, for work or for pleasure, it is now impossible. Bus journeys to remote parts of the district are also a thing of the past. As Dhulikhel is the district headquarters, many government buildings have been the target of Maoist bombs – telecoms, water, electricity, education offices. Initially, the bombs were made like Molotov cocktails, in Horlicks jars, the bigger ones in pressure cookers. Now that the security forces are receiving foreign aid to purchase more modern weapons, these are finding their way into Maoist hands, and attacks on buildings, as well as ambushes of army and police, buses and hospital vehicles, are more brutal.

Since King Gyanendra took control of the country on 4 October, some statues of royalty have come under attack; each now has its own armed guard. Travelling out and in to the Kathmandu valley to work, I'm aware of the government's 'fortress' policy. There are increasingly rigorous police and army checks on all vehicles as they enter and leave the valley. In this poor, mountainous country it isn't possible properly to defend every vulnerable spot from attack by insurgents. Are all the hundreds of footpaths over the valley rim watched? Of course not – and the Maoists know it. Even in the city, late at night patrols go home now it's colder, so bomb-making equipment still makes its way into the capital. You hear explosions early in the morning or late in the evening that are rarely accounted for in the media.

The state of emergency was lifted in the autumn of 2002 to enable free and fair elections to be held in November but freedom of the press doesn't seem to have been restored. Or is there self-censorship? Several hundred journalists have been imprisoned since the start of the insurgency in the mid-1990s [see *Index Index* for this period]. There have been atrocities on all sides but only the Maoist ones are reported.

At this week's Kathmandu International Mountain Film Festival (5–8 December), we learned of Jogimara, a small village from where 17 labourers were contracted to work on the new runway at Kalikot airport in the far west of Nepal. After the brutal attacks on government forces at Achham a year ago, the army set out to find the Maoists who had so humiliated them. They shot these innocent labourers because some Maoists were said to have hidden among them. The postscript of the film, *Jogimaraka Jyundaharu (The living of Jogimara)*, explained that the villagers petitioned the government via their MP for compensation, heard nothing and were eventually told that their papers had been lost.

A similar incident occurred a year later, in October 2002, when security forces killed seven villagers in Angapani, Bajura district, thinking they were Maoists when they were actually members of an anti-Maoist resistance force. The locals understand the security forces made a mistake but so far there has been no admission. Until there is, the families of those killed will be regarded as relatives of terrorists.

Ironically, the season of goodwill is starting in expat circles. As a volunteer I'm barely on the edge, but as a friend of a teacher at the British

Dhulikhel, Nepal: women working through the tension.
Credit: Frances Platt

School, I am invited to their Christmas performance. Year 4D considered the special gift they would give to the world was the gift of friendship so there would be no more wars and killing. Out of the mouths of babes . . .

It has been reported that the government and the Maoists are to start talks but still the insurgents are bombing in remote areas. Can the centre control the periphery? Will there be a repeat of the ceasefire nearly two years ago when the government was duped into thinking peace could be negotiated, while the Maoists were simply using the lull to regroup and rearm? [A ceasefire was signed on 29 January 2003 and peace talks are scheduled for mid–March. Ed]

Other concerns are on my mind now that winter's here. When I lived and worked in Dhulikhel, I passed the jail on my daily journey to work. This is the prison with a dedicated psychiatric unit, the only one for mentally ill men in Nepal. Before the growth of the insurgency, I visited the jail to take clothes and books to those prisoners whose families can't visit because of the distance and expense of travel. I recently attempted to visit again, aware that clothing for the cold weather would be needed. I met an insurmountable wall of bureaucracy. My unofficial enquiries revealed that some Maoist prisoners are being held in this jail and, as extra punishment, are held in the psychiatric unit. This gross abuse of human rights is astonishing enough, leaving aside the inadequate conditions in which these 30 vulnerable mentally ill prisoners are kept on remand indefinitely because there are no laws under which they can be tried.

Those of us in Kathmandu with enough to eat feel as though we are twiddling our thumbs while Rome burns – it has been frequently reported that famine is imminent in the far west of Nepal because Maoists are stealing what little food is available. Security forces are too thin on the ground to protect roads into these areas, so donors have stopped deliveries of food aid. What kind of socialist revolution is it that destroys the livelihoods of the poorest? For all their rhetoric, the Maoists have created a following from fear. Daniel Lak, a BBC World Service correspondent based in Kathmandu, talked to some villagers in Humla, between Simikot and the Tibetan border. In answer to the question: 'So what's the situation around here?', they said: 'You tell those people back in Kathmandu the truth: you tell them how Nepalis are feeling. If the Maoists come and we feed them, 40 or 50 at a time, we watch our food supplies dwindle, but what can we do? We know the next day the army and the police will come and accuse us of being Maoists. They insult us and look at our possessions. Does anyone care about us? We're all alone out here.'

PS Chatting to a friend who went to see the second showing of *Jogimaraka* at the film festival, it seems the police tried to stop it being shown. The start was delayed, the film was eventually shown with 'cuts' and the projector was stopped on the pretext it had broken down. According to *Himal Khabarpatrika*, a local bi-monthly: Groups of uniformed policemen made their presence felt at the festival venue. There was a demand for the tape and plain-clothes policemen were asking questions. Finally, a phone call from a higher-up authority directed the film not be shown at all.' During the following week, our English-language daily reported a government announcement that next year all films to be shown at the festival would be subject to prior censorship. ❏

Frances Platt *is now working in Tibet*

Support for

It is the generosity of our friends and supporters which makes *Index on Censorship*'s work possible. *Index* remains the only international publication devoted to the promotion and protection of that basic, yet still abused, human right – freedom of expression.

Your support is needed more than ever now as *Index* and the Writers & Scholars Educational Trust continue to grow and develop new projects. Donations will enable us to expand our website, which will make access to *Index*'s stories and communication between free-speech activists and supporters even easier, and will help directly with our Sponsored Subscriptions Programme which provides free copies of the magazine to activists in the developing world and the former Soviet states.

Please help *Index* speak out.

The Trustees and Directors would like to thank the many individuals and organisations who support *Index on Censorship* and the Writers & Scholars Educational Trust, including:

IF YOU WOULD LIKE MORE INFORMATION ABOUT INDEX ON CENSORSHIP OR WOULD LIKE TO SUPPORT OUR WORK, PLEASE **CONTACT HUGO GRIEVE, DEVELOPMENT MANAGER, ON 020 7278 2313 OR EMAIL HUGO@INDEXONCENSORSHIP.ORG**

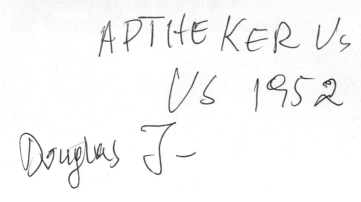

APTHEKER Us
Us 1952
Douglas J-

WWW.INDEXONCENSORSHIP.ORG
CONTACT@INDEXONCENSORSHIP.ORG
TEL: 020 7278 2313 • FAX: 020 7278 1878

SUBSCRIPTIONS (4 ISSUES PER ANNUM)
INDIVIDUALS: BRITAIN £32, US $48, REST OF WORLD £42
INSTITUTIONS: BRITAIN £48, US $80, REST OF WORLD £52
PLEASE PHONE 020 8249 4443
OR EMAIL TONY@INDEXONCENSORSHIP.ORG

Index on Censorship (ISSN 0306-4220) is published four times a year by a non-profit-making company: Writers & Scholars International Ltd, Lancaster House, 33 Islington High Street, London N1 9LH. *Index on Censorship* is associated with Writers & Scholars Educational Trust, registered charity number 325003 **Periodicals postage:** (US subscribers only) paid at Newark, New Jersey. Postmaster: send US address changes to *Index on Censorship* c/o Mercury Airfreight International Ltd Inc., 365 Blair Road, Avenel, NJ 07001, USA